Tackle Your Toddler's Behaviour

Kelly Beswick

Baile Áth
Dublin C

D

For UK order enquiries: please contact Bookpoint Ltd,
130 Milton Park, Abingdon, Oxon OX14 4SB.
Telephone: +44 (0) 1235 827720. *Fax:* +44 (0) 1235 400454.
Lines are open 09.00–17.00, Monday to Saturday, with a 24-hour
message answering service. Details about our titles and how to
order are available at www.teachyourself.co.uk

For USA order enquiries: please contact McGraw-Hill Customer
Services, PO Box 545, Blacklick, OH 43004-0545, USA.
Telephone: 1-800-722-4726. *Fax:* 1-614-755-5645.

For Canada order enquiries: please contact McGraw-Hill Ryerson
Ltd, 300 Water St, Whitby, Ontario L1N 9B6, Canada.
Telephone: 905 430 5000. *Fax:* 905 430 5020.

Long renowned as the authoritative source for self-guided learning –
with more than 50 million copies sold worldwide – the **Teach Yourself**
series includes over 500 titles in the fields of languages, crafts, hobbies,
business, computing and education.

British Library Cataloguing in Publication Data: a catalogue record
for this title is available from the British Library.

Library of Congress Catalog Card Number: on file.

First published in UK 2008 by Hodder Education, part of Hachette UK,
338 Euston Road, London, NW1 3BH.

First published in US 2008 by The McGraw-Hill Companies, Inc.

This edition published 2010.

The **Teach Yourself** name is a registered trade mark of
Hodder Headline.

Typeset by MPS Limited, A Macmillan Company.

Printed in Great Britain for Hodder Education, a Hachette UK Company,
338 Euston Road, London NW1 3BH, by CPI Cox & Wyman,
Reading, Berkshire RG1 8EX.

The publisher has used its best endeavours to ensure that the URLs
for external websites referred to in this book are correct and active
at the time of going to press. However, the publisher and the
author have no responsibility for the websites and can make no
guarantee that a site will remain live or that the content will remain
relevant, decent or appropriate.

Hachette UK's policy is to use papers that are natural, renewable
and recyclable products and made from wood grown in sustainable
forests. The logging and manufacturing processes are expected to
conform to the environmental regulations of the country of origin.

Impression number   10 9 8 7 6 5 4 3 2 1

Year   2014 2013 2012 2011 2010

To Sam, for being behind me all the way, Kit and Natasha, whose own toddler years have been my inspiration, and Mum for loving my children almost as much as me.

Image credits

Contents

Meet the author   viii
Only got a minute?   x
Only got five minutes?   xii
Only got ten minutes?   xiv
Introduction   xviii

1 **Toddlers: the facts**   1
   What is a toddler?   1
   The toddler years: a time of incredible development   2
   The not so 'terrible twos'   3
   Why your toddler's behaviour is natural and normal   5
   Your super-brainy toddler   6
   Toddler milestones: what to expect and when   7
   Six things your toddler could teach you   15

2 **Understanding your toddler's personality**   19
   Your one-of-a-kind toddler   19
   The nine toddler temperament traits   21
   The three toddler temperament types   22
   The importance of avoiding labels   29
   The importance of self-esteem   30
   Alike and different: making family comparisons   32
   Personality surprises   33

3 **The push for greater independence**   37
   Your toddler's instinctive desire for independence   37
   How your toddler's independence develops: what
       to expect and when   38
   The dos and don'ts of dealing with separation anxiety   43
   Toddler-proofing your home to enable independence
       to flourish   46
   Helping your toddler make decisions through choice   49
   Limiting the use of 'no' to retain its effectiveness   50
   Choosing your battles wisely   53
   Why a routine helps your toddler and you   55
   Establishing a good routine for you and your toddler   58

4   Typical toddler flashpoints   67
    Why certain situations throw toddlers into a tailspin   67
    The emotions behind a flashpoint   68
    The common toddler triggers   70
5   Temper tantrums and how to survive them   82
    What is a tantrum?   82
    The tantrum-prone toddler   85
    Food for thought: the link between additives
        and tantrums   87
    Types of tantrums   88
    Signs of a tantrum   88
    The tantrum spectrum   89
    Ways to avoid tantrums   91
    Coping with tantrums   94
    How to deal with public tantrums   101
    Keeping a record   103
    How to handle your toddler's tantrum around a sibling   104
    Tantrums and twins   105
    Other toddlers' tantrums   106
    Tantrums: the myths   107
    Outgrowing tantrums   108
    When to seek help   109
6   The secrets of toddler discipline   113
    Why discipline is important   113
    How discipline is different from punishment   114
    Why disciplining a toddler is not easy   115
    How to discipline a toddler effectively   118
    Methods of toddler discipline   124
    The behaviours you cannot ignore   131
    Your embarrassing toddler   133
    Smacking: is it ever the answer?   136
7   Encouraging toddler talk   139
    How speech and language develop   139
    The difference between expressive and receptive
        language   141
    Your toddler's language milestones   142
    Ways to get your toddler talking more   144
    Common toddler speech problems   153
    Fascinating talking facts   155

8   How to handle a fussy eater   158
    Why most toddlers are fussy about their food   158
    Personality and fussiness   161
    Offering new foods   163
    Practise what you preach: how you affect your
        toddler's eating   165
    What should a toddler eat?   167
    Foods to be careful about   170
    Toddler drinks   172
    Keeping mealtimes calm and relaxed   173
    Knowing when your toddler has had enough   174
    The vegetarian toddler   175
9   Getting your toddler to sleep better   179
    Why toddlers often struggle with sleep   179
    Why a baby who sleeps well can become a
        wakeful toddler   180
    Understanding your toddler's sleep   181
    How much sleep should your toddler have?   182
    Ways you can help your toddler to sleep better   183
    Typical toddler sleep problems   186
    Why naps matter   190
    The difference between nightmares and night terrors   191
    The move from cot to bed   193
    There were three in the bed: how to encourage your
        toddler to remain in their bed and out of yours   195
10 Tricks to successful toilet training   199
    Waving goodbye to nappies   199
    Is your toddler ready?   200
    Are you ready?   204
    Potty versus toilet   205
    On your marks: preparing your toddler   206
    Get set: getting your toddler familiarized   206
    Go: the start of toilet training proper   207
    Accidents and underwear   208
    Rewards and incentives   209
    Toilet training away from home   210
    Common toilet training problems   213
    When to call a halt   216

	How boys and girls differ	217
	Achieving dry nights	218
11	**Fun and games with your toddler**	**222**
	Why your toddler's play is so important	222
	How play helps your toddler's development	223
	Free play versus structured play	225
	Tips on playing with your toddler	227
	The different types of play	229
	Playing with other children	232
	Top ten toddler toys	234
	Gender and toy choice	235
	Toy safety	236
	Eight everyday objects that make great toys	237
	Great games you can play with your toddler	238
	Ways to turn everyday activities into a game	240
12	**Helping your toddler cope with change**	**243**
	Why change cannot be avoided	243
	What change means to your toddler	244
	Helping your toddler adjust to a new sibling	245
	Moving house with your toddler	249
	Choosing the best childcare	254
	Helping your toddler through a family break-up	265
13	**Toddler troubleshooting**	**272**
	20 of the most frequently asked questions answered	272
	Taking it further	**278**
	Index	**281**

Meet the author

Welcome to *Tackle Your Toddler's Behaviour*!

I have been working as a parenting journalist for many years now and one of the most frequent questions I get asked by parents of babies who are just about to enter the toddler years is: is it really so terrible? I think they expect their previously docile little angel to suddenly mutate into some horrific, tantrum-throwing monster. Of course this isn't the case. I'd be lying, however, if I said the toddler years were a complete breeze – there will be challenges and sometimes your child's behaviour will test you to the limit. But always running parallel with this will be your toddler's incredible sense of joy and unbridled enthusiasm for life. It's impossibly infectious and will make you see the world through new eyes.

My own two children are now past the toddler stage, and when I look back, I do so with immense fondness. I know there were tantrums aplenty (they are twins!) and moments when I would quite literally be tearing my hair out, but do you know what? I can hardly remember those times. It's the wonderment and the fun that I remember the most – they really are the most magical years.

Yet I do remember feeling a low-level sense of anxiety throughout some of that period. Everywhere I looked there were so-called parenting gurus, claiming to know exactly how you should be tackling your toddler's behaviour. Yet their supposedly fail-proof methods frequently didn't work on my children, leaving me feeling a failure as a parent. When did it all get so difficult, this parenting malarkey? It took a while for me to realize that parenting hadn't got difficult, we had just made it so by looking too far outside ourselves for the answers. My children are quirky, cantankerous, wonderful individuals and I was afraid they weren't ever going to slot into a one-size-fits-all style of parenting. Once I stopped trying to force square pegs into round holes and realized that no one knew my children better than me, it was as if a dark cloud had lifted.

It is with the benefit of hindsight that I have written this book – it's the manual I wish I'd had when my children were just entering the toddler stage. Rather than telling you what to do, I show you the options available to you and how they may (or, indeed, may not) work with your individual child. All the major areas have been covered, in what I hope is an accessible, easily digestible form, enabling you to pick and choose the best methods and strategies to assemble a bespoke way of managing your toddler's behaviour – i.e. one that is right for you and for your child. Above all, I hope this book takes some of the angst out of the toddler years, freeing you up to fully enjoy them in all their spontaneous, excitable and boisterous glory! Have fun.

Only got a minute?

- The toddler years are a time of tremendous growth and change as your child begins to make sense of the world and their place within it.

- This process can be a struggle for your child, as they start to exert their independence. They may experience situations that provoke strong emotions, while not being mature enough to deal with them.

- Overwhelmed and frustrated, your toddler's behaviour can deteriorate, sometimes resulting in tantrums. They are not being deliberately naughty – often they simply do not know how else to respond.

- It is largely from you, their main role model, that your toddler will learn how to react in ways that are more appropriate and socially acceptable.

- How you go about achieving this will depend both on the personality of your child and on what you feel comfortable with.

- Setting clear and consistent ground rules, through whatever routines and discipline methods you choose, has been proven to help in this tricky phase. It will help your toddler to understand what is expected of them and what their place is within the family and society.
- Your toddler will test those limits, as part of their need for greater independence, but if you stand firm, they will eventually learn that they do have freedom, but that it has set boundaries.
- This knowledge is extremely reassuring to a toddler, when so much else is still so confusing, and it will help them cope better in the wider world.
- It will also help you feel more confident in dealing with all aspects of your toddler's life, from feeding and sleeping to toilet training and starting childcare.

5 Only got five minutes?

▶ The rapid pace of your toddler's development can result in behaviour that is difficult to manage. Remember this is not a sign of bad parenting, but a perfectly normal stage that your toddler needs to go through in order to get to the next one.

▶ Nobody knows your child better than you. By recognizing their unique personality you can work with them rather than against them in order to find strategies that succeed. It will take time and energy, but at the end of the day you will have developed a parenting style that's right for you and your toddler.

▶ Your toddler's natural urge to exert their independence can be tricky to handle. Young toddlers can become oppositional and negative while older ones may begin to push boundaries and insist on doing things themselves. One effective technique to give more independence is to allow your toddler a limited choice.

▶ It is possible to avoid many tantrums by learning to recognize the signs of frustration in your toddler, giving your toddler a choice whenever possible, choosing your battles wisely and, for the younger toddler, employing distraction techniques. When a tantrum does occur, stay calm and in control.

▶ Disciplining a toddler is not easy, but it is necessary if they are to eventually become an emotionally mature adult who functions successfully in society. To discipline effectively you should set limits and establish boundaries which are age and stage appropriate and be consistent. Methods of discipline include positive reinforcement and Timeout.

▶ Praise your toddler when they say a word, then repeat it back to them but add an adjective. This will enlarge their vocabulary and teach word combinations. When your toddler says something wrong, don't say so. Just say the word back correctly. This is known as modelling.

- If your toddler refuses to try new foods, don't give up, as it can take many attempts before a new food is accepted. Because toddlers have tiny tummies, but need lots of energy, they can't get all the nutrition they need in just three meals, which is why healthy snacks are so important.
- Toddlers have shorter sleep cycles than adults, surfacing from a deep sleep into a lighter one approximately five times a night. Establish a good bedtime routine and teach your toddler to settle themselves through a sleep training programme that's acceptable to you. If problems persist, be firm and consistent.
- Signs that your toddler is ready to start toilet training include regular bowel movements, staying dry for several hours at a time, showing an interest in the toileting process and knowing when they need to go. Involve your toddler as much as possible, from buying the potty/trainer seat to choosing their underwear. Try not to make a fuss when an accident happens.
- Play is an essential part of your toddler's development. If you overly structure your toddler's play they don't get to practise their decision-making skills. When playing with your toddler let them be the leader while you are the follower.
- With a bit of thought and planning the negative impact of any unsettling changes in your toddler's life can be considerably lessened. If a new sibling is about to enter your toddler's world, involve them from the outset. Also set aside some special time for just you and your toddler once the baby's born. If you are moving house, reassure them that while things will be different, much will still be the same. If starting childcare, be positive and upbeat about it and ease them into it very slowly. If you are splitting from your partner, try to keep things civil for the sake of your child.

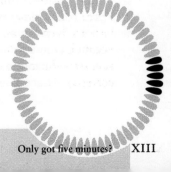

10 Only got ten minutes?

▶ Toddlerhood is a time of phenomenal development when your toddler's exuberance and wonder at the world are a joy to witness. Rather than dreading the toddler years, try to embrace them in all their spontaneous, fun-filled glory – all too soon this magical, innocent time will have passed.

▶ No two children are the same – which may sound obvious, but we often seem to forget this when it comes to managing their behaviour. Nobody knows your child better than you, and while you might not realize it, you are the expert at managing your toddler's behaviour. Whatever your toddler's personality, remember that every type has its advantages and blind spots, and by appreciating your toddler for who they are and making them feel comfortable and relaxed in their own skin, you will be helping to build their self-esteem.

▶ As soon as your child begins to understand that they are a separate entity from you, the urge to exert their independence begins to kick in. One of the most effective ways to enable your toddler to enjoy their burgeoning independence is by ensuring that your home is completely toddler-proof so that they can explore their environment safely. Another tried and trusted technique is to allow your toddler a limited choice. Establish a routine to give your toddler a solid, predictable structure around them as they take their first tentative steps in the world.

▶ There are certain environments and situations that can provoke extremely strong emotions in a toddler. These are known as flashpoints, and often they can be anticipated. It will help to put yourself in your toddler's shoes so you can understand why these situations are so intolerable to them. As far as sibling squabbles are concerned, it is worth noting that a certain amount of arguing is healthy and will teach your children some valuable lessons, such as how to deal with peers, how to negotiate and when to compromise.

▶ As unpleasant as tantrums are, they are perfectly normal and very common. When a tantrum does occur, it's important you stay calm and in control. If necessary, walk away and collect yourself in another room. Coping strategies include completely ignoring the tantrum (easier said than done, especially in public places), holding your toddler close until the tantrum passes or, for the older toddler, practising some Timeout. Don't try to reason with your child mid-tantrum and don't punish them for the tantrum – it should change nothing, for the better or worse. If a tantrum does occur in public, stay calm as this will help your toddler to calm down. Also, try to remember that most people will look on your plight sympathetically.

▶ Discipline is not punishment. To discipline a toddler effectively you will need to set limits and establish boundaries, make the discipline age and stage appropriate and factor in the importance of your toddler's personality. Consistency is crucial, as is your position as your toddler's biggest role model. One method of discipline is positive reinforcement, whereby you give your toddler praise for the things they do right, taking the emphasis off of what they are doing wrong. Reward charts can be a good way to encourage positive behaviour. Timeout is another popular method whereby your child is given a bit of time and space to cool down and reflect on their behaviour. Behaviour you should never ignore is that which hurts others, such as kicking and biting.

▶ Your toddler's growing verbal skills mark an exciting step in their development. To encourage your toddler to talk more give them a choice and name the objects they can choose between as this will expand their vocabulary. Praise your toddler when they say a word, then repeat it back to them but expand on it with an adjective. Other ways to encourage talk include providing a running commentary, or just knowing when to listen, reading to and singing with your toddler, switching off the television and getting your toddler to ditch their dummy. Don't worry if your toddler mispronounces certain words or talks with a lisp. These problems are very common and usually rectify themselves by the age of three.

▶ Being picky about food is a normal part of development and even has a name – neophobia, or fear of the new. It can be upsetting for a parent, but if you look at your toddler's food consumption over the course of a week, their diet is probably a lot more balanced than you think. Don't make a big deal about new food and don't try and disguise it by mixing it in with a favourite one. Simply serve the new food alongside an established one and praise your toddler even if they only eat a tiny morsel. To ensure that toddlers get everything they need, top them up with healthy snacks. Foods to be careful about with your toddler include salt, additives, sweeteners and raw eggs.

▶ Many toddlers struggle with aspects of sleep, whether going to bed, staying asleep or waking too early. On average, your toddler needs between 12 and 13 hours sleep over a 24-hour period, with one to two hours taken as a nap. Establish a good bedtime routine and teach your toddler to settle themselves through a sleep training programme that's acceptable to you. If problems persist, be firm and consistent. Don't be tempted to stop your toddler's nap in the hope they'll sleep better at night. A young child cannot get all the sleep they need during the night alone.

▶ Getting your toddler out of nappies is a significant rite of passage, but one that should not be hurried. Signs of readiness usually surface around two to three years of age and include regular bowel movements, staying dry for several hours at a time, showing an interest in the toileting process and knowing when they need to go. Involve them as much as possible, from buying the potty/trainer seat to choosing their underwear. A reward chart can often help keep a toddler interested and motivated. When it comes to dry nights, again don't rush things, just let your toddler lead the way.

▶ Play is an essential part of your toddler's development, teaching them important physical, mental, social and emotional skills in the process. To get the maximum benefit from play a toddler needs to be in charge of the activity. When you structure your toddler's play they use less imagination and creativity and don't get to practise their decision-making skills.

▶ Even if much of your toddler's life is predictable and well regulated, there will be elements that can't be controlled, resulting in changes that can be unsettling. But with a bit of thought and planning the negative impact of these changes can be considerably lessened. If a new sibling is about to enter your toddler's world, involve them from the outset, from letting them feel the baby move to joining in the name-choosing process. Once the baby's arrived, keep reassuring your toddler of your love and offer lots of praise when they do something right. Also set aside some special time for just you and your toddler. If you are planning to move house include your toddler as soon as possible, reassuring them that while some things will be different, much will still be the same. To help them settle in, make sorting out their room a priority and continue with their usual routine as best you can. If starting childcare, look at your options carefully and choose the one that feels right for you and your child. Be positive and upbeat about your childcare arrangements around your toddler and ease them into it very slowly. If you are splitting from your partner, prepare your toddler for the break-up by telling them about it together, keeping your explanation simple and non-condemnatory, and once the split has taken place, try to keep things civil for the sake of your child.

Introduction

As the parent of a toddler you are no doubt aware that this stage in your child's life can be absolutely amazing but also very challenging – after all, why else would you have picked up this book! Your toddler's job over the next few years is to push boundaries, test limits and generally make sense of the world around them. It's an incredibly important and incredibly difficult task and as they undertake it, their behaviour may deteriorate, becoming difficult and problematic. You must allow them to explore, to learn and to grow, but at the same time you must guide them, steering them away from the dangerous and the unacceptable. That is your task – and it is not always an easy one.

This book is designed to help you in that endeavour, not by telling you what to do, but by showing you the various options that are available, because despite what some experts would have you believe, there really isn't one fail-proof method of managing a toddler's behaviour as so much depends on the child. Your toddler is an individual, with their own unique personality, so why should a technique or method that works on one child necessarily work on them?

The fact of the matter is you are the expert when it comes to managing your toddler's behaviour because no one knows your child better than you do. You might not realize it, but you do have all the skills necessary to successfully see your child through the toddler years, it's just a question of recognizing those skills and putting them into practice. And that really is the purpose of this book – to put you firmly back in the driving seat, confidently doing what's right and what's best for your toddler.

This book will therefore show you how to work with your toddler's personality, rather than against it, when managing their behaviour over some of the key issues you are likely to experience during the toddler years – from tantrums and discipline to fussy feeding and poor sleeping.

As well as detailing the various strategies available, so you can decide what to try and see what works best, the book is also peppered with case studies, where real parents talk candidly about their experiences and the various ways they've tried (sometimes successfully, sometimes not) to manage their toddler's behaviour. Through these, you'll hopefully feel reassured that your toddler's behaviour is perfectly normal, and in some cases, perhaps better than their contemporaries! In addition, you might just pick up on a tactic you hadn't thought of before.

Also throughout the book you'll find plenty of tips for getting the behaviour you want from your toddler, as well as ways to better manage your own. There are also lots of fascinating toddler facts that hopefully serve to remind you of what a truly incredible stage of development your child is going through.

How you read this book is, of course, entirely up to you. It can be read cover to cover, but as a parent of a demanding toddler, the chances are you'll be dipping in and out. As such, it has been written to enable you to troubleshoot a particular problem or concern as and when it arises.

Finally, it is hoped that this book will not only help you better manage your toddler's behaviour, but also to better enjoy the precious toddler years, which are such a short and spectacular part of your child's journey into adulthood.

Please note: this book offers advice for dealing with behaviours associated with your normal, average toddler and does not tackle toddlers with specific medical conditions or with special needs.

1

Toddlers: the facts

In this chapter you will learn:
- *what constitutes a toddler*
- *the signs that your baby is becoming a toddler*
- *why the 'terrible twos' is a misnomer*
- *why toddler defiance is a crucial part of development*
- *tips on staying positive*
- *how your toddler's brain develops*
- *why repetition helps brain development*
- *about your toddler's physical development*
- *about your toddler's mental development*
- *about your toddler's social and emotional development.*

What is a toddler?

Typically, a baby becomes a toddler at around the age of one, when they start to take their first faltering steps, or toddle – hence the name. But the term toddler is applied far beyond that relatively short period of learning to walk and has come to embody an entire stage in your child's development. Generally, a child is considered to be at the toddler stage until approximately three years old. But as with all stages your child goes through, it is often difficult to pinpoint precisely when they move from one stage to the next. So, for example, while some ten-month-olds are still clearly babies, others may already be showing signs of entering the toddler phase (see below). Similarly, it is not uncommon to witness four-year-olds throwing spectacular tantrums and behaving in a manner that would shame a two-year-old.

FIVE SIGNS THAT YOUR BABY IS BECOMING A TODDLER

1 *They have become much more interested in their surroundings.*
2 *They are starting to explore their world more, either crawling or shuffling, or perhaps 'cruising' by holding on to the furniture or your hand.*
3 *They can say one or two words, usually 'mama' or 'dada'.*
4 *They know the meaning of several words, especially 'no'.*
5 *They become grumpy when forced to do things they don't like or want.*

The toddler years: a time of incredible development

One thing is certain, however: the toddler stage, for whatever length it lasts in your child, will be a time of incredible physical, mental and emotional development. It will be a time of much fun and laughter as your child develops their sense of self and begins to exert their independence. Their unique personality will come to the fore and you will increasingly see glimpses of the adult they will eventually become.

At the same time, you will undoubtedly face challenges. Toddlers are notoriously oppositional – not as an act of whim, but as an extremely important part of their learning process. With their growing independence, your child will need to push the boundaries, to insist on making their own choices and to be their own person. Of course, for a choice to be their own it will need to be different from yours, and herein lies the problem. Sometimes raising a toddler can feel like a huge battle of wills.

Case study

Jamie really was such an easy baby. Right from the outset, he fed well and we quickly got him into a routine – in fact he was sleeping through the night at six weeks. People used to comment on what a contented and happy little boy he was, and I must say, I did feel a teensy bit smug. So when, at about 11 months, Jamie suddenly started screaming and wailing every time I tried to strap him in to his pushchair, I thought there must be something wrong. It got so bad that I didn't leave the house for several days. If I tried forcing him in, he'd go as stiff as a board and even if I did manage to close the straps, he'd cry so much that I'd end up getting him out. I was so concerned, I eventually spoke to the health visitor, who gently explained that Jamie was behaving like a typical toddler and letting me know, in no uncertain terms, that he didn't like being constrained in his buggy. Until she said it, I honestly still thought of Jamie as a docile baby. It was a bit of a shock to realize that he'd suddenly evolved into this little person with a mind very much of his own. He's since forgotten that he hates the pushchair – probably because he's realized it usually takes him to the park. But he's now developed a dislike of wearing his coat!

The not so 'terrible twos'

If ever there was an expression guaranteed to raise the pulse of parents entering the toddler stage, then the 'terrible twos' is it. The idea that an entire year of your child's life is categorized in this negative way is of course profoundly daunting, but in truth, whoever coined the phrase was doing neither parents nor their offspring any favours. Yes, there will be run-ins as your increasingly strong-willed toddler attempts to make sense of their world and their place within it – one minute wanting to 'do it myself' and the next needing comfort and reassurance. Tantrums and whining will sometimes be par for the course. But so too will love, laughter and moments of such pure joy that you will remember them for the rest of your life.

WAYS TO EMPHASIZE THE POSITIVE

It is important in the toddler years to emphasize the positive, and there really is a lot worth considering:

▶ *Your toddler thinks you are the greatest person in the whole wide world and as far as they are concerned, you are the centre of their universe. Relish this – it will not last forever.*

▶ *Babies cry for an average of three hours a day. Toddlers cry a lot less.*

▶ *You probably have a bit more time to yourself than you did when your toddler was a baby.*

▶ *Affection is never in short supply when there's a toddler around.*

▶ *Every day your toddler is learning and discovering new things, which is an amazing thing to witness.*

▶ *A toddler's love of life and enthusiasm is infectious and will reinvigorate your view of the world.*

▶ *At the toddler stage, your child will start to develop their sense of humour. Toddlers love to laugh – up to 300 times a day, while adults laugh on average only 15 times a day.*

▶ *A toddler's strange observations and funny expressions are a constant source of amusement, and will probably go down in your family's folklore – re-lived and repeated many times in years to come.*

Top tip

Why not write a list of the things that make you smile about your toddler (the feel of their little hand in yours, the way they greet you when you have been away from them) and take a look at it the next time the going gets tough.

Why your toddler's behaviour is natural and normal

Another thing about the misnomer of the 'terrible twos' is that it makes this period sound like an aberration and one that ideally would be best avoided. But the fact is, without displaying the egocentric and sometimes challenging behaviour associated with this stage, your child would miss out on a crucial part of their development.

It is essential that toddlers start to get to grips with the world around them, to begin to understand what is acceptable, what is unacceptable and where they fit in. The toddler years are a child's proving ground, where they will develop the skills to cope with the frustrating challenges and dilemmas of adult life. However, unlike you, they are not yet capable of rational thought and are unable to fully vocalize their anxieties and concerns. Is it any wonder that it can sometimes all become too much? But this period of sweeping change is the beginning of your child's transition into a social human being, and the trick is learning how best to manage and nurture this wonderful, magical time.

STEP INTO YOUR TODDLER'S SHOES

Sometimes it really helps to see things from your toddler's point of view. Whereas once they were a babe in arms and their every need was catered for, suddenly, and unexpectedly, things have changed – for example, now they might have to wait a moment for your full attention, or maybe you've gone back to work and are no longer a constant presence. Also there are new rules: for example, prodding food with their fingers was once acceptable, but now they are expected to use a spoon. It is no wonder toddlers sometimes struggle to make sense of it all.

Insight

I know that lots of parents start questioning their parenting ability when their toddler's behaviour deteriorates. The chances are you're doing nothing wrong; it's simply the stage that your child is at.

A toddler judges the seriousness of their behaviour in terms of the immediate impact of an event, not the intention. For example, they think it is worse to spill a lot of paint accidentally than to spill a little bit deliberately.

Your super-brainy toddler

Just because your toddler isn't capable of rational thought just yet, that doesn't mean that their brainpower is in any way inferior to yours. In fact, a toddler's brain is twice as active as an adult's, with double the amount of connections – that's more connections in total than are made at any other time in a person's life.

In the toddler years, it is these connections between brain cells that are turned, through repetition, into networks. Networks are what allow your toddler to think and learn and this is why so many basic skills are developed during the toddler years. Indeed, such are the learning abilities of an average two-year-old that even a sophisticated computer simulation would struggle to match them.

So, as you can see, the toddler brain really is something quite phenomenal as it forges the pathways that will be used for the rest of your child's life.

Top tip

It is worth listening to your toddler the next time they plead with you to 'do it again'. Repetition is the key to your toddler's brain development, so while singing 'The Wheels on the Bus' for the tenth time (yes, they really do go round and round and round...) might be boring for you, your toddler will love the familiarity and it will help build important connections in their brain.

FOOD FOR THOUGHT

A daily dose of the essential fatty acids, in particular omega-3 and omega-6, has been proven to boost toddlers' brainpower. These fatty acids make up a quarter of the brain's grey matter, and are critical to the growth and maintenance of brain cells. They can be found naturally in oily fish, soya beans, rapeseed oil and walnuts, and are also available in supplement form. In a recent study of 65 children aged between 18 months and three years, a daily dose of a combined omega-3 and omega-6 supplement was given, and after five months, 79 per cent of the toddlers showed significantly improved concentration and behaviour.

Did you know?

By their third birthday, your toddler's brain will have tripled in size and have formed about 1,000 trillion connections.

Toddler milestones: what to expect and when

Because a toddler's brain is primed to learn, over the next few years you will witness remarkable growth in all areas of your child's development – such is the rate of learning that sometimes it will feel like your toddler is acquiring a new skill every single day. Of course, each child is an individual and they will develop at their own pace, so while one toddler may be able to recite a favourite nursery rhyme at 18 months, another might still not have said their first word. In the vast majority of cases there is absolutely nothing to worry about and the child will reach each developmental milestone when they are good and ready. If, however, you are concerned about your toddler's development in any area, consult your health visitor or GP for advice.

Top tip

Try not to compare your toddler with others developmentally as it can cause unnecessary anxiety to both you and your child. Remember:

▶ *Toddler development isn't a race. Of course every parent is proud of their toddler's achievements, but try to avoid being competitive.*
▶ *Toddlers often leapfrog each other when it comes to reaching the various milestones, so the child that may seem a little behind one moment, may well be out in front the next.*
▶ *Toddlers have a remarkable in-built capacity to concentrate on one developmental milestone at a time. So the toddler who is busy mastering walking may well do so temporarily to the neglect of another area, for example, language.*

Insight

I've found that parenting can be highly competitive, and it's worth bearing this in mind when you next hear someone boasting about their toddler's amazing achievements or angelic behaviour. Take such claims with a pinch of salt.

PHYSICAL DEVELOPMENT

Physically your toddler will progress over the next few years from those first faltering footsteps to running, jumping and kicking a ball. Suddenly, from crawling around the sandpit, they will be hurtling down slides and clambering to the top of the climbing frame. Their increased strength and agility will bring a new-found confidence and your child's body shape will slowly begin to transform. That rounded baby belly will begin to flatten out, while chubby, dimpled limbs will start to elongate as muscles develop. At the same time, your child's fine motor skills are being slowly perfected and you will begin to notice them becoming far more dexterous with their fingers. Soon your toddler will be scribbling with a crayon (and not necessarily just on paper), holding a paintbrush and carefully placing building blocks on top of each other. By the time they are three years old the physical capabilities of your toddler will render their fumbling, stumbling one-year-old self barely recognizable.

Insight

As your toddler develops physically, I know it's tempting not to always trust their new-found abilities, for example using the pushchair when they're perfectly capable of walking to the shop. Whenever possible, allow them to show off their emerging skills.

Did you know?

At a year old, your child has already tripled in size. Thankfully, weight gain slows down considerably in the toddler years, otherwise, by the time your child was four, they'd weigh almost as much as a blue whale!

Physical milestones

At 12 to 15 months your toddler will probably be able to:

▶ *stand on their own*
▶ *perhaps walk with one hand held*
▶ *crawl down stairs*
▶ *kneel.*

At 15 to 18 months your toddler will probably be able to:

▶ *walk well alone*
▶ *possibly bend down and stand up unassisted*
▶ *use their fine motor skills to hold a crayon and scribble and build a tower from play blocks*
▶ *lift a cup to their mouth and drink*
▶ *climb onto furniture*
▶ *maybe dance to music.*

At 18 to 24 months your toddler will probably be able to:

- *feed himself or herself with a small spoon*
- *run*
- *perhaps kick a ball*
- *walk up stairs*
- *climb into a small chair.*

At 24 to 36 months your toddler will probably be able to:

- *dress themselves*
- *open doors and lids*
- *ride a tricycle*
- *throw and catch a ball.*

Did you know?

The reason most toddlers learn to walk at around a year old is because it is only then that their skeleton's soft cartilage has been fully turned into hard bone and can support their body weight.

Case study

By 17 months Mathilda still wasn't walking and I must confess, I was starting to worry as all my friends' children of the same age were toddling around. But she was perfectly happy shuffling about on her bottom and seemed in no rush to stand on her own two feet. I even took her to the doctors, where I was told there was absolutely nothing to be concerned about. My GP explained that as long as Mathilda was mobile, either crawling or bottom shuffling, then she was physically fine for her age and that she would no doubt start walking when she was ready. I was amazed when just a few weeks later, without any warning, Mathilda stood up. Admittedly, she immediately started to wobble and fell back down again, but after that there was no stopping her. To look at her now, you'd never guess that she's only been walking a few months – she's completely caught up with the other children and has even overtaken a few, and I mean that quite literally, because she's just started to run, too.

MENTAL DEVELOPMENT

Over the toddler years, your child's mental skills will come on leaps and bounds. The most obvious manifestation of this will be their mastering of language, with their vocabulary increasing dramatically over this period from one or two simple words to learning, on average, ten new words a day by the time they are two years old. By three, your child will probably be speaking clearly and in sentences, and don't be surprised if they are even capable of answering you back. Accompanying this language development will be a huge increase in your toddler's level of understanding as they become capable of following simple instructions. Questions will start coming thick and fast as your toddler attempts to make sense of the world. Indeed, 'why?' will come to replace 'no' as a favourite word.

Insight

From my experience, some toddlers are naturally little chatterboxes, while others are more reticent. If your toddler is the latter, don't worry; it's probably just their personality to be a bit more introvert.

Mental milestones
At 12 to 15 months your toddler will probably be able to:

▶ *use four to six words*
▶ *follow a simple request, such as 'sit'*
▶ *possibly follow a more complex command when accompanied by a gesture; for example, they might bring a cup to you if you point at it and say: 'Please bring me the cup'*
▶ *begin to realize that an object still exists even though it is out of sight, for example a toy in a box*
▶ *possibly point to a body part when asked.*

At 15 to 18 months your toddler will probably be able to:

- *use 10 to 20 words, but will understand more*
- *follow a story*
- *fetch objects from another room*
- *follow a command without a gesture.*

At 18 to 24 months your toddler will probably be able to:

- *use around 20 to 50 words, but will understand many more*
- *use two-word sentences*
- *talk a lot and more clearly*
- *know the names of some animals*
- *start to understand cause and effect*
- *begin to understand limits*
- *ask 'why?'*
- *search for a hidden object*
- *scribble well*
- *'read' board books on their own.*

At 24 to 36 months your toddler will probably be able to:

- *easily learn new words, places and people's names*
- *make longer sentences*
- *speak clearly most of the time*
- *name at least six body parts*
- *possibly name one colour*
- *attempt to sing in time with songs*
- *begin to understand abstract concepts like 'soon' and 'later'.*

SOCIAL AND EMOTIONAL DEVELOPMENT

It is in a toddler's social and emotional development that parents are likely to experience the most challenges and also, it must be said, the greatest joy. As your child struggles to learn the boundaries of social exchanges and to learn to control their emotions, especially the angry ones, they will also learn how to respond to others – spontaneously giving you a cuddle, sharing a toy with a playmate, showing empathy to others when they are hurt or upset, and discovering the dos and don'ts of everyday life. And it is through the maze of social and emotional milestones that your toddler will need you the most. You are their guide, their first and favourite role model, and although there will be much testing of limits during this period, the deeper the emotional bond between you and your toddler, the easier they will find the gradual move towards effective social and emotional skills.

Insight

As a mum, I know how difficult it can sometimes be to get out and about with your toddler, but if you are sociable your toddler is more likely to be sociable too.

Social and emotional milestones

At 12 to 15 months your toddler will probably be able to:

▶ *enjoy gazing at their reflection in a mirror*
▶ *try to make their needs known, for example, pointing to a cup if they are thirsty*
▶ *raise their arms when they want to be picked up and cuddled*
▶ *imitate others and mimic actions, for example, covering their eyes while playing peek-a-boo.*

At 15 to 18 months your toddler will probably be able to:

▶ *greet people with a 'hello' and enjoy waving*
▶ *mimic things they see you doing on a daily basis, for example, sweeping the floor or talking on the telephone*
▶ *play alongside other children but not with them – they will only interact if their space is invaded*
▶ *show a preference for certain soft toys and dolls.*

At 18 to 24 months your toddler will probably be able to:

▶ *role play, for example, dressing up or playing tea parties*
▶ *mimic social behaviour, such as hugging a teddy bear or feeding a doll*
▶ *begin exerting their independence, possibly by saying 'no' or throwing a tantrum*

- *express more complex emotions such as jealousy, affection, pride and shame*
- *have a greater sense of self, but will possibly experience greater anxiety when separated from you.*

At 24 to 36 months your toddler will probably be able to:

- *begin interacting with other children*
- *play turn-taking games*
- *start to understand the concept of sharing, although may not be very good at it yet*
- *be apart from you without feeling such anxiety*
- *know the difference between boys and girls*
- *realize it is okay to make a mistake or not be able to do something*
- *show preferences for certain clothes, books, DVDs, etc.*
- *be sympathetic and understanding if someone is hurt or upset.*

IF AT FIRST YOU DON'T SUCCEED...

... try and try again. Yes, that old adage is never truer than when applied to a toddler. At all key stages of your toddler's development they will inevitably struggle to master certain skills. This can be frustrating for a toddler, and it may take several attempts before they finally learn how to do a specific thing. Despite the setbacks, it is important that your toddler feels confident and capable. Encourage them to try again, and explain how they will sometimes need a lot of practice before they get it right. Also, try not to always step in when your toddler is struggling – give them the freedom to fail, as sometimes this is the only way to learn to succeed.

Case study

I'm very close to my mum and I usually chat on the phone to her a couple of times a day, often on my mobile, which I have tucked in the crook of my neck while I'm busy doing something else, like tidying up or making Ellie's tea. The other day I was in the kitchen and I could hear Ellie in the front room playing, and it really sounded like she was deep in conversation with someone. I peeked through the doorway to see what she was doing, and there was my little girl, pacing up and down, pushing her dolly in the pushchair with her toy phone to her ear. I had to laugh, because not only did she look just like me, she sounded like me too, going, 'Mmmm..., mmmm..., yes', as if the person at the other end was telling her some fascinating story. When I asked her who she was talking to, she said 'Nana', and passed me her phone so I could have a chat too.

Top tip

A toddler's emotional and social development isn't always linear, with young children having a tendency to slide back into a previous stage if they feel upset or unsettled by events in their life. For example, your two-year-old may start asking for a bottle again with the arrival of a new sibling. Don't tell your toddler they're too old. Maybe they have seen the attention the new baby with the bottle is receiving, or perhaps they just need extra comfort during what is for them a stressful time. With patience and love, your toddler will soon resume their more mature behaviour.

Six things your toddler could teach you

Over the toddler years your child will look to you for much help and guidance, but remember, there's quite a lot you can learn from them, too.

1 **To persevere.** *A toddler rarely gives up. Sometimes for a parent this tenacity can be a bit annoying, especially when they're asking you for the twentieth time that day: 'Please can I have an ice cream?' But the drive of the headstrong toddler is truly amazing and sometimes, as adults, we would do well to be as focused as they are.*

2 **To live in the here and now.** *Toddlers don't worry about what went on yesterday and rarely concern themselves with what is going to happen an hour hence. As such they are utterly engaged in the present, enjoying the actual moment, which is something we adults often struggle to do.*

3 **To forgive and forget.** *Toddlers do not bear malice. Something that has thrown them into a complete state of apoplexy one moment will be quickly forgotten the next. Sunshine quickly follows storm clouds in a toddler's life, but as adults, we tend to find it much harder to move on.*

4 **To be spontaneous.** *A toddler acts upon their impulses. They lack premeditation and as such their behaviour is natural and unrestrained. All too often as adults we are weighed down by the possible consequences of our actions.*

5 **To love unconditionally.** *Few relationships in adult life are based on unconditional love, but that is exactly what your toddler feels towards you. There are no limits or conditions to a toddler's love, whereas an adult's love often comes with strings attached.*

6 **To learn from mistakes.** *As adults, we tend to fear failure and easily give up or prefer not to try something if there's a risk of not succeeding. Toddlers, however, have no such concerns. Their inherent desire to learn overrides any fear of failing and, of course, they eventually cut down on the mistakes by learning what not to do.*

10 THINGS TO REMEMBER

1 *Don't dread the onset of the toddler years. It truly is a time of incredible development. The phase 'the terrible twos' is in fact a misnomer, as there is so much to enjoy about this short and magical stage in your child's life.*

2 *Your toddler's more challenging behaviour shouldn't be seen as some sort of aberration, but instead viewed as an important part of their development. Without the tantrums and the pushing of boundaries, your toddler would miss out on a crucial part of their development.*

3 *Your toddler might sometimes behave in an irrational manner, but don't underestimate them. Their brain is in fact twice as active as yours, busily making connections that will eventually form the networks that enable your toddler to think and learn.*

4 *Repetition is the key to forming these networks, which is why your toddler loves doing the same things over and over again.*

5 *Milestones mark exciting new stages in your toddler's development, but don't be overly concerned if they reach a particular milestone slower than their peers. Toddler development isn't a race and every child is different.*

6 *Your child's growing physical prowess is a result of their gross and fine motor skills continuing to improve, along with an increase in strength and agility.*

7 *Mental development will most obviously manifest itself through the mastering of speech and language.*

8 *The deeper the emotional bond between you and your toddler, the easier they will find the gradual move towards effective emotional and social skills. Just expect lots of testing of limits along the way.*

9   *Unlike physical and mental development, your toddler's emotional and social development may not always be linear. They may slip back a stage if they feel upset or unsettled.*

10   *If your toddler is struggling to master a certain skill and gets frustrated, try not to step in. Giving your child the freedom to fail is sometimes the only way for them to learn to succeed.*

2

....

Understanding your toddler's personality

In this chapter you will learn:
- *why personality is key to managing toddler behaviour*
- *what the basic temperament traits and types are*
- *how better to understand your toddler's personality*
- *ways to bring out the best in your toddler*
- *how to avoid labelling*
- *techniques to boost your toddler's self-esteem*
- *the pros and cons of family comparisons.*

Your one-of-a-kind toddler

Even when they were a newborn baby, the cornerstones of your child's personality and temperament were very much in evidence – whether grizzly and fretful or easily soothed, perhaps happy to be handled or unsettled in unfamiliar arms. And as the months pass, the uniqueness of your child's character begins to emerge. Indeed, by the time they are hitting the toddler stage you have got a proper little individual on your hands.

Over the next few years, as your toddler becomes better at expressing themselves – their likes and dislikes, how certain people and situations make them feel – their distinct personality will become even more prominent.

WHY ONE SIZE DOES NOT FIT ALL

When it comes to managing your child's behaviour over the toddler years, a good understanding and appreciation of that unique personality will really hold you in good stead.

All too often, in our quick-fix society, it is assumed that parenting techniques can be applied across the board, and that every child will respond and react in the same established way. Of course, this approach does not take into account the individual personality and temperament of the child involved. What works for one child will not necessarily work for another and by recognizing this fact, by not trying to force a square peg into a round hole, much distress and frustration can be avoided on both sides.

To best manage your toddler, it really helps if you can respect, accept, accommodate and celebrate the child you have, to work with their personality, not against it. In doing this, you will be far more sensitive and intuitive to your child's needs and, in turn, your child will gradually become more sensitive and intuitive to yours.

Insight

In the past many parenting experts have completely overlooked the personality of the child when dealing with their behaviour, but I've recently noticed that a more holistic approach has started to emerge where the child's character is taken into account.

Case study

For Christopher life is a bit of a breeze. He's a really robust little lad who's always taken new situations in his stride. If I take him to a birthday party, he'll soon be charging around the house with the best of them. He loves being around other children and is quickly accepted as part of the gang. He's also happy at nursery and barely glances back when I drop him off in the morning. As far as discipline goes, if I place Christopher on the naughty step, he'll sit there obediently for the allotted time and invariably says sorry afterwards.

My daughter, Amelie, however, is a totally different child. At any social gathering, you'll find her clinging to my leg. She won't let go of me. If I try to prise her away and leave her for a moment, just to pop to the loo or whatever, she'll insist on going with me. On the few occasions she has lost sight of me, she has burst into tears. If another child approaches, unless she knows them really well, she'll studiously ignore them. As you can imagine, settling her into nursery has been a bit of a challenge. What's more, the naughty step simply doesn't work for Amelie, and the few times I have tried to enforce it she's gone berserk. Yet if I reason with her and explain clearly why whatever she is doing is upsetting me, I usually get the desired result. Of course it goes without saying that I adore both my children, but I really do have to manage them so completely differently.

Insight

I've often noticed how siblings can be almost polar opposites in terms of personality and that it's usually evident from birth, which just goes to show how powerful nature is in terms of temperament.

Top tip

There is no right or wrong, no better or worse personality type. All types are equally valuable, with their own natural strengths and potential blind spots.

The nine toddler temperament traits

Psychological research into the temperament of toddlers has identified the following nine traits that exist to varying degrees (mild to intense) in all children. Take a look at the traits listed below and consider them in terms of how your child expresses them.

1 **Activity level.** *Is your toddler usually calm and relaxed and quite happy to sit still for long periods, OR are they constantly on the go and have to be doing something all the time?*

2 **Rhythmicity.** *Is your toddler a creature of habit who thrives on routine and has always had regular eating and sleeping patterns, OR are they more unpredictable in their daily routines?*

3 **Approach/withdrawal.** *Does your toddler move easily into new settings and quickly feel comfortable with new people, OR are they wary around strangers and find unfamiliar situations uncomfortable?*

4 **Adaptability.** *Can your toddler easily adjust to sudden changes in plan and disruption to routine, OR do they resist and find it hard to adapt to transition?*

5 **Intensity.** *Do you find that you often have to guess your toddler's feelings, OR does the whole world know when they are happy or angry?*

6 **Mood.** *Does your toddler generally have a sunny disposition and an even temper, OR are they sometimes anxious and prone to changing their mood quickly?*

7 **Persistence and attention span.** *Will your toddler normally stick at a task until it is completed, even if it takes a long time, OR do they tend to quickly become frustrated and move on to something else?*

8 **Distractibility.** *Can your toddler become so absorbed in an activity that they shut out all distractions, OR will they be unable to concentrate if something else is going on in the room?*

9 **Sensory threshold.** *Is your toddler unconcerned by such things as loud noises, bright lights, clothing or food textures, OR do you find they can get quite bothered by these things, for instance becoming distressed by a misplaced sock seam?*

The three toddler temperament types

It is the combination and level of these individual traits that make each toddler who they are. But for ease of definition, three basic types of temperament have been identified as follows:

1 **The easy/flexible toddler.** *These children are generally calm and happy, with regular eating and sleeping patterns. They are also very adaptable and not easily upset.*
2 **The active/feisty toddler.** *These children are often bundles of energy, who do not slot easily into routines and can be fussy when it comes to feeding. Their sleeping habits are usually quite erratic, too. They can become anxious in new situations and around strangers.*
3 **The slow-to-warm-up/cautious toddler.** *These children usually appear quite passive and will often withdraw when presented with an unfamiliar scenario. But once they become better acquainted with a situation or person they react positively.*

Did you know?

According to research, approximately 65 per cent of all toddlers will more or less fit into one of the above three temperament types, with 40 per cent falling into the easy/flexible category, ten per cent into the active/feisty category while the final 15 per cent are regarded as slow to warm up/cautious. As for the remaining 35 per cent, they are a mixture of all three.

Insight

In assessing their toddler's personality, I've found that parents can get overly concerned, thinking certain traits will hinder their child's progress through life. This is rarely the case. In fact, it is by recognizing these traits and accepting them that you are likely to get the best out of your child.

TODDLER PERSONALITY QUIZ

Having established the various traits and temperament types, the following fun quiz is designed to help you to better determine your child's personality. Simple and quick to do, it will only paint a broad picture of your toddler's personality, directing you to the temperament that is most dominant and leaving you to fill in the gaps.

Tick the answer that most applies to your toddler and add up your scores to find the temperament type that is most applicable.

1 *You take your toddler over to a friend's house. Do they:*
   a *play happily on the floor*
   b *whine loudly to go home*
   c *stick firmly at your side until they have got the lay of the land?*
2 *Which of these activities would your toddler enjoy the most?*
   a *drawing pictures*
   b *jumping on the furniture*
   c *helping you cook.*
3 *In the playground, your toddler would be happiest:*
   a *playing in the sandpit alongside the other children*
   b *clambering to the top of the climbing frame*
   c *being pushed on a swing.*
4 *During playtimes with other children, what is your toddler most likely to be doing?*
   a *They'd probably be happily and actively involved.*
   b *They'd be right in the thick of things, but woe betide any child that tried to take something they were playing with.*
   c *They'd be on the sidelines, watching what is going on.*
5 *The most noticeable thing about your toddler is:*
   a *how laid-back and adaptable they are*
   b *how much energy they have got*
   c *how sensitive they are.*
6 *If a stranger were to say 'hello' to your toddler, what would they be most likely to do?*
   a *politely say 'hello' in return*
   b *run off in the opposite direction*
   c *hide behind your leg.*
7 *If your toddler feels hurt or upset, do they:*
   a *tend to keep it to themselves*
   b *shout at full volume about what is troubling them*

c   *take the time to find exactly the right words to describe how they're feeling – and will then need to have your undivided attention to tell you?*

If your child scored mostly 'a'
THE EASY/FLEXIBLE TODDLER

Your toddler appears already to understand the meaning of Zen, being a calm, easy-going, go-with-the-flow sort of child. But as you probably already know, easy children aren't all smooth sailing. Sometimes it can be hard to get their attention, and they still need a lot of love and reassurance.

HOW TO BRING OUT THEIR BEST:
- *Accentuate the positive. Don't forget to praise your toddler when they do what you ask. It is important to reinforce positive behaviour even in obedient children.*
- *Be realistic. The sunny-natured toddler can still throw a spectacular wobbly should the mood take them, but don't come down harder on them just because it's so unusual.*
- *Read the signs. Just because your toddler's feelings aren't always obvious, it doesn't mean that things don't upset them. It is important to tune in to their subtle signals and know when things aren't right with them. Perhaps set aside special times to talk about your toddler's frustrations and hurts – it will help you to find out what they are thinking and feeling.*
- *Play with them. It sounds obvious, but often it is easy to leave mellow toddlers to their own devices, as they seem perfectly happy. But interactive play is important for learning, so give them plenty of options and choices.*

Case study

Tommy is our fourth child and he really is the most placid and easy-going of the lot. He's the youngest by five years, so while the other children do fuss over him, he's had to make do with just my company for much of the day. But he loves sitting looking at picture books and will happily play with his toys for hours at a time. Because he so rarely makes a fuss about anything, I have sometimes found myself leaving him to his own devices while I have got on with the household chores, which is something I could never have done with my other children when they were his age – they would have demanded my attention in no uncertain terms! But just because Tommy's not a demanding child, that doesn't mean he feels things less strongly. I recently had to leave him for a couple of hours with our next-door neighbour to take my eldest daughter to an appointment. When I got back, the neighbour said Tommy had been the perfect little angel, but I just knew from the look in Tommy's big brown eyes that he'd missed me dreadfully and when I picked him up for a cuddle, he squeezed me really tight and said: 'love you mama'.

If your child scored mostly 'b'
THE ACTIVE/FEISTY TODDLER
Joyful, energetic and entertaining, your toddler knows how to have fun, but they will also let you know very loudly and very clearly when they are not happy, and they can be hard to fit into a routine and quite obstinate when pushed.

HOW TO BRING OUT THEIR BEST:
- *Understand their triggers. If your toddler struggles with sharing, then try and steer them away from the toy box when other children are around and instead involve them in a group activity.*
- *Insist on naptime. If your toddler is still young, don't be tempted to abandon their afternoon nap just because they resist. Your toddler is prone to getting over-tired and without that daytime sleep their little body won't be able to cope and they will become hard to manage and difficult to calm down.*
- *Break the boredom. Your toddler is probably in constant motion and thrives on new situations and challenges. Don't be tempted to plonk them in front of the TV – much better to take them out in the fresh air.*
- *Be a calming influence. Your toddler can easily be over-stimulated. Try and recognize the signs and then step in and offer some quiet time, perhaps reading a book or listening to soothing music together.*

► *Give clear instructions. Your toddler is a whirling dervish and such is their impulsive nature that they sometimes struggle to pay attention. Get down to their level and make eye contact when you want them to listen to what you are saying.*

► *Prepare them for change. Your toddler sometimes finds it a struggle to make the transition from one place or activity to another, but if you give them warning, they will resist less.*

Case study

At first I thought it was probably because I'm an older mum that I was struggling to keep up with Sophie – I had her when I was 38 – but having got to know other mums of a similar age I have realized that it's not so much me, it's her! My little girl doesn't sit still from the moment she wakes up in the morning until she finally conks out – we joke that she's like one of the bunnies in that Duracell battery advert. I honestly don't know where she gets her energy from – she's such a tiny little thing. Most days I have to take her to the park to run off some steam, because if I didn't she'd cause complete devastation in the house. If for some reason we do end up being cooped up indoors, she starts getting really restless, emptying out cupboards and throwing her toys all over the place. I did wonder whether perhaps she was a bit hyperactive, but my mum says that I was exactly the same as Sophie when I was her age and that they used to call me The Whirlwind because I was constantly dashing around here, there and everywhere, creating havoc in my wake. In fact, my mum jokes that I have finally got my comeuppance.

If your child scored mostly 'c'
THE SLOW-TO-WARM-UP/CAUTIOUS TODDLER
Your toddler can be shy and sensitive on unfamiliar terrain and may be more of an observer than a joiner. Since new situations can cause them anxiety, give them time to find their feet and feel at ease.

HOW TO BRING OUT THEIR BEST:
► *Hold them close. When your toddler is meeting someone new, draw them in to you and speak in a soothing, calming voice.*

- *Take it slowly. Your toddler won't enjoy being fussed over by people they don't know. Gently suggest to friends and relatives that they back off a bit initially. If your toddler is given ample time to establish relationships in new situations, their confidence will begin to grow.*
- *Mix the old with the new. If you are going somewhere unfamiliar with your toddler, take their favourite toy for comfort.*
- *Prepare them beforehand. Before doing anything that your toddler might find daunting, tell them what to expect; for example, if you are going somewhere where there is a dog, forewarn them. The more your toddler knows, the more comfortable they will be.*
- *Whenever possible, stick to a routine. Your toddler feels at their most safe and secure when they know what is going to happen next and will get upset and anxious when things suddenly become unpredictable.*

Case study

Last week was my husband's birthday, so we arranged for Jack's childminder to come over and babysit while we went out for a quick meal at the local Italian. I did debate whether to tell Jack beforehand, but because he's quite an anxious little boy I didn't want to worry him unduly. And besides, he's usually a very good sleeper and would be soundly tucked up in bed by the time we left. Anyhow, all went according to plan and we'd just ordered our food and were toasting our good fortune when my mobile phone went off in my handbag. I fished it out and immediately saw the word 'Home' flashing on the screen. Yes, you've guessed it – Jack had woken up calling out for us. The childminder had gone up to re-settle him, but Jack was definitely having none of it and was screaming the house down as we spoke. Of course we had to abandon the meal and dash home to comfort our little lad, who was beside himself. I felt absolutely awful because I know what Jack's like – he really needs to know what's happening and can't bear to be thrust into a new situation without warning. I can only imagine how upset he must have been at suddenly finding his childminder in his bedroom, especially since she's never even been to our house before. The next time we plan an evening out, I'll make sure Jack knows exactly what's happening well in advance.

The importance of avoiding labels

Whatever your toddler's personality type, rejoice in their individuality, and try to avoid using labels when describing your child as these can be self-fulfilling. For example, if your toddler is shy and they hear you describe them as such, they are likely to think there is something wrong with them and as a result may become even more shy. If a situation requires you to describe your child in front of them, choose your words wisely. Here are some suggested label swaps:

SHY – CAREFUL
A shy child retreats from life, while a careful one is aware of potential dangers and takes steps to avoid them.

WILD – ENERGETIC
Wild suggests unruly and out-of-control, while energetic implies a toddler who is brimming over with enthusiasm.

FUSSY – SELECTIVE
A fussy toddler sounds picky and faddy, while a selective one only wants what is best.

STUBBORN – TENACIOUS
A stubborn toddler will dig their heels in without rhyme or reason, while one who is tenacious is a fighter who won't give in easily.

DEFIANT – COURAGEOUS

A defiant toddler refuses to do what is asked, while a courageous one sticks up for what they believe in.

The importance of self-esteem

Today it is generally recognized that a child is largely born with a certain temperament, that nature slightly outweighs nurture in this instance, but that is not to say that you cannot guide and influence your toddler to ensure that they achieve their maximum potential.

As a parent, you can have a huge impact on your toddler's behaviour and development just by making them feel comfortable and relaxed with who they are – in other words, by building your child's self-esteem regardless of whether they are cautious, exuberant, intense or laid-back by nature.

WHAT HAVING GOOD SELF-ESTEEM MEANS TO A TODDLER

Insight

Our busy lives can sometimes make it hard to carve out the time to give your toddler your undivided attention, but I don't think you should underestimate what it does for your child's self-worth. It doesn't have to take a lot of time, but it sends the clear message that you think they're important and valuable.

Toddlers with high self-esteem will probably:

▶ *like themselves and feel good about who they are*
▶ *know that they are valued, worthwhile and likeable*
▶ *have the confidence to try new challenges*
▶ *feel they can achieve most of the things they set out to do*
▶ *not be afraid to keep on trying even if things go wrong and they fail occasionally.*

WAYS TO BOOST YOUR TODDLER'S SELF-ESTEEM

Here are ten ways you can help to build your toddler's confidence in themselves.

1 *Tell your toddler you love them as often as possible.*
2 *You can never be too affectionate with a toddler. Cuddles and kisses are the physical manifestation of your love for them.*
3 *Let your toddler know that you think they are marvellous. Tell them how proud you are of them, praise their imagination and applaud their successes, but don't forget to praise their efforts and attempts, too.*
4 *Let your toddler know that you find them great fun to be with and that you like nothing better than spending time with them.*
5 *Talk to your toddler as much as possible. Chatting to your child will further push home the message that you really do enjoy their company.*
6 *Listen to what your toddler has to say. Let them know that you find their opinions and observations interesting and that they are someone worth listening to.*
7 *Everyone responds well to encouragement, so let your toddler hear you acknowledging the small things they do throughout the day, whether getting dressed by themselves or picking up their toys.*
8 *Let your toddler try out lots of activities and find something that they enjoy and feel they are good at. Perhaps it is building a tower out of blocks or singing a favourite nursery rhyme – whatever it is, let that become your toddler's 'special something'.*
9 *Encourage friendships. In the early toddler years, your child might not show much interest in other children, and will prefer playing on their own. But the seeds of sociability are being sown, and being able to eventually make friends and get on with others will really help build self-esteem.*
10 *Create your own family rituals. Whether it is a morning snuggle in bed with your toddler or a special way you have of saying goodnight, these little rituals will re-affirm your toddler's special place in the family.*

Alike and different: making family comparisons

As a parent, it is very easy to have preconceived notions and make assumptions about your child's personality based on your own temperament and perhaps that of your partner and immediate family. How often have you heard someone say: 'She's so like me – really stubborn and headstrong', or 'Look at him, he's just like his father, he loves being the centre of attention'. Of course, viewing your child as an extension of yourself is completely natural. But there are pitfalls to this approach and it might be worth bearing in mind the following:

▶ *Your toddler's impulses, drives and desires, the way they process information and why they express themselves the way they do cannot, by the very nature of genetics, be a carbon copy of either you or your partner. Your child is unique.*

▶ *At the same time, however, you will inevitably catch glimpses of something in your toddler that reminds you of part of yourself or your partner. Most of the time these similarities will make you proud, as you revel in the fact that your toddler is a 'chip off the old block'. But sometimes you may see something in your toddler that you don't particularly like in yourself and would like to change, or it might be something in your partner. If this happens, try to be objective. Again, your toddler is unique and each trait is just a small part of the whole package. Also, as a parent, the only person you can change is yourself.*

▶ *What if your toddler displays traits that are very different from yours? For example, you may feel pleased that they are outgoing and extrovert when you have always suffered from being shy and withdrawn. Or the difference may cause you discomfort – perhaps you are by nature someone who needs time alone, while your sociable toddler wants to be with you and talking to you throughout the day, in which case, work out a way that acknowledges your needs, but allows your toddler fully to be who they are.*

Case study

From the moment Sidra was born everyone kept saying how much she looked like me, and my mum even came to the hospital armed with photos of me as a newborn to prove the point. I think it was therefore expected that Sidra would also be similar to me – I've always been a bit of a tomboy and loved playing rough and tumble with my three brothers. The exact opposite is true, however. We jokingly call Sidra The Little Princess as she is the girliest little girl in the world. She loves playing with her dollies, which is something I hated – in fact, when I was given one once for Christmas I cried, as I wanted an Action Man like the boys. Sidra also insists on wearing only pink and floats around most of the time dressed as a fairy. I've really tried to get her into jeans and T-shirts but she point-blank refuses – she totally knows her own mind in this respect. Sometimes I half wonder if she's really my daughter, our personalities are so different. But then I only need to look at her, with the same curly hair and same oval-shaped face, to know that there's absolutely no doubt there.

Personality surprises

No matter how consistent your toddler's personality may appear to be, sometimes they can – and will – catch you completely off guard by behaving in a way that you least expect. For example, a toddler who is usually wary of strangers might suddenly start showering someone they have just met with affection, while a highly vocal child may suddenly internalize a problem. But the fact that your child can surprise and contradict himself or herself in this respect is what makes being the parent of a toddler so stimulating and exciting.

Also keep in mind that the characteristics you might find the most challenging in your child's toddler years may very well turn into their most positive qualities as they grow. For example, intense, feisty toddlers often become passionate and creative children who are good at asserting themselves and making things happen, while cautious toddlers, who prefer to hold back and take things slowly, can develop into very thoughtful and sensitive children who are good at listening and empathizing with others.

10 THINGS TO REMEMBER

1 *Each toddler is a unique individual and when it comes to managing behaviour, a good understanding and appreciation of this fact will hold you in good stead. Work with your toddler's personality, not against it.*

2 *Don't assume that some personality types are better than others. They are all valuable, offering different qualities and attributes. As the saying goes, wouldn't it be boring if we were all the same.*

3 *An easy/flexible toddler may sound like a dream, but it's important to recognize that just because their feelings aren't always obvious, it doesn't mean that things don't upset them. Learn to spot the subtle signs that things aren't right with them.*

4 *For active/feisty toddlers, over-stimulation can be a problem. If your toddler is still young, stick with a lunchtime nap. For the older toddler, it will help to insist on some quiet time.*

5 *Forewarned is forearmed for the slow-to-warm-up/cautious toddler, so before doing anything that your toddler might find daunting, tell them what to expect beforehand. The more they know, the more comfortable they will be.*

6 *Try to avoid using labels when describing your toddler, especially if it's in front of them, as doing so can act as a self-fulfilling prophecy.*

7 *To help bring out the best in your toddler, and ensure that they reach their maximum potential regardless of their personality type, make them feel comfortable and relaxed with who they are.*

8 *By helping to instil a healthy sense of self in your toddler you will make them more resilient and unafraid to try new things even if they do go wrong.*

9 *One of the most effective ways to boost a toddler's self-esteem is to simply spend time with them, talking and listening, and letting them know how much you enjoy their company.*

10 *No matter how set in stone your toddler's personality appears to be, sometimes they will completely take you by surprise by behaving in the way you least expect. Don't worry – it's just such contradictions that make toddlers so exciting.*

3

The push for greater independence

In this chapter you will learn:
* *how your toddler's independence develops*
* *how to ease separation anxiety*
* *tips on toddler-proofing your home*
* *about the importance of offering a choice*
* *ways to limit the word 'no'*
* *ways to avoid power struggles*
* *how to establish a good routine*
* *what to do when routines break down.*

Your toddler's instinctive desire for independence

Not so very long ago, just a year or so in fact, your child was a helpless babe in arms. As a newborn, they looked to you to meet their every need. Indeed, such was their reliance on you that in your baby's first few months of life, they were completely unaware that you and they were separate beings.

At around six to seven months old, your child probably first began to realize that they were separate from you, and that you could go away and leave them. Soon after that discovery came the knowledge that they were their own person, with their own body, thoughts and feelings. And now, as your child enters the toddler years, they want to put this new-found knowledge to the test – and that means increasingly wanting to do things for themselves, to do things their way and to exert their independence whenever and wherever possible.

Of course, this desire for independence is instinctive and perfectly natural and it will be present throughout your child's journey into adulthood. But it first becomes really apparent during the toddler period and then later, in adolescence. Indeed, some child behaviour experts have dubbed the toddler years 'the first adolescence' for exactly this reason.

How your toddler's independence develops: what to expect and when

Here's how you can expect your toddler's need for independence to manifest itself over the coming months and years:

12 TO 18 MONTHS

During this crucial six-month period your toddler will undergo an astounding transformation from near helplessness to burgeoning independence and as a result they will probably:

▶ *become increasingly oppositional. In trying out their new-found will, your toddler may go through a period during which their behaviour is unreasonable and negative. Perhaps they refuse to be strapped in their car seat, or maybe they turn their nose up at food that was a firm favourite just a day or so ago. Another common way this negativity manifests itself, particularly in younger toddlers, is by constantly saying 'no' to practically every single request.*
▶ *develop a strong desire to explore. Having acquired the physical and mental capacity to explore on their own, your toddler is now eager to go off on all sorts of adventures. It is at this stage that you should seriously consider*

toddler-proofing your house (see page 46), as your toddler will quite literally be into everything, with a very limited understanding of what constitutes a danger.

▶ *realize the limits of their powers. Having briefly thought of themselves as invincible, toddlers will quickly realize that they still have much to work out, whether that's how to put on their coat properly or how to get down from the settee onto which they have just so cleverly climbed up. This realization can both frighten and lead to frustration in a toddler.*

▶ *suffer separation anxiety. Your toddler now knows that they are a separate entity from you and that you can go off and leave them. But each time you go, they are unsure whether you will return. This fear of abandonment – or separation anxiety – reaches a peak at around 18 months old, and gradually decreases as your toddler becomes increasingly confident that you will always come back (see page 43 on the dos and don'ts of dealing with separation anxiety).*

Insight

I've found that a lot of parents are reluctant to let their toddlers explore outside, fearing for their safety. Check out your local parks as many have special fenced-in toddler areas.

Did you know?

In Italy the terrible twos are known as the *fase del no*, which roughly translated means the 'phase of saying no'.

Case study

It really came on so suddenly. One moment Lottie was a happy-go-lucky little baby, doing everything I asked her, then, as if overnight, she found the power of the word 'no' and she has not stopped using it since. From the moment she wakes up everything is a negative. 'Would you like some milk Lottie?' 'No.' 'Let's put on your tights Lottie.' 'No.' Even a 'Would you like to go to the park Lottie?' elicits that same familiar response, and that is despite the fact that she absolutely adores going to the park and feeding the ducks. Thankfully, having been through the same thing at a similar age with her big sister Lydia, I know that this stage is usually relatively short-lived. In fact, in Lydia it disappeared almost as quickly as it started, when one day I asked her if she'd like to do some painting, and instead of the customary 'no', she thought for a moment and then replied 'maybe'. At that point I knew we'd turned the corner.

Top tip

As well as exerting their independence, another reason toddlers say 'no' so much is because they don't know very many words yet. Help your toddler expand their vocabulary by turning 'no' into a game. See if your toddler knows the opposite of 'no'; ask them what comes between 'no' and 'yes' and teach them the words 'maybe', 'possibly', 'perhaps' or 'I don't know'. Also teach them nicer ways to say 'no', such as 'no thank you'.

18 TO 24 MONTHS

By the time your toddler is approaching their second birthday, they will have a much stronger sense of self-awareness and the fact that they are an individual person. Over this period, your toddler will probably:

▶ *largely overcome their separation anxiety. Experience has shown your toddler the reliability of your coming back and, while they may still get upset when being dropped off at nursery or left with a childminder, your toddler will quickly calm down, secure in the knowledge of your return.*
▶ *become increasingly assertive. At this age your toddler will probably be determined to take charge and show you that they are in control of their lives. They will insist on having a say*

in everyday decisions, from what they will eat to what they will wear. Of course, they are too immature to always make the right decision, which is why it is so important to offer your toddler a choice, wherever possible (for more on offering choices see page 49).

Insight

In my experience, the best way to drop your toddler off at childcare is quickly and without fuss. The longer you prolong the situation, the more likely your toddler is to kick off.

Did you know?

Research shows that your toddler's self-awareness turns an important corner at the 18- to 24-month-old stage. A study discovered that a baby under one does not understand that they are seeing a reflection of themselves when placed in front of a mirror, and when red paint was daubed on their nose, the baby would always reach out to touch their reflection's nose rather than their own. By the age of 21 months however, a toddler has become aware that the reflection they see when looking in a mirror is their own, and indeed, when red paint was put on the nose of a child this age, they would automatically touch their own nose when they saw the red-nosed image in the mirror.

Case study

As a baby Kieran would eat whatever was placed in front of him. He's always had a healthy appetite and enjoyed quite a wide variety of food for his age. But just lately he's started refusing things that previously he would have gobbled down without a moment's hesitation. For instance, he used to love fish pie, but

CASE STUDY

when I tried to give it to him the other day, he refused to take a single mouthful. I was so angry, having spent a good hour in the kitchen preparing it from scratch. I felt like prising open his mouth and forcing him to at least taste it, but of course, you can't. I did draw the line when about half an hour later he started asking me for fromage frais. I explained that as he hadn't eaten his dinner he wasn't having any fromage frais which, along with Babybels and cream crackers, seems to be the only thing he will eat at the moment. I know that Kieran's just going through a stage of wanting his own way, even if it means cutting off his nose to spite his face, and that he'll eventually grow out of it. But I must say, when you're going through it, it can really wear you down.

Top tip

When your toddler is asserting themselves in a difficult or frustrating manner, try to remember that without this stage of independence, they would not be able to develop into a person who knows what they want and can think for themselves.

24 TO 36 MONTHS

Between the ages of two and three, your toddler will continue to struggle for greater independence while at the same time pushing the boundaries. During this often challenging period your toddler will probably:

▶ *test limits. Your toddler needs to find out what is acceptable and what is not – to discover how far they can go with their behaviour. For example, you tell your toddler to only use the crayons on the paper, but then as soon as your back is turned, they deliberately colour on the walls. They want to see your reaction, and being firm and consistent is the key here.*

▶ *insist on doing things themselves or their way. 'Me do it myself, me do it myself' can be the constant refrain of toddlers in this age group. Sometimes your toddler's demands will be reasonable, for example, wanting to do up their own coat, while at other times it might be dangerous to give in to your toddler's demands, like not wanting to hold your hand while crossing a busy road.*

Top tip

As your toddler strives for greater independence, try to focus on the behaviour you want from them, rather than calling attention to the behaviour you don't want. So, for example, if your child keeps running ahead of you, rather than saying 'Stop running', try to say, 'I really like it when you walk beside me'.

Case study

We went through an odd period with Natasha when she was just a few months shy of her third birthday. She's always loved her soft toys and right from a baby she'd insist on taking her Mr Spooky, a funny little comforter, to bed with her. As she'd got older Mr Spooky was joined by an ever-growing band of bears, bunnies, pandas, etc. until there was barely enough room left in the bed for her. Then one night, completely out of the blue, she insisted that I take every single toy out of her bed, even her beloved Mr Spooky, and refused to sleep with anything whatsoever for weeks after that. It was almost as if she was testing herself to see whether she could do without them, which of course she could. Once she'd realized this, the toys slowly returned. But not poor Mr Spooky, who has now been firmly relegated to the bottom of the toy box as something 'for babies'.

The dos and don'ts of dealing with separation anxiety

Even the most secure toddler will probably suffer from separation anxiety at some point. Don't worry – it is a perfectly natural stage in your toddler's development, and while it normally reaches its peak at around 18 months and then eases off, don't be surprised if it resurfaces again occasionally, especially if your toddler finds themselves in a new environment, perhaps a change in childminder or starting nursery, or if they are concerned about something at home, such as the arrival of a new baby. Here are a few dos and don'ts to help you both cope better when you have to be apart.

DO:	DON'T:
▶ Keep your goodbyes short and sweet. There is no point in prolonging the agony, and by being firm and to the point you are giving your toddler the message that you have confidence in their ability to cope.	▶ Hover around, or keep returning to check whether your toddler has settled. They will sense your anxiety and will probably find it even harder to calm down afterwards.
▶ Give your toddler a little reminder of you, perhaps a handkerchief they could look after for you until your return.	▶ Sneak out when you think your toddler isn't looking. You want your toddler to know that they can trust you.
▶ Keep a smile on your face, however upset you may feel inside. Your toddler needs to see that you are fine with the situation.	▶ Try and bribe your toddler with treats or presents. It is a slippery slope and besides, your toddler needs to express their feelings.
▶ Send clear messages. Your toddler needs to know that no matter how much they cry or stamp their feet, you still have to leave them.	▶ Suddenly change your mind because of your toddler's protests. If you do, your toddler will get the message that if they create enough fuss you won't go.
▶ REMEMBER: Separation anxiety means that a strong and loving bond exists between you and your toddler.	▶ Finally, don't be surprised if your toddler's separation anxiety disappears, but then comes back during times of change or after holidays or sickness.

I know of one mum who gave her child a photograph of them together to keep in his tray at nursery. If ever the toddler got anxious he would take it out to remind himself that he'd soon be back with mummy.

Case study

Grace has been attending a local nursery since she was nine months old and she'd always been very happy there. When I'd drop her off in the morning, she'd kiss me goodbye and toddle off to play. But a few weeks ago she suddenly started getting really upset when I tried to leave, saying 'no go mummy', and clinging to my leg. On several occasions one of the teachers had to come over and carry her off, which provoked even more screaming and tears. It's been absolutely awful and has really broken my heart, but when I called the nursery to check whether she'd calmed down, they told me that she'd been perfectly fine within a couple of minutes of me going. Then, last week I took her in, dreading the hysterics, but she was completely back to her normal self – no crying, no pleading, just a quick kiss and cuddle and off she went. I've since found out that there's a new person working in Grace's room, so I'm wondering whether that's what caused her reaction. Thankfully, whatever the reason, it seems to have disappeared as quickly as it came.

Top tip

You can help a young toddler learn to cope with separation through short practice sessions at home. Separation will be easier on them when they initiate it, so when your toddler goes to another room (one that's toddler-proofed), don't follow them right away – wait for one or two minutes. When you have to go to another room for a few seconds, tell them where you're going and that you'll return. If your toddler fusses, call to them instead of running back. Gradually they will learn that nothing terrible happens when you're gone and, just as important, that you always come back when you say you will.

Toddler-proofing your home to enable independence to flourish

When your baby started crawling, you probably looked at your home with new eyes, seeing all the possible hazards in simple, everyday situations and objects. Suddenly the vase on the coffee table became a potential lethal weapon, while that gap behind the sideboard became a possible death trap. But having only recently baby-proofed your home, you must now cast your concerned gaze higher, wider and further afield, because your baby is now a toddler with the ability to walk, run and climb, which means they can reach cabinets, drawers, saucepans, etc. better than ever before. To enable your toddler to enjoy their increasing independence and explore their environment safely, take a look at the following checklist detailing, room by room, the simple measures you can take to keep them out of harm's way. Not only will these measures protect your precious toddler, they will give you peace of mind, and protect your precious objects, too.

IN THE LIVING ROOM...

▶ *Cover all electrical sockets. Plastic covers are cheap and readily available.*
▶ *Make sure lamp cords are secure and can't be pulled.*
▶ *Remove floor lamps unless they can be easily anchored.*
▶ *Cushion sharp corners of tables, hearths, etc. Corner cushions or guards are sold in many stores and are available over the Internet.*
▶ *Place all breakables out of your toddler's reach. Safer still, put them away for a few years as your toddler may start using anything they can stand on to reach things ever higher up.*
▶ *Move house plants out of reach as many are poisonous.*
▶ *Avoid strangulation hazards by ensuring that curtain and blind cords are tucked up where little hands can't reach.*

IN THE DINING ROOM/EATING AREA...

▶ *Push chairs all the way up to the table to discourage climbing.*
▶ *Put toddler-proof latches on drawers and cabinets that contain breakables.*
▶ *Push items on the table into the centre.*
▶ *If using a tablecloth, make sure you tuck the corners out of grabbing distance.*

IN THE KITCHEN...

▶ *Keep all sharp knives in a secure place, well out of reach.*
▶ *Store all cleaning supplies, including washing powder, dishwasher tablets, etc. on a high shelf or locked in a cabinet.*
▶ *Keep all household products in their original containers to limit confusion and also, if poisoning were to occur, so that you know exactly what was consumed.*
▶ *Always unplug kitchen appliances after use and make sure cords are not left dangling.*
▶ *When cooking on the hob, always use the back rings, and turn saucepan handles towards the wall.*
▶ *Keep lighters and matches in a safe place.*
▶ *Use toddler-proof latches on easy-to-reach kitchen cupboards. But to keep your curious toddler happy, leave one cupboard accessible containing unbreakable items that you don't mind being played with.*
▶ *Store plastic bags out of reach.*
▶ *Don't leave hot drinks on the edge of the kitchen worktop. Push them right back.*

IN THE BATHROOM...

▶ *Always keep the medicine cabinet locked.*
▶ *Make sure razors, scissors, nail polish, etc. are placed well out of reach.*

- Use mats with non-skid backings on the floor and use a non-slip bath mat in the bath.
- Use a plastic toothbrush holder and soap dish, rather than glass or ceramic ones.
- Get into the habit of keeping the toilet seat down as the sight of water can be very tempting to a toddler. Besides being unhygienic, the toilet bowl can also be dangerous as a young child can drown in just a few inches of water.

UPSTAIRS...

- If you haven't installed a stair gate already, you might wish to consider one now, although some parents choose not to use a stair gate with their toddler, instead preferring to teach them how to get up and down the stairs safely on their own (but always under supervision).
- Move chairs and other furniture away from upstairs windows.
- Put locks on all upstairs windows.
- To avoid tipping, attach tall dressers and wardrobes to the wall and don't store heavy objects on top of these pieces of furniture.

OUTSIDE THE HOME...

- Make sure that your toddler cannot get access to the street and that all gates are secure and locks are in full working order.
- Fence-in ponds or, better still, fill them in until your child is older.
- Driveways and garages are dangerous places for toddlers, so make sure your toddler cannot wander onto the driveway and that the garage is kept locked.

Top tip

When visiting friends and family who don't have small children, be extra vigilant as their homes are unlikely to be toddler-proof. Do a quick sweep of the house, removing obvious breakables and hazards, and try to keep your toddler in sight at all times.

Choose your toddler-proof locks and latches carefully. I've found that some types not only make it impossible for your toddler to open, they make it very difficult for you too, which is very annoying when trying to open a much-used kitchen cupboard.

Helping your toddler make decisions through choice

As part of the push for greater independence, your toddler increasingly needs to feel that they are making their own decisions, and one of the easiest ways to help them feel this is to give them some choice. By giving your toddler a choice and allowing them to be part of the decision-making process, they will feel a sense of control that will sidestep potential power struggles. You aren't making them do something – they are choosing to do it. Besides, no one likes to be forced to do something, so if given a choice your toddler is much more likely to co-operate. Also, choices are part of life, and making the right ones, understanding that choices have consequences and discovering their own preferences are all skills that your toddler needs to learn.

Here are four simple ways to make giving choices work well for both you and your toddler.

1 **Give limited choices.** *For a toddler, it is probably best to limit the choices offered to just two. Any more and your toddler will probably become confused. So, for example, rather than asking your toddler what they would like for lunch, offer a choice of say pasta or pizza.*
2 **Eliminate any options that are unacceptable to you.** *This helps you stay in control of the bigger issues. So, for example, while your toddler might not want to clean their teeth, this is not an option as far as you are concerned. Therefore, give them the choice of cleaning their teeth now or after they have had a story.*

3 **Offer an either/or choice.** *Keep instructions as simple as possible. For example, 'Do you want to put your shoes on yourself or do you want me to put them on for you?' will be better understood than 'Shall we put your shoes on? I can do it if you like.'*

4 **Stick to what has been chosen.** *A toddler needs to learn that if they have made a bad decision they have to live with the consequences. For example, perhaps your toddler has chosen cereal for breakfast, but then turns their nose up and demands egg. Try not to bow to pressure. Understanding the consequences, both good and bad, that come with independence is an important life lesson and slowly, through experience, your toddler will become better at decision-making.*

Insight

One way I've found that will help your toddler to make the right choice is to resist the temptation to hurry the decision-making process and take the time to explain to them what each option entails.

Limiting the use of 'no' to retain its effectiveness

Toddlers are notorious copycats and the fewer times you say 'no' to your toddler, the less they will scream back 'no' to you. Also, the more you use the 'no' word with a toddler, the less effective it becomes. If your child hears you saying 'no' 20 or 30 times a day, they will inevitably start to tune out and the word will lose its power. As such, it is worth saving 'no' for when your toddler's behaviour is completely non-negotiable, for example, if they are about to put themselves or others in danger. Toddler-proofing your home, as discussed previously, is one of the most effective ways to avoid overusing 'no', as you will have created an environment that gives your toddler scope to explore without having their actions constantly vetoed. Here are some other ways to limit your use of the word 'no'.

- ▶ **Explain.** *Give your toddler a reason why you want them to comply and not just an order. So, for example, if your toddler is reaching for the litter tray, your first reaction will probably be to bark 'no', but try to resist the urge and explain why the litter tray is out of bounds instead, for example, 'Dirty. Cat's poo.'*
- ▶ **Personalize.** *Try including your toddler's name into the request, for example, if your toddler has grabbed something off the table that you don't want them to eat, say, 'Not for…' (insert your child's name). It will make your toddler feel that there is a valid reason that specifically applies to them and you are far more likely to receive the co-operation you want.*
- ▶ **Pre-empt.** *If you know you will be going into a situation that is likely to require you to refuse your toddler's request, try to explain why beforehand. For example, you may be about to set off for your weekly trip to the supermarket, and inevitably your toddler will demand sweets at the checkout which, equally inevitably, you will decline to buy. Before you go, tell your toddler that you are going to the shops to buy food and not sweeties. If they still have a tantrum at the till, remind them of what you said.*
- ▶ **Soften the blow.** *If you offer your toddler a positive, alongside the negative, it will make your directive far more palatable. For example, if your toddler is about to pull all the books off the bookshelf, a 'Please don't do that. Why not come here and I will read to you' sounds like a much more attractive alternative than just a simple 'no'.*
- ▶ **Be descriptive.** *Your toddler really won't understand why they are being told 'no' most of the time, but if you try to be descriptive they will have a far better understanding of why they shouldn't be doing something. For example, if your toddler is trying to grab your mug of tea, say 'hot' or 'ouch' and they will be more likely to move away.*
- ▶ **Get 'the look'.** *Try to master a stern expression, one that says you mean business, and use it the next time your toddler is doing something that you don't want them to do. The look should convey that you disapprove of their behaviour and that you don't like what they are doing.*

Correctly mastered, it can also suggest that you know they know better than that.

▶ **Use alternatives.** *Here are four more simple alternatives to no:*
  1 *Stop...*
  2 *Please don't...*
  3 *That's not okay.*
  4 *I want you to...*

Case study

It wasn't until Sammy hit the toddler years that I remembered 'that look'. It was the face my mum would pull when one of us kids was playing up. Her head would tilt to one side, her eyes would narrow and her lips would purse slightly. Just that expression would stop us in our tracks – she honestly didn't need to say a single word. We just knew. Along with 'that look', her other tactic was to use 'that voice'. It wasn't a shout, just firm, calm and measured, but by her mere tone, it was obvious that she wasn't best pleased. Now that I'm finding myself constantly having to say 'no' to Sammy and telling him not to do things, I've decided to take a leaf out of my mum's book and develop a stern look and voice that lets Sammy know that Mummy means business. It's funny, because I always used to swear that I'd do things completely differently from my mum, but I now realize that she knew a trick or two.

Top tip
Limiting your use of the word 'no' does not mean accepting the unacceptable from your toddler. What it does mean is being a bit creative and finding new and interesting ways to get them to co-operate.

Insight
One fun way I've discovered to make your toddler aware of their use of the 'no' word and indeed your own is to turn it into a game. Every time either of you say it you have to do a silly forfeit.

Choosing your battles wisely

As mentioned previously, sometimes raising a toddler can feel like a huge battle of wills. But as the adult, you can choose when to engage or withdraw. For example, what if your toddler is insisting on wearing their wellies even though it's not raining, and you really want them to look smart for a visit to Grandma's? Okay, so they might not look as aesthetically pleasing as you would have liked with their somewhat eccentric choice of footwear, but in the big scheme of things, does it really matter? On the other hand, what if your toddler is refusing to put on their coat and the conditions outside are Arctic? Well this is a battle in which you probably will choose to engage, as it is one that could potentially put your child's health in jeopardy. When it comes to looming battles with your toddler, you basically have three choices, as listed here.

1 **Backing off.** *Choosing not to engage in a power struggle with your toddler doesn't mean you have given in or that your toddler has won – it really isn't about winning or losing. It just means that you have made a choice, and that the control your child wants, be it wearing those wellies or walking to the shops instead of going in the pushchair, is one that is appropriate to your toddler's age and skills and that the issue at stake is sufficiently trivial that ultimately it doesn't really matter. It also makes sense to back off over issues which you are not going to win on, no matter what you say or do. For example, you cannot physically force your toddler to go to sleep during their lunchtime nap, and your cajoling will in all likelihood exacerbate the situation. What you can do is tell them that if they won't go to sleep then fine, they can just lie there. In all probability, they will doze off eventually.*

2 **Lay down the law.** *Insisting that your orders are followed despite your toddler's furious protestations should be saved for the truly important things – situations where the lesson your toddler might learn from not heeding your advice is outweighed by the danger in doing so. For example, if your toddler is insisting on taking their shoes off in the sandpit,*

they will probably get cold feet and want to keep them on next time. If, however, your toddler wants to take their shoes off in the park and there is broken glass around, this really is not an option – you simply will not give in.

3 **Negotiate, compromise, give choices.** *These are all ways of meeting a wilful toddler half way. For example, perhaps your toddler doesn't want to leave the playground. Realistically, offering ten more minutes on the swings and slides is unlikely to throw out your schedule, while your toddler gets some additional time, although not as much as they probably would have liked.*

Whatever way you choose to deal with a potential power struggle, try to stay calm and focused. If you become highly emotional, the chances are your toddler will too. The best first step to take when a battle begins to loom is simply to pause. Stopping your agitated response will encourage your toddler to stop too, because there is no argument going on. Then decide on the best course of action.

Case study

I think I've definitely become better at picking my battles, and I now turn a blind eye to things that I never would have tolerated with my eldest child. When Molly was a toddler, we used to have run-ins on a daily basis, from what she'd wear to what she'd eat – you name it, we fought over it. Looking back I think I felt this stupid need to be in control and that included controlling Molly. If she wouldn't do something I said, I felt that I was somehow failing as a parent and I would then get really upset. I can now see this was ridiculous. When number two came along, I simply had to let go of the reins a bit, and when I did, I realized that everything didn't come tumbling down around me. Now I have three young children to chase around after, and unless it's something really major, like they're in danger of hurting themselves or others, I'm not going to get into a fight. Just last week I took my two-year-old, Flynn, to playgroup in his big sister's fairy dress, which he had insisted on wearing. Rather than look at me aghast, the other mums said how cute and that he was obviously in touch with his feminine side!

Why a routine helps your toddler and you

Maybe you were keen to establish a strict routine from the moment your baby was born, and quickly had them feeding regularly, napping three times a day and sleeping through the night. Or perhaps you have been more of a go-with-the-flow sort of person who has been happy to let your baby feed on demand and fall asleep whenever and wherever. It is more likely that you have been a bit of both, mostly adhering to a routine but happy to break it when circumstances required.

Whatever your attitude to a routine in that first year, by the time your child is entering the toddler stage, it becomes less about the pros and cons to you of having such a daily structure and more about the needs of your toddler. And the fact of the matter is, whatever your child's temperament – flexible, feisty or cautious – all toddlers thrive on routine. At a time when they are going through so much change, and so much in their world is new and frightening, your toddler finds incredible comfort in the predictability of a routine. It makes them feel safe and secure, while offering freedom within boundaries – all of which are very important as your toddler becomes more independent and struggles to manage their emotions and strong impulses.

Here are three reasons why a routine is good for toddlers.

1 **It gives your toddler a sense of security.** *Your toddler is taking their first tentative steps into the world, and by creating a solid, predictable structure around them they will feel less fearful.*

2 **It will lessen separation anxiety.** *If your toddler knows that every morning, at roughly the same time, they will be taken to nursery, for example, this will help them to anticipate the situation and be less prone to fretting about your departure. Meanwhile, the consistency of collecting them will soon make your toddler realize that no matter what, you will always return.*

3 **It will help your toddler to learn.** *As stated previously, toddlers learn through repetition, and the familiar phrase 'do it again' is part of this process. So by doing the same things, day in and day out, you naturally create an excellent learning environment for your toddler.*

Here are three reasons why a routine will also benefit you.

1 **It will reduce power struggles.** *By providing your toddler with a regular pattern to their day, when they have their meals, what time they take their nap, when bath time is, etc. they will know exactly what to expect. And because your toddler always knows what is happening next, you will be far less likely to encounter resistance from them.*

2 **It will help you set clear boundaries and be consistent.** *Because a routine establishes a framework and sets limits, you will find it easier to be consistent about what is and is not acceptable behaviour and you will also be less likely to cave in under pressure.*

3 **It will give you the time to do the things you need to do.** *A routine better structures your day, and makes more efficient use of your time. This will enable you to do necessary chores during the day and thus prevent them from eating into your time in the evening.*

A ROUTINE DOESN'T HAVE TO BE BORING

For some people, the very mention of the word routine sends them running for the door. To them it implies a dull rigidity – an inflexibility where each day merges into the other, with little contrast or colour. But the fact is, a routine can be as strict or as loose as you like. It really can be tailored to what suits you, your toddler and the rest of the family. For example, some parents of toddlers will insist that breakfast is served at 7.30 a.m. precisely every single day. Perhaps their toddler wakes up ravenous and will start acting up if not fed immediately, or maybe the early start is dictated by the work patterns of the parents. Others, meanwhile, will happily pour out the cornflakes anytime within an hour of waking. Perhaps their timetable is less pressing or their child is simply more able to wait.

Top tip

The effectiveness of a daily routine is not based on doing something at exactly the same time each day, it is more about doing that something at around the same time each day.

Case study

For a long time, I really shunned the idea of a routine. My partner and I have always prided ourselves on being very easy-going and spontaneous. The idea of having to adhere to a daily timetable of events just felt so alien and went against everything we believed in. But they say a baby changes you, and in this respect Kalifa has most certainly changed us. While the idea of taking her to the restaurant with us of an evening was all very appealing, we soon discovered that the reality was quite different. Kalifa is now 18 months old and we call her our little routine queen. She's the sort of child who really needs her naps and if she's not tucked up in her cot by 7.30 p.m. at the latest, then all hell breaks loose. We try not to let Kalifa's routine rule us though. So if we want to go out for the day, rather than waiting until after Kalifa's nap, we'll simply time the journey so it coincides with it and she'll then nod off in the car. I'm now pregnant with our second child, and we'll definitely be following a routine from the outset with this baby.

CASE STUDY

Establishing a good routine for you and your toddler

Here are two examples of a toddler's routine. As you will see, Routine A is quite structured while Routine B is more flexible and loose. In both cases the toddlers were a little over two years old and no longer had a morning nap.

Routine A

7.00 a.m.	wake up
7.30 a.m.	get up, get dressed, have breakfast
8.30 a.m.	go for a walk
9.00 a.m.	play
10.00 a.m.	morning snack
12.00 p.m.	lunch
1.00 p.m.	nap
3.30 p.m.	afternoon snack
4.00 p.m.	outside play
5.00 p.m.	dinner
6.30 p.m.	bath, stories
7.00 p.m.	bed

Routine B

8.00–8.30 a.m.	wake up
9.00–10.00 a.m.	get up, get dressed, have breakfast
12.30–1.30 p.m.	lunch
2.00–4.00 p.m.	usually naps at some point
5.30–6.30 p.m.	dinner
7.00–7.30 p.m.	bath, stories
8.00–8.30 p.m.	bed

Top tip

If you want to establish a good toddler routine, one of the best places to start is with a list. Write down everything you have to get done in a given day, for example work, shopping, washing, cooking, etc. Then make a separate list of your toddler's needs – mealtimes, snacks, naps, playtime, bedtime (in as little or as much detail as you wish). Now examine the two lists and work out how you can best meet both sets of requirements over the course of a 12-hour day.

RULES ARE MADE FOR BREAKING, SOMETIMES

Remember that much of your toddler's routine is self-imposed and the world isn't going to cave in if the schedule isn't always kept. Okay, so your toddler might get a little hungry and whiny if you find yourself still dashing around the supermarket at dinnertime, but a late meal isn't going to cause anyone any lasting damage. Similarly, staying up late on the odd special occasion will have no long-term impact on your toddler's sleeping habits, although you might find they are a little cranky the next day.

Top tip
It will really help get your morning routine off to a better, less stressful start if you get up half an hour before your toddler. This way you can get yourself ready without any disturbance and then, when your toddler does get up, you can give them your undivided attention.

THE MOST COMMON ROUTINES

At its most basic, a routine need only accommodate mealtimes and bedtime, as these really are the most crucial elements of your toddler's day. Just by establishing regular times for breakfast, lunch, dinner and snacks and setting a time for bath, story and bed will ensure that your child's two most intrinsic needs are met – they will be eating and sleeping properly.

The mealtime routine
Here are five points to consider.

1 *It helps to forewarn a toddler that a mealtime is coming up, as they will then know that it will soon be time to stop what they are doing and come to the table.*

2 *The mealtime routine is about consistency. It is not about forcing your toddler to eat. You, as the parent, decide what and when food is served, your toddler will decide whether and how much to eat.*

3 *Sit down with your toddler to eat, even if you will be having your meal later. It will help make mealtimes a more sociable event.*

4 *As part of the mealtime routine, let your toddler have their own special eating chair and their own plate, cup and cutlery. This will all help to reinforce the familiarity and predictability of the situation.*

5 *Establish a clear signal for when the mealtime is over and it is okay for your toddler to get up and leave the table. It might take some time to achieve this goal but, through persistence, you will get there in the end.*

Did you know?

Studies have shown that having the same mealtime routine every day will enhance your child's willingness to try new foods.

Case study

Getting Xavier into a good mealtime routine hasn't been easy. I always try to serve his meals around the same time each day and, on the whole, he's a pretty good eater. But the problem is actually getting him to the table. He's often so engrossed in his play that making him stop and come and wash his hands results in a massive strop, with him throwing himself on the floor and refusing to budge. After much coaxing, he does come eventually, but the whole process is stressful and exhausting. Then, the other day, I decided to try something different. Rather than calling him to the table, I told him that we were going to play a game. He had to listen very carefully and when he heard me clap my hands that would mean that his food was ready. He was immediately captivated and as soon as I clapped, he was straight in the kitchen. I can't believe how much he loves this new 'game', and now he claps himself to let me know when he's finished eating.

The bedtime routine
Here are four points to consider:

1 *The bedtime routine can start immediately after dinner has finished, by choosing a quiet activity that you and your toddler can do together. This will help them to slowly wind down.*
2 *Giving a toddler a bath is an established part of most bedtime routines. It is the perfect signal that the day is drawing to a close and that it will soon be time to go to sleep.*
3 *The bedtime story is another common factor in the bedtime routine. Decide ahead of time how many books you are willing to read to your toddler (or how many times you will read them the same one) and let them know beforehand. Then stand firm, despite the inevitable pleas.*
4 *When it comes to the actual goodnights, some parents prefer to keep it short and sweet, while others are happy to linger until their toddler falls asleep. There is no right or wrong way – it is whatever works best for you and your toddler.*

Did you know?

A 2007 study of babies and toddlers found that those who had a consistent bedtime routine fell asleep faster, slept for longer stretches and woke less often during the night than those that were not in a routine.

Case study

While our bedtime routine takes an hour in total, the actual saying goodnight bit has always been pretty quick. We have this thing where we say goodnight to her toy animals. So after we've said: 'Goodnight Mr Monkey, goodnight Mr Bear', etc. I then say goodnight to Emily, give her a kiss, switch off the light and leave the room. That's it. No dragging it out. My brother and his family were staying with us a couple of weekends ago and he and his wife couldn't believe that Emily went down so quickly. All of their three children have insisted that either mummy or daddy lay with them until they fall asleep, which can sometimes take a good half an hour. I don't mean to sound harsh, but I honestly wouldn't have the patience. I don't mind devoting my entire day to Emily, but when it comes to the evening, well that's my time and I want to spend it with my husband, Gary. It's the only time we actually get to talk and find out what the other's been up to.

Insight

In my experience, many parents move the goal posts of a routine often without even realizing it, and are surprised when their toddler then pushes boundaries. Remember it is by doing the same thing over and over again that your toddler will learn to accept a situation and it becomes part of their everyday life.

THE RITUALS THAT BECOME PART OF A ROUTINE

Family life is made up of lots of little rituals, and as your child moves through the toddler years you will undoubtedly develop many more of these, which then become part of the fabric of your day-to-day life. Some of these rituals will evolve from health and hygiene issues, for example, washing hands before mealtimes and cleaning teeth before bed. Others will be more personal to you and your toddler, for example, perhaps you like to sing a lullaby to your toddler before tucking them in and saying goodnight, or maybe your toddler jumps into your bed for a quick cuddle first thing in the morning before getting up and dressed. These more personal rituals are what make your relationship with your toddler so special and unique. They also re-affirm to your toddler how much you love them and that their world is safe and secure, and in their push for greater independence the importance of this cannot be overestimated.

HELPING YOUR TODDLER COPE WITH
A BROKEN ROUTINE

A broken routine will not harm a toddler but it can be quite unsettling. Suddenly what they thought they could take for granted no longer seems to be the case.

Here are four things you could try to help lessen their distress:

1 *If possible, give your toddler warning that the routine is going to be broken. So if you usually go to the park in the afternoon, but won't be going today because the car is broken, let them know.*
2 *Try not to overcomplicate your explanation. A simple, 'No park today. The car is broken,' will suffice.*
3 *Say that you understand your toddler's upset. 'You feel really sad because we can't go, don't you?' will acknowledge your toddler's feelings.*
4 *Change little things every now and then in your toddler's routine. This will help your toddler be better able to deal with a more extreme break in routine during a crisis.*

GETTING A ROUTINE BACK ON TRACK

As stated previously, the occasional minor blip in your toddler's routine will not cause any real problems. But what to do when a routine completely falls to pieces as a result of extraordinary circumstances, such as through illness or while on holiday? Here are a few things to consider when trying to re-establish a routine.

▶ **Don't panic.** *Try calmly to re-establish the routine at the next appropriate opportunity. So, for example, if your toddler has been poorly and off their food, wait until they are feeling better and their appetite has returned before offering regular sit-down meals. As long as they are getting sufficient liquids, they will be fine.*
▶ **Be patient.** *It might take your toddler a day or two to get back into their routine. For example, going on holiday with a toddler*

is bound to throw them off balance as they become accustomed to their new environment. Equally it might take a few days to get back on track afterwards. But if you think about it, that is the same for everybody.

▶ **Be consistent.** *Once you decide that the time is right to re-establish the routine, stick with it. Perhaps your toddler has grown unused to sleeping in their own bed after an illness or a family holiday. Reassure your toddler that they will be fine sleeping in their own bed, just like before. They might be a bit unsettled for a couple of nights, but try not to waver – your toddler will soon realize that sleeping in their own bed is the norm.*

Case study

We'd had a wonderful holiday in France, staying at a friend's *gîte*, but because the place was quite small, we all shared a bedroom, which is something we've not done at home since Ryan was about two months old. Of course Ryan absolutely loved it, waking up beside Mummy and Daddy every morning. But the night we got back was awful. Ryan did not want to sleep in his own bedroom and kept saying, 'me sleep with you, me sleep with you'. After much toing and froing, he eventually dozed off, only to wake up a few hours later crying. I must say, none of us got much sleep that night, and I was tempted at one point just to give in and let him come in with us, which is something we've really tried not to do in the past. But we managed to resist and I'm so glad we did, because the next night we only had a few minor grumbles and the night after that he slept right through without a murmur. He's now completely back in synch, which is a massive relief. I'd definitely recommend staying firm and focused when trying to re-establish a routine.

10 THINGS TO REMEMBER

1 *Once your child begins to realize they are a separate person from you, the instinctive need to exert their independence kicks in. This becomes very pronounced in the toddler years and again in adolescence. As a parent, it isn't always easy to accommodate this desire for independence, but remember, it is a perfectly natural one.*

2 *Your toddler's need for independence will manifest itself in increasingly oppositional behaviour, for example refusing to do what you ask and repeatedly saying 'no' to any request.*

3 *To reduce the number of times your toddler says 'no', teach them alternative words, and also try to limit your use of the word too. Save 'no' for the times when there really isn't an alternative, such as when their welfare or safety is at stake.*

4 *In tandem with your child's burgeoning independence will usually be a marked increase in separation anxiety. This tends to reach a peak at around 18 months, and tapers off as your toddler comes to realize that you are a permanent presence in their lives, albeit one that will have to leave them occasionally.*

5 *Part of your toddler's push for independence is testing limits and pushing boundaries. They need to see that what you say really is the case, and that if they do continue to misbehave there will be consequences.*

6 *To counterbalance some of the more challenging behaviour you're likely to encounter with your toddler, try to focus on the behaviour you want from them, rather than drawing attention to the behaviour you don't. For example, rather than saying 'stop jumping on the couch', say 'I really like it when you sit down nicely beside me'.*

7   *To enable your toddler to enjoy their increasing independence and explore their environment safely, it will really help to toddler-proof your home.*

8   *Allowing your toddler to feel that they are making their own decisions by giving them a limited choice is a very effective way of staving off power struggles. Remember to stick with what your toddler has chosen as they need to learn to live with the consequences of their decisions.*

9   *Another highly effective way of dealing with power struggles is to simply not engage. Obviously this won't be possible all of the time, but by choosing your battles wisely you will save yourself an awful lot of aggravation.*

10 *Toddlers tend to thrive on a routine. Being able to predict what is going to happen in their lives makes them feel safe and secure at a time of incredible upheaval.*

4

Typical toddler flashpoints

In this chapter you will learn:
- *what causes a flashpoint*
- *the emotions behind a flashpoint*
- *common toddler triggers*
- *ways to avoid battles when getting dressed*
- *techniques to make shopping easier*
- *tips for surviving long car journeys*
- *ways to avoid car sickness*
- *how to handle squabbling siblings*
- *ways to cut down on rivalry.*

Why certain situations throw toddlers into a tailspin

In the previous chapter we looked at your toddler's natural desire for greater independence and how, by structuring their environment to feel as safe and secure as possible, you can allow your toddler to push the boundaries in a way that is acceptable to you both.

But of course, no one's environment can be perfectly regulated at all times. The reality of life is that sometimes circumstances and situations will conspire to throw your toddler into a tailspin. These inevitable flashpoints provoke such strong emotions and/or sensations in toddlers that it is almost impossible for them to control themselves. At these times you are likely to see a sudden deterioration in your toddler's behaviour which, at its worst, can lead to a full-blown tantrum (see Chapter 5).

The good news is that these flashpoints can invariably be anticipated and, with a bit of foresight and careful handling, the reaction they arouse in your toddler can be greatly reduced and sometimes avoided completely.

The emotions behind a flashpoint

Before looking at specific flashpoints, it helps to examine some of the strong emotions or sensations that your toddler is likely to be experiencing during such an episode.

1 **Frustration.** *Your toddler is still trying to get to grips with their world, and when they find they are incapable of doing something it comes as a huge blow. Perhaps your toddler is struggling to do up the buttons on their coat, or maybe they cannot make you understand what it is that they want, such as their yellow cup and not the blue one.*

2 **That desire for independence.** *Your toddler may begin to find any form of restraint upsetting, for example, you may suddenly find it a battle getting them into their high chair.*

3 **Hunger and/or tiredness.** *It sounds obvious, but a hungry and/or tired toddler is a grumpy toddler and, as such, much more liable to mood swings. In this state your toddler is more likely to become fractious and less able to cope with everyday situations.*

4 **Being denied something.** *A toddler doesn't understand abstract concepts such as tomorrow or later, and they certainly don't understand when something might not be suitable for them. This is why when your toddler is refused something it is such a big deal – they can feel like their whole world has just collapsed. Similarly, sharing is a completely alien concept. For example, if your toddler is forced to share a favourite toy with*

a playmate, for them that is tantamount to it being taken away from them.

5 **Jealousy and competitiveness.** *Another reason why your toddler is not yet able to process the concept of sharing is because they are unable to see another person's point of view. For example, the said playmate with whom they have had to share their toy has now become a rival. Jealousy in a toddler is also very common when they have to share their parent with one or more other children.*

6 **Wanting attention.** *Toddlers love being the centre of attention, so when you are preoccupied or busy doing something that doesn't involve them they can often feel very aggrieved. For example, perhaps your toddler has a tendency to behave badly when you are chatting on the phone.*

7 **Feeling bored.** *An under-stimulated toddler can be just as challenging as an over-stimulated one, especially if your child is of an active disposition. For example, a toddler who has been cooped up indoors all day will become increasingly irritable and short-tempered. They will have an excess of energy with no way of properly expending it.*

8 **Becoming overwhelmed.** *On some days and in certain situations, things can simply become too much for a toddler. They are overloaded with emotions, many of them conflicting, and it reaches a point when they simply can't cope. For example, perhaps your toddler has spent an afternoon at a children's birthday party, and the mixture of excitement, occasional anger, frustration and eventual tiredness tips them over the edge.*

Top tip

Take another look at the above list of emotions and sensations, one or more of which your toddler is likely to experience when they hit a flashpoint. Now, instead of reading 'toddler', read 'yourself', because as an adult, these are probably exactly the same emotions and sensations that provoke, upset and distress you. The difference is that you have learnt to control your reaction to them, while your toddler has just started to learn.

The common toddler triggers

There are many situations that can trigger a strong reaction in a toddler, and here are four of the most common.

GETTING YOUR TODDLER DRESSED

Maybe your toddler starts running away from you when you suggest putting their clothes on, or perhaps they refuse to wear what has been chosen or insist on wearing something totally inappropriate. Sometimes actually keeping a toddler's clothes on once dressed is the challenge. Whatever the problem, dressing a toddler can be a minefield and for some parents it becomes a daily battle, and one that both they and their toddler dread.

What is going on?
For your toddler, the process of getting dressed can feel very restrictive. They are being forced to stand still and then have their body manipulated into clothing. In addition, they may feel unhappy with what they are being made to wear, all of which goes against your toddler's desire for greater independence and can lead to anger and frustration on their part and yours.

What you can do
It is time-consuming, but let your toddler help you get them dressed. For example, they can put on their socks while you can do the more difficult job of putting on their trousers. As your toddler gets older and more dexterous, you can encourage them to dress themselves. To better do this, try choosing clothing that slips on or has an elastic waistband or Velcro, as your toddler will find this far easier than zips, buttons, straps and hooks. If your toddler wants a say in what they wear, whenever possible let them. This is where offering a simple choice really proves effective. So, for example, your toddler can choose either the stripy T-shirt or the bright green one, and both of these options are perfectly acceptable to you.

If you know you're going to be in a mad rush in the morning, I've found that it helps to go through clothing choices the night before, and explain to your toddler clearly and firmly that what they've chosen is what they will be wearing in the morning.

Did you know?

A toddler sits with their knees turned out and naturally puts shoes on with the fastenings on the inside where they can see them, although most shoes are designed to have the fastening on the outside. This is why your toddler will invariably put their shoes on the wrong feet.

Case study

Oscar is quite a headstrong little lad and every morning I was having this huge battle getting him dressed. Basically he point-blank refused and when I tried to take his pyjamas off he'd run away. During the week I'm normally in quite a rush to get out of the house to drop Oscar off at the childminder's and get into work, so as you can imagine, the last thing I wanted to be doing was chasing around trying to catch a two-year-old. Then when I did finally catch him, I had this ridiculous struggle putting the clothes on him, with Oscar immediately trying to take them off again. When I told the childminder what was happening, she suggested that I save myself the aggro and bring Oscar to her in his pyjamas and she'd help him put his clothes on later. But when I tried this Oscar was beside himself. He did not want to still be wearing his pyjamas in the car and got really upset. Since then though, it's been amazing – Oscar actually wants to get dressed in the morning. As far as he's concerned, anything's better than wearing his pyjamas in the car!

GOING SHOPPING WITH YOUR TODDLER

Look around any supermarket on any given day and the chances are you will find a protesting toddler. Perhaps they are throwing a tantrum, prostrate in the middle of the aisle, or maybe they are screaming for sweeties which their parent is steadfastly refusing to buy. Shopping in general, and in supermarkets in particular, seems to have an incredible ability to bring out the worst in a toddler.

What is going on?
If you think about it, it is hardly surprising that a shopping trip is such a common toddler flashpoint. Your toddler usually needs to be strapped in and/or restrained and, as a result, they are being denied the opportunity to run around and touch all the lovely goodies so temptingly on display. What is more, you are also probably denying them sweets or whatever else has taken their fancy, which is causing even more anger and frustration. Add to this the fact that your attention is usually elsewhere (Have you remembered the soap powder? What shall we have for tea tonight?), plus the sheer boredom factor – then you can see it is a combustible combination of emotions and one that frequently leads to an eruption.

What you can do
Timing is important when taking a toddler shopping. Try to go after naptime and make sure they have recently been fed. If possible, it is also worth avoiding the weekends and going mid-week when it is much quieter. Once there, try to involve your toddler in the shopping process. For example, pretend you are lost and ask them to help you find a certain aisle, or let them choose which food they would prefer and allow them to hold some of it or help put a few items in the shopping trolley. If you make doing the shopping as much like a game as possible, your toddler will be having far too much fun to start playing up. Also, take a few of their favourite toys along with you and pull them out when you can see they are starting to get bored. Finally, try to be as organized as possible when doing the shopping. If you go about your shopping systematically you will get through it much faster.

Insight

A game that I've found to really captivate and engage toddlers when shopping is the silly mummy game, where you say 'look at these delicious bananas', while holding a bunch of grapes. They'll love constantly correcting you as you go down the aisles.

Top tip

Writing a shopping list will really help speed up the shopping process. Try organizing your list according to where each item is located in the store, so you don't have to waste time going back and forth with your protesting toddler.

Case study

Shopping with Eliza used to be awful. The first ten minutes or so would be okay, but then she'd get restless, stuck there in the seat of the shopping trolley, and would start whining to get out. I'd then get her out and let her walk beside the trolley, but she soon got bored and would run off and grab things randomly off the shelves, causing absolute havoc. If I then tried to put her back in the trolley, she'd start kicking and screaming and refuse to go back in. As you can imagine the weekly supermarket shop soon became my idea of hell, and I'm sure Eliza wasn't enjoying it much either! But then our local supermarket introduced these kids' trolleys and I can honestly say they have transformed our shopping experience. Now Eliza loves pushing along her little trolley and putting things in it. She feels that she's helping me and I'm just so relieved not to have a crying toddler on my hands. The only downside is that I sometimes get to the checkout and find a strange item in her trolley – last week it was a tin of dog food and we haven't got a dog!

Insight

I'd recommend taking a stash of healthy snacks, such as carrot sticks or a small box of raisins, on supermarket trips and using them as a form of distraction or offering them up as an alternative to the sweeties they're bound to spot.

Did you know?

According to research, the average mum faces a challenging episode with their toddler as often as once every three to nine minutes when at home, while that figure rises to once every 48 seconds when in a supermarket.

TAKING YOUR TODDLER ON LONG CAR JOURNEYS

Sitting in the confines of a big metal box for several hours with little to do or see would not be many people's idea of fun. But for a boisterous toddler it can be pure torture. No wonder they keep asking you: 'Are we there yet?' Your toddler is just desperate for the ordeal to end. Tempers then become frayed – theirs as well as yours – and by the time you do finally reach your destination, everyone is at the end of their tether. Add to this the fact that many toddlers experience travel sickness, and it is easy to see why a long journey is such a common flashpoint.

What is going on?
A car really is like a prison to your toddler. Not only are they stuck in a confined space, they are also strapped into a car seat with very little room for manoeuvre. This doesn't sit well with a newly independent toddler, who may start protesting at the very prospect of going in their car seat, getting things off to a stressful start before the journey has even begun. As with the supermarket experience, a lengthy car journey will also provoke extreme boredom in your toddler, while again your attention is likely to be elsewhere, especially if you are driving.

What you can do
Whenever possible, try to time your car journey to coincide with a nap, or you could consider travelling at night if you are planning on stopping over. This way your toddler is likely to spend most

of the journey sound asleep. And at these times the roads will probably be emptier too. If this isn't possible, then distracting your toddler is your best bet. Songs and story tapes are great for this, as are crayons and paper, or better still, why not buy a magnetic drawing board that is compact and portable, and can be used over and over again? Meanwhile, a good supply of healthy drinks and snacks will stop them becoming dehydrated and stave off hunger and boredom, while regular stops will allow your toddler to have a run around and will make them feel like they are on a day out instead of just a boring journey from A to B.

Insight

If your toddler is a really terrible traveller, I think it's worth considering taking the train instead of driving. Children love train journeys as there's much more to see and do, and it will give you the opportunity to spend some quality time together.

Coping with travel sickness

If your toddler suffers from travel sickness, the most likely cause is that their brain is receiving conflicting signals. Their eyes are sending messages to their brain that are different from those being reported by the delicate balance mechanisms of the inner ear. So, for example, your toddler may be looking at a board book and their eyes are seeing the motionless book, but the balance mechanisms are saying that they are moving. If your toddler starts feeling sick, try to get them to focus forwards on objects a distance ahead, for example a lorry or tractor, or even a tree, as this will help to get the conflicting signals back in synch.

Other causes can include:

▶ *strong smells in the car, such as a heavy perfume or an air freshener*
▶ *routes that have lots of windy roads or bumps and cause your toddler's head to jerk back and forth.*

Case study

My mum and dad live about 100 miles in one direction while my
husband's parents live about the same distance the other way.
We really want our two sons, Fin, three, and Max, 18 months, to
be close to their grandparents, so we try to visit both sets at least
once a month. You'd think, therefore, that we would be pretty
good at long car journeys, but up until recently the exact opposite
has been true. At the outset the boys would be fine, but soon the
backseat would turn into a battleground, and I would spend the
rest of the drive constantly turning around, telling them to stop
fighting. By the time we finally arrived, my husband and I would
be in foul moods, while the boys would be grizzly and exhausted,
neither of which made for a very pleasant start to our visit. Then
my husband came up with the idea of travelling at night and it's
been a complete revelation. I get the boys bathed and ready in their
pyjamas and dressing gowns and they're usually both fast asleep
by the time we hit the motorway. Then when we arrive we simply
carry them straight up to bed, leaving us free to enjoy the rest of
the evening with our folks. Perfect!

MANAGING SIBLING SQUABBLES

Whether in the toddler years or older, sibling squabbles are
an inevitable fact of family life. But what makes them such a
flashpoint with toddlers is their reluctance to share and their
inability to view a situation from another person's perspective.
Around a sibling, one of your toddler's most used words will
probably be 'mine' as they fiercely protect what they perceive to
be their property. In addition, an argument with a sibling can

quickly escalate into physical aggression when a toddler is involved because, without the vocabulary, they are unable to express their anger and frustration in any other way.

What is going on?
When siblings argue they are in fact learning quite a few valuable lessons, including how to deal with others of a similar age, how to negotiate, when to compromise, how far they can go with the physical aggression and what it is like to feel anger towards someone they love. In short, the bickering and jockeying for position that goes on between siblings is all part of your toddler's development into a social being.

What you can do
While you won't be able to stop your children from arguing with each other completely, you can certainly avert many brewing battles by teaching them to take turns. This doesn't mean that they always have to play together – sometimes they will want to do their own thing. Also, when learning to take turns your toddler may initially feel that because they have not got something immediately, be it a disputed toy or a favoured seat, they will never get it. But persevere, as they will eventually grasp the concept. And while they are waiting for their turn, why not suggest another activity for them to do?

When your children are bickering, try to resist the urge to immediately step in and resolve the conflict for them – it is important that they start learning how to sort out issues on their own. If, however, the same squabble is occurring again and again or they begin hitting, biting, smacking, etc. then of course you will need to intervene. Probably the best tactic is to separate them. Everyone needs a little space and time alone, and toddlers in particular are often unaware of that need or lack the skill to articulate it.

Did you know?

On average, siblings spend more time together during childhood than they do with their parents.

Four ways to cut down on the sibling rivalry

1 **Try not to make comparisons.** *For example, perhaps your eldest child could dress themselves by the time they were three years old, while your younger one is still struggling at this age. Pointing out this fact to them in the hope of chivvying them along will only aggravate feelings of jealousy. Although your intentions may be innocent, a child is likely to hear the message, 'You love them more than me'.*

2 **Remember, every child is a unique individual.** *Children have their own temperament and personality. Perhaps one prefers their own company while the other is a far more social creature. It is important to respect these differences. You can also help to bring out the best in them by encouraging their unique qualities. Try promoting their different interests so that each child excels in their own way. When a child's special talents are recognized, it sets them apart from their siblings and builds up their self-esteem.*

3 **Set aside special one-to-one time with each child.** *Whether it is doing a specific activity together, such as going swimming or simply snuggling up on the couch for a story, these are the times when you can really focus on each child, without interruption from a sibling. And by doing this you will greatly diminish their battle for your attention.*

4 **Try not to apportion blame.** *When your children are fighting it is tempting to take sides, to try to assess who started it, and blame one child. But when siblings fight, it is often hard to sort out who really did what. Instead of taking sides, allow each child to tell their side of the story and listen. If you are impartial when your children squabble they will be less likely to use it as a way of getting your attention.*

Insight

I'd recommend encouraging your children to do separate activities at as early an age as possible as not only will it give them their 'special thing' that distinguishes them from their sibling, it will also give them space and time apart.

All siblings squabble and siblings between the ages of two and four will, on average, have a conflict about once every nine minutes.

Case study

Corey and Kelsy are only a little over a year apart in age. I wanted to have them as close together as possible so they could be friends. There was a four-year age gap between my sister and me and when I was little she didn't want anything to do with me – I was considered far too much of a baby, and by the time we were both teenagers, we hated each other's guts. But I'm starting to question my thinking because at the moment my pair are fighting like cat and dog. If Corey puts down a toy and Kelsy picks it up, there are screams and tantrums from Corey. Even though he's stopped playing with it, he'll say: 'It's my toy!' Then there are the arguments over who is sitting on what chair – it really gets ridiculous. And just the other week in the car Kelsy started moaning that Corey was looking out of her window! I must admit, I did laugh at that one. When the bickering gets unbearable I try to remind myself that they'll probably be fine when they're older. Just look at my sister and me – since we've both left home and established our own lives we really have become the best of friends.

CASE STUDY

10 THINGS TO REMEMBER

1   *Because it is impossible to always regulate and control your toddler's environment, they will inevitably face situations that provoke strong reactions. These situations are known as flashpoints and the good news is that they can usually be predicted.*

2   *There are many emotions behind a flashpoint, ranging from attention seeking to boredom, but perhaps the most prominent is frustration from failing to be able to do something or feeling that they have no choice or are being denied.*

3   *Many toddler flashpoints also cause frustration and upset in you, but the difference is that you have learnt to control your reaction, while your toddler has not.*

4   *If getting your toddler dressed is proving to be a daily flashpoint, it will help to give them a sense of control if you offer them a simple choice of what to wear and then let them help you put their clothes on.*

5   *Shopping is one of the most common toddler triggers, so try to time your supermarket trip so that your toddler isn't tired and/or hungry and get them involved in the whole shopping process.*

6   *Write a shopping list before you go, organized according to where products are located. You'll be amazed at how much time this can save.*

7   *If long car journeys are your toddler's biggest bugbear, try timing your trip to coincide with their nap or perhaps consider driving at night.*

8   *Songs and story tapes, crayons and paper, and even a special little travelling bag filled with unexpected knick-knacks will all help take your toddler's mind off a long journey.*

9 *Toddlers invariably struggle in their dealings with siblings, largely because they have yet to grasp the concept of sharing. Persevere with teaching your children to take turns as it will eventually pay dividends.*

10 *Remember, however, that a certain number of sibling squabbles are inevitable and do in fact provide your children with invaluable life lessons.*

5

Temper tantrums and how
to survive them

In this chapter you will learn:
* *why tantrums occur*
* *when they are most frequent*
* *why some toddlers are more prone to tantrums*
* *about different tantrum types and different tantrum levels*
* *techniques for avoiding tantrums*
* *what to do when a tantrum strikes*
* *how to handle public tantrums*
* *what to do when your toddler has a tantrum in front of a sibling*
* *how to deal with twins having a tantrum*
* *tips on handling other people's toddlers.*

What is a tantrum?

A temper tantrum is the behaviour that parents of toddlers dread the most. To witness a temper tantrum is a bit like watching the human equivalent of a volcanic eruption. You have heard the initial grumblings that have gradually grown from a whine to a cry, and now things have reached boiling point. The toddler in question has become completely incapable of containing their anger and/or frustration any longer, and it all comes spewing out in a totally uncontrollable manner, be it throwing themselves on the floor, screaming, kicking, hitting, breath-holding or perhaps a combination of all of these. To see such intense, raw emotion and obvious distress in any child, let alone your own, can be very upsetting. No wonder tantrums have an almost mythical status, for a full-blown temper tantrum is indeed a force of nature.

WHY TANTRUMS HAPPEN

Despite their near mythical status, there is no real mystery as to why tantrums occur so frequently in toddlers. It is simply an immature response to feeling cross or thwarted. Just as we adults can become exasperated and angry when our plans go awry or our needs are not met, so does your toddler. But whereas we have developed the skills to express our anger and emotions in a relatively controlled manner – although most of us are still prone to the occasional bit of door slamming or cursing under our breath – young children have not. Their ability to reason is very restricted. A toddler is still learning concepts such as time and patience and lives for the here and now. The words 'soon' and 'later' have little meaning for them. In a toddler, it is little wonder that frustration can build up very quickly and may then be expressed in the only way they know how – by having a tantrum.

Insight

When your toddler has their first few tantrums, I've found that parents are often left feeling upset and confused, wondering what they could have done differently. It's important not to blame yourself. In time you will realize that tantrums happen and it's no one's fault.

Did you know?

Tantrums most often happen in the presence of a toddler's main carer. This is because the child feels safe and confident enough of that person's reactions to be able to behave in such a way. So the next time your toddler is throwing a

(Contd)

tantrum in front of you, try viewing it as a compliment, although it probably doesn't feel like one!

WHY TANTRUMS ARE NORMAL

As unpleasant as a tantrum is for both you and your toddler, it is worth remembering that it is a perfectly normal part of your child's development. Through tantrums, your toddler is starting to learn how to regulate and control their emotions. It is a process that takes many years, but once learnt, your toddler will be able to:

▶ *recognize what they are feeling*
▶ *show those feelings in ways that don't hurt themselves or others*
▶ *cope with their emotions.*

In short, tantrums often mark your child's first step on the road to becoming a caring, sharing, compassionate human being.

HOW COMMON ARE TANTRUMS?

It is estimated that 83 per cent of all two-year-olds have temper tantrums, so it is quite rare for a child to go through the toddler years without ever having one. Tantrums generally begin at around the age of 12 to 18 months, peak between two and three years, before tapering off considerably by the age of four, and becoming virtually non-existent in most five-year-olds. But while most toddlers have tantrums, some may only ever have one or two, while for others it can become a regular event.

Did you know?

One in five two-year-olds is estimated to have two tantrums a day – but remember, this means four out of five don't!

84

The tantrum-prone toddler

So what makes one toddler more prone to tantrums than another?
As with much of understanding your toddler's behaviour, your
child's individual personality is partly the key. It is generally
recognized that the following four characteristics can make a
toddler more prone to tantrums:

1 **High activity levels.** *The toddler who is in perpetual motion is
   burning so much energy that they can easily become depleted
   and this is when tempers can become frayed and tantrums
   become more likely.*
2 **Low rhythmicity.** *If a toddler has irregular patterns and finds
   it difficult to slot into a routine, then their sleeping and eating
   are likely to be affected. Tiredness and/or hunger are major
   contributory factors when it comes to toddler tantrums.*
3 **Low adaptability.** *A toddler who struggles to adjust to change
   and finds it hard to cope with a disruption in routine is more
   prone to meltdowns when things do not go according to plan.*
4 **High intensity.** *When a toddler has intense emotional reactions
   they can display tremendous exuberance. But the flipside is
   that they can also throw huge tantrums.*

Knowing whether your toddler has some, or perhaps all, of these
characteristics will place you in a better position to cope with
their tantrums and work out effective strategies to avoid them.
For example, if your toddler is the sort of child who never sits
still, then pre-empt the energy slump at the tail end of the day by
insisting that they do take a lunchtime nap or even just half an
hour's quiet time. Similarly, the toddler who has difficulty adapting
to transition may need extra explanation and more reassurance
than one who adjusts easily.

Case study

At 14 months old I don't think Lois has had a full-blown tantrum
yet, but over the past few months she certainly seems to be working

herself up to one. I must admit, I laugh when she throws herself on the floor when I tell her she can't have something. But I don't think my husband found it particularly funny when she recently decided to lie prostrate in the supermarket aisle, kicking and screaming. Last weekend, however, she took us both by surprise. We'd spent the whole day at the zoo and she really had the loveliest time. We'd done all the things she'd wanted and had spent ages in the animal petting area, letting her stroke the bunnies. So when it was time to go, we thought she would come easily. But oh how wrong can you be! Lois had been having such a lovely time that she simply didn't want to leave and no amount of coaxing and persuading could convince her otherwise. In the end we had to forcibly carry her out. She really was hysterical and by the time we'd got her to the car, her eyes were red and swollen from all the crying. Thankfully she sobbed herself to sleep on the journey home. But both of us were slightly taken aback by the ferocity of her reaction, and I guess that's just the beginning.

Top tip

Try to get into the habit of giving your toddler a signal that you will be packing up, going out, moving on or whatever, about five minutes before you plan to do so. At first they won't understand what five minutes is, but after a while they will get used to it and many tantrums will be averted. Nobody likes to drop everything at a moment's notice, especially when they are enjoying themselves – and yet we often expect toddlers to do just that!

OTHER CONTRIBUTORY FACTORS

As well as your toddler's temperament, other factors that contribute to a child's tendency to have tantrums include:

▶ *tiredness*
▶ *hunger*

- ▶ *your toddler's age and stage of development*
- ▶ *stress in your toddler's environment*
- ▶ *underlying behavioural, developmental or health conditions (see page 109 for when to seek help).*

Insight

Making sure your toddler gets enough sleep, including their afternoon nap, is, I believe, one of the best ways to limit tantrums. An over-tired toddler is like a ticking time bomb, with the slightest upset setting them off.

Food for thought: the link between additives and tantrums

If your toddler seems particularly prone to tantrums, it might be worth double-checking the labels of the food and drink you are giving them. A government-funded study found a definite link between certain food colourings and preservatives and a deterioration in toddler mood and behaviour. The findings were based on reports from parents after 277 three-year-olds from the Isle of Wight took part in the month-long study, in which for the first two weeks they consumed a juice drink that contained additives commonly found in popular crisps, sweets and fizzy drinks. For the remaining two weeks, the toddlers drank a placebo fruit juice, identical in appearance, but without the additives. Indeed, it was found that consuming the food additives resulted in tantrums in as many as 25 per cent of toddlers, which is one in four! These are the names and E numbers to watch out for:

- ▶ *Tartrazine = E102*
- ▶ *Sunset Yellow = E110*
- ▶ *Carmoisine = E122*
- ▶ *Ponceau 4R = E124*
- ▶ *Sodium Benzoate = E211.*

Types of tantrums

When tantrums do strike, as they almost inevitably will, it is possible to identify two distinct types:

1 **The frustration tantrum.** *This occurs when your toddler does not get the result they want or they fail to achieve something quickly enough. For example, your toddler is not able to carry out a task or is not able to make their needs known. The frustration tantrum tends to occur more frequently in younger toddlers who are still mastering their verbal skills and manual dexterity.*
2 **The demanding tantrum.** *This will tend to happen when your toddler has been denied something that they want, such as sweets at the supermarket checkout or that extra half an hour playing in the park. There can be little doubt that your toddler does genuinely want what they can't have and is terribly upset at being denied it, but the fact remains that this tantrum is also about pushing the boundaries, and testing your resolve. As such, the demanding tantrum is far more prevalent in the older toddler.*

Did you know?

The average tantrum lasts approximately 11 minutes, although they can be as short as 30 seconds or as long as 25 minutes.

Signs of a tantrum

Some signs of a tantrum are more common than others.

Common signs
The three most common signs that your toddler is having a tantrum are:

1 *Your toddler is crying, screaming or shouting.*
2 *Your toddler is arching their back or tensing their body.*
3 *Your toddler is flailing their arms around.*

Less common signs
These signs are more extreme, but are thankfully less common:

1 *Your toddler is kicking, biting, scratching, hair-pulling or pinching other people.*
2 *Your toddler is throwing or breaking things.*
3 *Your toddler is head-banging, breath-holding or inflicting self-injury.*

Insight
In my experience, breath-holding can be one of the most worrying signs of a tantrum for parents, with some toddlers fainting as a result. This looks far worse than it is, because once the toddler has passed out their breathing will resume normally.

The tantrum spectrum

Having looked at the various causes and types of tantrum, as well as the more and less common signs, you can see that one toddler's tantrum can be very different from another's. And indeed, your toddler may throw wildly different tantrums depending on age and circumstances. The fact is, the word 'tantrum' encompasses quite a wide spectrum of toddler reactions and emotions.

THE TRAFFIC LIGHT SYSTEM

To help manage your toddler's tantrums, it is good to have an understanding of the level of tantrum you are dealing with, and this is where the traffic light system of classification proves very useful. Perhaps your toddler will move through the various levels of tantrum, i.e. from green (moderate) to amber (average) to red (extreme), as their anger and/or frustration grows, or maybe they are the sort of child who rarely ever goes beyond green. Some toddlers, however, can hit red almost from the outset. Take a look at the different levels of tantrum below to help you better assess your toddler's tantrums.

GREEN This is really the mildest form of tantrum, where your toddler is showing clear signs of brewing anger and frustration, perhaps through grizzling, whining and crying, and bucking their body in remonstrance, but they are still receptive to the world around them.

AMBER This level of tantrum is far more vocal and much more physical, with your toddler perhaps hitting you, throwing themselves on the floor, screaming and shouting. But despite their evident fury, they are still conscious of their actions.

RED Otherwise known as the full-blown tantrum, this is the emotional equivalent of the previously mentioned volcanic eruption. Your toddler is completely overwhelmed by their own internal rage, their eyes are glazed over and they quite literally shake with anger. They are oblivious to what is happening around them. This last level of tantrum can be extremely distressing to witness, but it is worth remembering that it is also very upsetting for your toddler, who is not doing it out of naughtiness, but because they have lost all their self-control.

Case study

CASE STUDY

I'll never forget the first time Kirsty had a full-blown tantrum. It was unlike anything I've ever seen before and it really took me by surprise. It happened one evening, shortly after we'd come back from holiday, so I think she was probably feeling a bit unsettled. She didn't want to go to sleep and started crying. But when I went in to calm her, Kirsty was having none of it. She started kicking and screaming and when I picked her up she even whacked me in the face. It was awful. Looking at her, I quickly realized that she honestly didn't know what she was doing – it was like she was possessed. She was shaking with rage and her eyes were totally unfocused, she was just completely consumed by her own anger. I tried walking her around the house in the hope that a change of scenery would snap her out of it, but none of the usual tricks would work. In the end I just sat, holding her tightly, while she wriggled and fought, until eventually the anger subsided. She then started sobbing. I think the whole experience had terrified her. I had to sit there for about 20 minutes, stroking her head and calming her down. Finally she dozed off in my arms and I popped her back into her bed, and to look at her lying there, you would never have known what had just happened.

Top tip

It is worth remembering that a full-blown temper tantrum is incredibly frightening for your toddler. They have completely lost control of themselves and the violent, screaming, furious creature they have become is someone they do not recognize and, as such, find profoundly shocking. There is no point in even attempting to reason with or discipline a toddler who is in the throes of a full-blown tantrum. It is simply a question of ensuring that your toddler is safe and waiting for the storm to pass.

Ways to avoid tantrums

One of the best ways to cope with a tantrum is to avoid it in the first place, which, with a bit of practice, isn't as hard as it sounds. It will help if you put the following strategies into place from the outset:

▶ **Be your toddler's role model.** *Try to set a good example – avoid getting angry or shouting in rage as this will only send the signal to your toddler that this is acceptable behaviour. If you can, whenever possible, keep calm and avoid raising your voice in anger when around your toddler, as this will show them that it is possible to control strong feelings, and they will eventually learn by example.*

▶ **Remember the importance of praise.** *All too often we lavish attention on a toddler who is misbehaving or having a tantrum, while a toddler who is quietly playing in the corner is all but ignored. Try practising positive reinforcement with your toddler by vocalizing your pleasure when they behave well. This will help to encourage more of the behaviour you want. For more on positive reinforcement, see Chapter 6.*

AVOIDANCE TECHNIQUES

As you move through the toddler years, you will find that you become increasingly adept at employing the following techniques:

▶ **Recognizing the signs of frustration.** *Over time, you will learn to pick up on the warning signs that your toddler is growing increasingly frustrated. For example, perhaps your toddler has a certain type of whine that often precedes an implosion. If you can spot these signs early enough, you will be able to step in and avoid trouble. Maybe your toddler is trying to do a puzzle that is too difficult for them and they are becoming upset that despite trying really hard, they simply cannot do it. Try offering them a helping hand, or suggest another activity they will be able to do.*

▶ **Knowing your toddler's flashpoints.** *If you know that certain things are likely to set your child off, for example boredom at the supermarket or vying for your attention while you chat on the phone, it might be worth avoiding these situations whenever possible.*

▶ **Giving a choice.** *As discussed in Chapter 3, giving your toddler some say in what is happening in their lives, be it what they wear, what they eat or perhaps where they go, greatly reduces their feelings of frustration and ultimately results in far fewer tantrums.*

▶ **Choosing your battles wisely.** *Again, this is a strategy that was explored in Chapter 3, and involves avoiding fights with your toddler over little things and saving your insistence on something for when it really does matter, for example when issues of health and/or safety are at stake.*

▶ **Distracting your toddler.** *One of the most effective methods of defusing a brewing tantrum in a younger toddler is by taking their mind off of whatever is upsetting them. Distraction can be as simple as pretending that something amazing has just happened outside the window to offering them something a bit strange or unusual to play with. You will find that once your toddler's attention has been diverted, they quickly forget whatever it was that was about to set them off.*

Insight

I've often witnessed experienced parents juggling several of the above techniques at once when attempting to head off a brewing tantrum. It's amazing how such strategies eventually become second nature and much of the time you'll probably not even be aware that you're using them.

Case study

Mealtimes often used to descend into a tantrum with Erin. She'd get bored and irritable at being made to sit at the table and she would then start grizzling and lose interest in her food. Fed up with the daily battle, I decided to try and lighten the atmosphere a bit and turn her bad behaviour into a story. So I started telling her about this little girl called Erica, who never, ever ate her breakfast and how her poor mummy would try to tempt her with more and more elaborate foods, such as boiled dinosaur eggs and bread especially toasted by a dragon's fiery breath. Erin became so engrossed in the story that she completely forgot she was about to throw a wobbly and I even managed to get her to finish off her bowl of cereal by insisting she take a mouthful before I would continue with the tale. I've since employed this distraction technique in all sorts of situations and it really does work. Just last week Erin started to lose it in a cafe when I told her that she couldn't have a cake. All I had to say was: 'Listen Erin, do you want mummy to tell you a story about the naughty little boy who gobbled up all the birthday cake?' and she immediately stopped whining and demanded to hear the story.

Top tip

To use distraction techniques with an older toddler, it helps to be a bit creative. Whereas once a: 'Look at that dickey-bird in the tree' would have made your toddler forget that they definitely didn't want to remain strapped in their pushchair, try it on the older toddler and you will get a look of 'so what?' and the grizzling will quickly resume. That is when a bit of creativity and imagination comes into play. 'Look at that bush. Do you think that's the sort of place where a Gruffalo would hide?' is far more likely to get the desired result.

Coping with tantrums

Sometimes, despite using the above avoidance techniques, a tantrum simply cannot be averted. Your toddler, for whatever reason, has gone into meltdown. How you choose to handle the tantrum obviously depends on what type of tantrum it is – frustration or demanding – and also at what level it is at – green, amber or red. In addition, your toddler's age and personality should be taken into account when choosing the best course of action.

Insight

From personal experience, I've found that the effect your toddler's tantrum has on you depends on your mood and circumstances on any given day. Often you'll handle it with grace and humour, while occasionally it might really get you down. Try not to dwell on the bad days.

Top tip

Try not to judge yourself as a parent based on how many tantrums your toddler has. Much better to judge yourself on how you respond to those tantrums, and even then remember that you are only human and are bound to make mistakes.

WHAT TO DO WHEN A TANTRUM HAPPENS

One of the most effective things you can do when a tantrum erupts is to keep your cool. Staying calm will help keep a lid on things. If you start shouting, smacking and losing control yourself, the situation will undoubtedly escalate. Here are three simple ways to help you stay in control:

1 **Walk away.** *Go into the kitchen, make a cup of tea, switch on the radio. Do whatever momentarily takes your mind off the situation and allows you to regain your composure.*
2 **Take a deep breath.** *It sounds obvious, but taking a deep breath and counting to ten really does have an immediate calming effect. You will also be able to see things a bit more objectively once the heat of the moment has passed.*
3 **Call someone up.** *When things are really reaching crisis point, reach for that telephone. It is amazing how a chat to a sympathetic friend or partner can restore sanity.*

Case study

It was Nathan's second tantrum of the day and I really was getting to the end of my tether. The first one had erupted because he hadn't wanted to get in his car seat and this one was because I'd stopped him from jumping on the couch. He was lying on the floor, kicking and screaming, and I must say, I felt like doing the same. But instead I simply walked out of the room and started busying myself in the kitchen. In no time at all, Nathan appeared in the hallway, where he again threw himself on the floor, sobbing. At this point, I had to laugh. He obviously wanted an audience and having a tantrum on his own, in the front room, just hadn't been the same. Realizing this completely calmed me down and I could finally see Nathan's tantrums for what they actually were. Yes my little boy was behaving ridiculously, but by nearly losing the plot myself, I'd been in danger of behaving even more ridiculously, and I was supposed to be the adult!

Walking away from your toddler when they are having a tantrum is sometimes referred to as 'parent timeout' because removing yourself, however briefly, from the situation, has given you the opportunity to calm down, and hopefully to regain some perspective on the situation.

Ignoring tantrums

It takes nerves of steel, but sometimes the best course of action when your toddler is having a tantrum is to simply ignore it. Of course this strategy is more effective with a demanding tantrum than a frustration one, and it is not to be advised if the level of tantrum is rising from amber to red and your toddler is in danger of harming themselves or others. Another factor, of course, is whether the tantrum is taking place at home or in public, with all eyes suddenly swivelled in your direction, wondering how you are going to handle things. But under the right circumstances, pretending to take no notice can really help to calm things down. By withholding your attention, you are sending a very clear signal to your toddler that tantrums will not get them what they want.

Ignoring is difficult though, because it doesn't come naturally. When your toddler is having a tantrum, your natural response is to do something about it, to respond in some way. In order to effectively ignore your toddler, you need to go against this instinct by doing the following:

- ▸ *Stay as calm and quiet as possible.*
- ▸ *Avoid commenting in any way.*
- ▸ *Keep your facial expressions neutral.*
- ▸ *Avoid all eye contact.*
- ▸ *Avoid all physical contact.*

It is also vital that you make sure other key family members and/or carers are aware that this is the course of action you have decided upon. For example, if your toddler throws a tantrum around you and you ignore it, make sure your tantrum-throwing toddler doesn't then get the attention or the desired outcome from this behaviour from somebody else.

Insight

When trying to ignore a tantrum, I'd recommend occupying yourself with something, perhaps pretending to study a magazine or rearranging the ornaments on the mantelpiece. This will help you to focus on something other than your toddler, while giving them the clear message that their behaviour is of no interest to you.

Top tip

If you do choose to go down the ignoring route, it is worth remembering that in about 75 per cent of cases, your toddler's tantrum will escalate or intensify before it stops. It is therefore important to stick with it, providing of course that your toddler poses no risk to himself or others. If you do capitulate while your toddler is upping the ante, they will naturally assume that by behaving even worse, they have made you give in, which obviously sets a dangerous precedent.

Holding close

If your toddler is in the throes of a tantrum, it might help to hold them tightly in your arms. The idea is that by drawing them in to you and holding them close and firmly (but not squeezing), your toddler is better able to remain rational, even though they are extremely upset. A tight hold can also help dissolve anger (both in the toddler and the parent), with the hold often turning into a hug as control and composure are regained. Whether this strategy works or not will largely depend on your toddler's temperament. For some it can be a great source of comfort knowing that they are in the safety of your steadfast arms, while for others it can feel like you are restraining them and as a result your toddler may become even angrier.

> ## Top tip
> If your toddler does respond well to being held, then you could also try talking to them very softly while they are in your arms. Tell them that you understand that they are upset, and speak in a soothing, convincing voice. In fact, you could carry on talking to your toddler about almost anything, provided you keep your voice calm and gentle.

Timeout

If you find it impossible to ignore your toddler's tantrums and holding them firmly in your arms only seems to make matters worse, then you might want to consider Timeout. This is currently a very popular method for dealing with tantrums and involves removing your toddler from an explosive situation to a safe place, for example, a corner in the sitting room or a specific step on the stairs, until they have calmed down. The general rule is that your toddler stays in Timeout for one minute for each year of their life, so for example, a two-year-old should be there for two minutes, a three-year-old for three minutes and so on. It is generally agreed that Timeout shouldn't be used for toddlers under two years of age as they simply won't understand the concept. In fact it is not usually until around the age of three that Timeout becomes really effective, as this is when your toddler becomes far more capable of sitting still and reflecting on the behaviour that has led to them being put in Timeout, and realizing that certain types of behaviour will have consequences. For more on the dos and don'ts of Timeout, see Chapter 6.

> ## Insight
> If using Timeout to cope with a toddler in a tantrum, I think it's important your child realizes that they are not being punished for the tantrum, they are simply being given the time and space to calm down. As such, don't march them off to the 'naughty corner', place them in the 'quiet corner' instead.

Did you know?

A recent poll of more than 8,000 parents asked whether Timeout worked on their toddlers: 32 per cent said it definitely did, 48 per cent said only sometimes, 17 per cent said no, with the remaining three per cent saying that they did not believe in Timeout.

Case study

I first tried using Timeout when Maisy was a few months shy of her second birthday. She'd been in a terrible mood for most of the morning, not wanting to get dressed, refusing to eat her breakfast, and then throwing a huge tantrum when I switched off the television. I decided it was time to create a naughty step and after several warnings, I put her on it, hoping it would give her a chance to cool off. But rather than calm the situation down it just made things worse. There was absolutely no way Maisy was going to sit on that step for a second, let alone the minute and a half she was supposed to. Of course I couldn't force her to stay, so I ended up abandoning the whole idea. I now realize that Maisy was far too young to understand what was happening. A year on, however, and the naughty step has proved a godsend. In fact, just the other day Maisy was getting herself more and more worked up over something until she finally went and plonked herself on the naughty step to calm herself down.

Top tip

When practising Timeout it is important to let your toddler know that you are not mad or angry with them – it is their behaviour that you dislike, not them. Even when you are putting your toddler in Timeout, try to let them know that you love them. And once Timeout is finished, give your toddler a kiss and a cuddle to let them know that there are no hard feelings – all is forgiven and forgotten.

WHAT NOT TO DO WHEN A TANTRUM HAPPENS

When dealing with a toddler tantrum, it will help to avoid the following:

Reasoning or explaining during a tantrum
Trying to reason your toddler out of their tantrum is a waste of time. For example, telling your howling toddler that they cannot have a toy because you bought them a present yesterday will fall on completely deaf ears. Similarly, explaining to your angry toddler that you have got to leave the park because it is time for lunch is unlikely to have any impact. Your toddler will not listen to any form of reason or explanation in the midst of a tantrum, and will actually be incapable of even hearing you if the tantrum is of the red variety. Save the reasoning and explanations for afterwards, when your toddler has calmed down and will be more receptive.

Throwing a tantrum yourself
As stated previously, keeping cool, calm and collected is vital when dealing with your toddler's tantrums. If you start screaming and shouting, and throwing a tantrum yourself, your toddler will simply think that such lack of self-control is acceptable behaviour.

Belittling your child
When your toddler is having a tantrum they have lost their self-control. This does not mean they should lose their self-respect, too. Try to avoid humiliating or disparaging your toddler when they are having a tantrum. Don't call them 'bad' or 'silly' and don't tell them how embarrassing they are or how ashamed of themselves they should be.

Raking up the past
Don't keep reminding your toddler of an earlier tantrum. What's done is done. It is important that your toddler can move forward with a clean slate, and in the knowledge that no one bears them any grudges.

Letting your toddler's tantrums change anything

Make sure that your toddler's tantrums achieve nothing. Everything should remain as it was before the tantrum. For example, if your toddler threw a tantrum because you wouldn't let them watch television, don't switch on the television now as a reward that the tantrum has stopped. Similarly, if you were going to take your toddler to the park before their tantrum, do not now withdraw that offer as a punishment for the tantrum.

How to deal with public tantrums

These are possibly the worst type of tantrum as they are so public and it is hard for parents not to feel embarrassed. Also, having an audience to witness your toddler's tantrum can make you feel like you are being judged. What must people be thinking of you? It can feel as if your parenting skills are being laid open for public scrutiny, and no doubt they are being deemed severely lacking. Yet public tantrums are extremely common. Many public places, such as shops, cinemas and amusement parks, are totally overwhelming to the toddler. Packed full of wonderful things, most of which they can't even touch, let alone have, it is little wonder that for many toddlers it all becomes too much. But what to do when the volcano erupts in the full glare of the public? Here are a few things worth considering:

▶ *As with a private tantrum, it is essential that you remain calm. Yet it is all too easy to overreact in front of an audience's watchful stares. You become so concerned about what other people are thinking, that the tantrum will probably provoke a far stronger response in you than one that takes place in the confines of your own home. Try to suppress this feeling, because if your toddler picks up on the fact that their tantrum is really getting to you, they are likely to react even more strongly. Your anxiety will feed your toddler's anxiety and the tantrum will escalate.*

▶ *If you manage successfully to keep a lid on your emotions, it is hoped that your toddler will begin to calm down. But if your* toddler is still very much in the grip of their tantrum or it is moving up a level from amber to red, you might want to consider removing them from the situation. Maybe that means leaving a friend's house and going home, or abandoning your supermarket shop and withdrawing to the car. If in a restaurant, the toilets may offer a more private space for your toddler to blow off steam. Sometimes just the simple act of taking your toddler away from the setting where the temper tantrum erupted can defuse it. Sometimes, however, you may not be able to remove your toddler from the situation, for example, if you are in an aeroplane with the seat belt signs on. When this happens, it really is a case of just gritting your teeth and waiting for the storm to pass.

▶ A public tantrum can be bad enough, but one in front of either your own parents or your in-laws can be even worse as you will probably feel even more scrutinized. In this circumstance, it will help to speak to the grandparents about the tantrums beforehand and the various ways you are trying to deal with them. This way they will be less likely to step in or offer counterproductive advice.

▶ Don't be tempted to give your toddler whatever it is they want just because a public tantrum looms. It might temporarily avert trouble, but you really will be setting yourself up for far greater difficulties in the long run. Stand firm, and again, do not be tempted to explain why they cannot have whatever it is that has triggered the tantrum.

▶ When your toddler is calm, you should speak with them about what started the tantrum, how it made them feel (do not get into the reasons why they were angry or frustrated), and what they could do the next time they encounter a similar situation.

▶ Finally, remember that most of the people you believe to be judging you are probably parents themselves, and they have in all likelihood been through exactly the same situation. As such, any looks you get when your toddler is throwing a tantrum in public are far more likely to be knowing glances and sympathetic smiles.

If you are unlucky enough to have a member of the public question your parenting skills during your toddler's tantrum, I would strongly advise resisting the temptation to bite their head off. Simply say: 'I am dealing with the situation thank you', and turn away.

Case study

I'll never forget Tabitha's 'Bus Tantrum' as it's now famously known by me and my husband. We'd been on a nursery outing to see a pantomime at our local theatre and we'd all had a wonderful time. As we were leaving the theatre Tabitha noticed that lots of the children had these glowing sticks that they'd been selling in the foyer, and she immediately started whining for one. I would have actually got her one – anything for a quiet life – but the shop had shut by the time we got there. Anyway, this sent Tabitha into a tailspin and as we boarded the bus with all the other mums and toddlers from the nursery, my little girl erupted into a full-blown tantrum, crying, screaming, and even hitting me. It was absolutely awful, and she kept it up for the entire 20-minute journey. All eyes were on me, and other than sit there, holding her, I didn't know what else to do. As she squirmed and kicked, I could see some of the other mums giving me sympathetic glances, as if to say, 'don't worry, we've all been there', but at the time it felt like little consolation. Looking back, I realize that Tabitha was over-tired, as she'd missed her afternoon nap, and also over-stimulated after such an exciting day, but while it was happening I just wanted the ground to swallow me up.

Keeping a record

Sometimes it really helps to keep a record of your toddler's tantrums. In the relief of the tantrum ending, it is all too easy to forget exactly what occurred and any lessons you could have learnt from the situation. A record will help you document the facts – it will give you a clear picture of what is happening to your toddler, helping you to establish patterns and providing pointers to ways to better avoid tantrum-provoking emotions and situations. What is more, a record will help you better understand your own reactions to your toddler's tantrums and, if necessary, find more effective strategies for coping.

Your record could include the following information:

▶ *What usually leads to your toddler having a tantrum?*
▶ *Where do the tantrums usually occur?*
▶ *Does it happen more around a particular person?*
▶ *How often do they happen?*
▶ *How long do they last?*
▶ *Describe your child's behaviour during the tantrum.*
▶ *Where would you place it on the tantrum spectrum?*
▶ *Describe what you typically do during the tantrum.*
▶ *How does your toddler's tantrum make you feel?*

How to handle your toddler's tantrum around a sibling

A younger sibling under a year old will be largely oblivious to your toddler's tantrum and will only be affected if it takes you away from them when they want or need you. Much older than this, however, and the sibling may start imitating their tantrum-throwing sibling's behaviour, especially if they can see that it gets results. Therefore it is important to make sure nothing whatsoever changes as a result of your toddler's tantrum. For example, you must not buy them the fluffy toy that prompted the tantrum in the first place.

The attention that your toddler's tantrum demands and the upset it can cause is likely to be an annoyance to an older sibling, who might be tempted to rile even further the tantrum-throwing toddler, as this will then turn the spotlight back on them. To avoid this, when possible remove your toddler to another room where you can take appropriate action away from the older sibling.

If your toddler is going through a particularly tantrum-prone phase, try to be sensitive to the impact this is having on an older sibling and make the effort to spend one-to-one time with them, when you can raise the subject of the toddler's tantrums and reassure them that you understand how they must be feeling and that it is just a phase that will soon pass.

Tantrums and twins

You have no doubt heard the expression 'double trouble', and if you are a parent of twins, it is something you probably hear on an almost daily basis. However, whether you experience it with regard to tantrums depends largely on the personalities of your twins. Some twins will never have a tantrum together. They prefer to take it in turns, so that when one twin is having a tantrum, the other becomes quiet and watchful. Indeed, in some cases the calm twin even begins behaving far better than they usually would, almost as if aware that they need to compensate for their twin's tantrum.

Other twins will take a very different tack, with one twin's tantrum provoking an even stronger response in the other. This is known as Twin Escalation Syndrome (TES) – the tendency of multiples to intensify and expand their behaviours in reaction to each other. So now, instead of one toddler throwing a tantrum, you have two. Usually there is no reason for the second tantrum, just that they want to do what their twin sibling is doing. Not surprisingly, when TES does occur with tantrums it can be very difficult to keep a lid on the situation. Here are some courses of action to consider.

> ▶ **Separate.** *This really is your first line of defence. As soon as you see a tantrum brewing in your toddler, remove them from their twin sibling. If the situation has already escalated and*

you use Timeout, designate a different location for each child, preferably in separate rooms.

▶ **Reduce competition.** *This is often at the root of TES, as your twins are in constant competition for resources, attention and approval. Diminish the rivalry by providing ample one-to-one time with each child.*

▶ **Remain calm.** *Easier said than done with two children going into complete meltdown, but it is vital that you keep out of the escalation and in control. If necessary, take a quick 'parent timeout' by removing yourself to another room and counting to ten.*

Other toddlers' tantrums

You have probably witnessed other toddlers' tantrums at a distance, for example at playgroup or in the supermarket, but what do you do if another toddler throws one in your home, in front of your child? The chances are the parent will be there, as a toddler will rarely have a tantrum without their main carer being present, and of course you must defer to them on how best to deal with it. But by all means suggest that they might like to take the toddler into another room. At least then your eagle-eyed toddler won't be able to pick up on any new tantrum tactics or decide to join in!

If a visiting toddler is being naughty or aggressive and the parent is not present, there are two possible courses of action:

1 *The same rules apply to the visiting toddler as to your own child. If you start bending your rules for guests you could cause confusion and resentment in your toddler. A verbal report is then given to the parent, stating just the facts, without complaining or passing judgment.*

2 *You consider that disciplining someone else's child is out of your domain. Unless they are doing damage or physically hurting your toddler, you are prepared to turn a blind eye, while making it clear to your toddler that such behaviour is not permissible from them.*

Tantrums: the myths

As already mentioned, tantrums have an almost mythical status, and certainly much misinformation and many myths exist about the toddler temper tantrum. Here, five of the most common myths are explained.

1. Your toddler's tantrum is 'manipulative' and 'attention-seeking'
This assumes that your toddler is a miniature adult, capable of being deceitful and deliberately behaving in a disruptive manner. In fact, there is nothing deliberate or deceitful about your toddler's tantrum – they are simply expressing a need. Sometimes that need can be very real, for example, the need for food, the need for sleep or the need for your attention. Other times the need can be more a question of want, for example, wanting the sweets in the supermarket, wanting to get out of the pushchair, wanting to stay in the park – but that doesn't make them any less real to your toddler.

2. Your toddler throws tantrums to wind you up and embarrass you
We all have a tendency to personalize things, but it is wrong to do so when it comes to your toddler's tantrum. A tantrum is not aimed specifically at you, and in no way is your toddler showing spite towards you – a tantrum simply reflects your toddler's immature emotional make-up. Yes, they may throw more tantrums in your presence, but as stated previously, this is because they feel a sense of safety and security around you that allows them to express strong emotions in front of you.

3. You are a bad parent because your toddler has tantrums
It is all too easy to start blaming yourself, especially if you have a tantrum-prone toddler. Of course a loving, stable and predictable environment will help cut back on the frequency of tantrums and it is always good to explore things you can do to improve the situation, for example, making sure your toddler eats regularly and has their naps on time. But as discussed earlier, your toddler's temperament is likely to play a more substantial role. Understanding and working with your toddler's temperament can reduce the intensity and length of the tantrums, but however

conscientious you are, it is unlikely that you will be able to prevent them entirely.

4. The best way to deal with temper tantrums is...
The fact is, there is no single best way to deal with a tantrum, as so many factors need to be taken into account. Again, as already discussed, several different approaches can be taken, depending on your toddler, you, the tantrum itself, the circumstances surrounding the tantrum and the setting in which it is taking place. Probably the best thing you can do is to listen to your instincts and act accordingly. And remember, what might be effective for one situation may not be effective in another.

5. Tantrums bother you more than they bother your toddler
Yes, you probably run the gamut of emotions when your toddler is having a tantrum, from concern to frustration to anger to perhaps embarrassment, but you, as the adult, are in control of those emotions. It is worth reiterating the fact that one of the strongest emotions your toddler is likely to be feeling when they are in throes of a tantrum is fear. No wonder your toddler turns to you for comfort after a tantrum. For them it has been a terrifying experience. Undoubtedly a tantrum does affect you, but it is important to remember what your toddler experiences as well.

Outgrowing tantrums

In reality the toddler years are only a short phase in your child's life. In no time at all, your headstrong toddler will be a preschooler, whose ability to use language, to reason and to solve problems will greatly reduce the need for tantrums. Physically, they will be bigger and stronger and much more able to withstand the sensations and emotions that could knock them sideways as a toddler. In short, the tantrums will slowly but surely decrease until eventually they become a distant memory. That is not to say you will look back on those tantrums fondly, but you will be better placed to see the funny side.

Case study

Now I can laugh about it – in fact it's become one of those stories that you end up telling at dinner parties, but at the time I was so upset. George was about 18 months old and he'd really hit the ground running with the tantrums. From a placid little baby, he'd suddenly become this puce-faced monster, complaining in no uncertain terms if I dared to make him do anything he didn't want to. Anyhow, on this particular day, feeling at the end of my tether, I decided to put George in his pushchair and stroll down the road to the Italian deli to pick up a few tasty bits for tea. But George didn't want to go, and started performing from the moment we left the house. By the time we reached the deli, he was screaming and shouting furiously. Determined to go through with my mission, I parked George up inside the doorway, as the aisle was too small to push the buggy through, and waited in line to be served. The next thing I knew, this old man had popped his head through the shop door, demanding to know what irresponsible person had left this poor baby on its own to cry. As you can imagine, I was horrified by his accusation and told him so in no uncertain terms. As the old man made a swift exit, I burst into floods of tears. Whether it was the sight of me sobbing, I don't know, but George then suddenly stopped.

When to seek help

While tantrums are a perfectly normal and common part of toddler behaviour, sometimes, just very occasionally, they can be a sign of an underlying problem. You need not worry about isolated or occasional extreme tantrums, where your toddler reaches level red and displays some of the less common, more severe signs associated with a tantrum. If, however, this becomes a common occurrence, you may want to talk to your GP or health visitor. Here are some possible signs that advice may be needed:

▶ *You have grown increasingly concerned about your toddler's tantrums.*

▶ *Your toddler's tantrums regularly escalate into violent behaviour that endangers others or results in self-inflicted injuries.*

▶ *You have problems handling your toddler's tantrums, especially if you are concerned that you might hurt your toddler in the heat of the moment.*

Top tip

There will be some days when you will be the perfect parent and others when coping with your toddler is more a matter of survival. When those difficult days come, remember that managing your toddler's behaviour is a learning process for both you and your toddler. As you help them to deal with their emotions, you will be setting up a relationship of love and trust that will extend from the terrible twos through the rest of their life.

10 THINGS TO REMEMBER

1 *A true temper tantrum is when your toddler becomes totally overwhelmed with feelings of anger and frustration and has no way of processing these feelings other than by going into a complete emotional meltdown.*

2 *In time your toddler will learn other, less disruptive ways to express their strong emotions, but until then, try to remember that tantrums are a sign that your child is developmentally on target.*

3 *Tantrums are incredibly common, occurring in more than 80 per cent of toddlers, but while some children may experience them nearly every day, for others it will be a less common occurrence.*

4 *Younger toddlers tend to experience frustration tantrums, where they are unable to do something or fail to make their needs known. These will lessen with growing verbal skills and manual dexterity.*

5 *The demanding tantrum is more evident in the older toddler and occurs when the child is denied something they want. This type of tantrum is more about pushing boundaries, and as such, you need to stand firm.*

6 *It is possible to avert many tantrums by recognizing the triggers, giving choices, choosing your battles, and by employing various distraction techniques.*

7 *When a tantrum does occur, however, one of the best things you can do is to keep your cool. If you start screaming and shouting and becoming upset, the situation will only escalate.*

8 *Ignoring tantrums, holding your toddler close and using the discipline method known as Timeout are other tactics you might want to try to calm things down.*

9 *Never belittle your child when they are having a tantrum. They have lost their self-control and they need your help in regaining it. They do not need to be humiliated or embarrassed and lose their self-respect too.*

10 *Public tantrums are undoubtedly the most difficult to deal with as you will feel that all eyes are on you, judging your every move. Try to remember that most people are sympathetic, and are probably just grateful it's not them.*

6

The secrets of toddler discipline

In this chapter you will learn:
- *why discipline is important to your toddler*
- *when to start discipline*
- *how discipline differs from punishment*
- *how personality will influence discipline*
- *ways to make discipline effective*
- *top toddler discipline techniques*
- *how to cope with aggressive behaviour*
- *tips on handling an embarrassing toddler.*

Why discipline is important

The word discipline is often seen as a negative one, conjuring up images of punishment and harshness. But 'discipline' actually stems from the word 'disciple', which means to teach or to train, and herein lies the secret of much toddler discipline. In the toddler years your child mostly needs to be taught what is correct and proper behaviour rather than be punished for failing to behave appropriately. Showing your toddler that certain rules need to be adhered to and that flouting these established rules is not acceptable makes it much easier for them to navigate the bigger, outside world.

Five reasons why toddler discipline is important
1 *It will help keep your toddler safe.*
2 *It will teach your toddler right from wrong.*

3 *It will help your toddler feel cared for and loved.*
4 *It will boost your toddler's self-esteem as they learn self-control and self-discipline.*
5 *It will help your toddler get along with other people.*

WHEN TO START DISCIPLINE

Taken in the context that discipline is gentle, helpful and supportive guidance that teaches your child what they should do as well as what they should not do – then the chances are that you have already started the process. At as young as six months old, a baby is aware of their behaviour and starts to become increasingly receptive to your response to it, be it encouraging or discouraging. But it is as your child approaches the toddler years and becomes increasingly mobile that discipline becomes more important.

How discipline is different from punishment

Although the two words are often used interchangeably, there are in fact some significant differences between discipline and punishment. These are detailed below.

Discipline:	Punishment:
▶ teaches your toddler self-control, confidence and responsibility.	▶ often involves simply telling your toddler what not to do, or to do something because you say so.
▶ fosters self-discipline as it requires your toddler to be responsible for their own actions.	▶ means that you, as the punisher, have become responsible for your toddler's behaviour.
▶ is an ongoing process. Effective discipline actually takes place all the time.	▶ usually only occurs when your toddler misbehaves.

- is positive and respectful.

- involves natural or logical consequences that are directly related to the misbehaviour. For example, if your toddler refuses to eat their dinner, then a natural consequence is that they go hungry. Alternatively, if your toddler refuses to pick up their toys, then a logical consequence would be that they are not allowed to play with them for the rest of the day. By imposing a logical consequence, if a natural one does not apply, then your toddler will eventually learn what is expected of them.

- involves your toddler following certain rules because you have talked about these rules beforehand and explained why they are expected to follow them.

- often attempts to shame or humiliate your toddler into submission.

- often consists of consequences that are illogical or unrelated to the misbehaviour that is carried out in the heat of the moment when tempers are running high. For example, forcing your toddler to sit at the table until their plate is clear will not teach them the natural consequence of not eating. Similarly, sending your toddler to their bedroom because they haven't picked up their toys will not teach them that they are expected to put away their toys.

- involves your toddler following rules, but only because they have been threatened or bribed to do so.

Why disciplining a toddler is not easy

It is generally agreed that effective discipline in the toddler years will set your child on the path to becoming an emotionally mature adult – one who is able to defer gratification, is considerate of the needs of others, is assertive without being aggressive or hostile and can tolerate discomfort when necessary. All of this is totally at odds with your toddler's natural disposition, which is why instilling discipline in a toddler is so difficult, but at the same time, so important. When it comes to toddler discipline, there are no shortcuts or quick fixes. It is time-consuming and requires a considerable amount of energy, but the benefits to you and your child will last a lifetime. Indeed, it is often said that after love, discipline is the most precious gift you can give a child.

Insight

I've noticed how parents often slip subconsciously into good cop/bad cop roles when disciplining their toddler. Try not to let this happen. If your toddler detects the merest hint of discord between your discipline styles they will play you off against each other.

Did you know?

It is perfectly normal for toddlers to misbehave. They are pushing boundaries, testing your limits and are of course naturally curious. As a result toddlers will frequently ask themselves, 'What will happen if I do this?' The answer to this question often leads to misbehaviour. For example, perhaps your toddler has put a toy down the toilet. This behaviour undoubtedly calls for discipline, as your toddler needs to learn that putting things down the toilet is not acceptable. But your toddler would not have learnt this lesson so effectively without putting the toy down the toilet in the first place.

Other common reasons why toddlers misbehave include:

▶ *illness*
▶ *boredom*
▶ *anger*

- *a need for attention or love*
- *low self-esteem*
- *anxiety*
- *confusion.*

Insight

When a toddler is being particularly fractious, I think it's always worth taking their temperature first so you can then rule out illness. Sometimes an undiscovered fever results in difficult behaviour as your toddler isn't yet able to articulate how they are feeling.

Case study

My dad was firmly of the 'spare the rod and spoil the child' school of thought when it came to keeping me and my sisters and brother in line. As a result, I swore I wasn't going to be a heavy disciplinarian when I became a parent. But since having Clinton and Theodore I've come to realize that there's a huge difference between the sort of punishment my dad regularly meted out (bearing in mind that this was nearly 35 years ago, and I honestly don't think his approach was unusual at the time) and the type of discipline that helps a child learn right from wrong and become a respectable member of society. I want my boys to be able to walk through life with their heads held high and to be able to comfortably fit into all sorts of social situations. Basically, I want them to be happy and well-adjusted young men, who are polite, kind and considerate to others. Therefore, I'm laying the foundations early, by teaching them how to behave. Sometimes, admittedly, it is an uphill struggle, but we're getting there. Clinton's now nearly five and Theodore will shortly turn three, and just the other week we were on the train when this woman came over and told me what beautifully behaved children I had. I nearly burst with pride.

Psychological studies have shown that discipline, especially in the toddler years, is the area of parenting that drags up the most memories from our own childhoods. Experts have dubbed these memories 'ghosts from the nursery' and they can subconsciously have a strong impact on how you choose to discipline your toddler, be it along the same lines, or the complete polar opposite.

How to discipline a toddler effectively

There are several factors to consider when deciding how best to discipline your toddler, and by thinking about these points beforehand, rather than just reacting to your toddler's behaviour as it happens, whatever method of discipline you decide to use is likely to be far more effective.

SET LIMITS AND ESTABLISH BOUNDARIES

Making your home safe and secure for your toddler to explore and having a good daily routine were topics discussed in Chapter 3, but it is worth reiterating here that it is by setting limits and providing structure that you will create the conditions that make it easier for your toddler to understand and follow the rules.

MAKE DISCIPLINE AGE AND STAGE APPROPRIATE

It is very important that you make sure the discipline is appropriate for your toddler's age and stage of development. For example, it is not realistic to expect a 15-month-old to eat their food without making a mess. At this age, they do not have the dexterity and muscle control required to hold a fork properly or drink from a cup without spillage. Similarly, most young toddlers will simply not understand the concept of 'Timeout'; but apply it to a three-year-old, who has developed the ability to reflect on their behaviour, and the technique can be very successful.

FACTOR IN THE IMPORTANCE OF PERSONALITY

How your toddler is best disciplined will also depend on their personality. For example, perhaps your toddler struggles to switch gears easily, and gets upset or angry if you try to force them to abandon an activity they have become engrossed in. Your toddler isn't being deliberately defiant, it is just part of their nature, and with a bit of advance warning, they will probably do your bidding. Discipline will be far more effective if you take into account your toddler's personality traits and characteristics. Similarly, it is worth bearing in mind that discipline techniques which work on one child will not necessarily work on another, and this includes close siblings. Again, this comes down to individual personality, and often you will need to adapt and tailor a different strategy for a different child.

Case study

Grant is naturally a very obliging child. At a very young age, if I asked him to do something he would invariably do it straight away. Gregory, however, will often pretend not to hear me, and I find myself having to repeat a request half a dozen times before he'll even acknowledge that I am talking to him. Oddly enough, though, I have found Gregory far easier to discipline. I think he's a much more straightforward little character, and if I tell him off about something, he's very quick to say sorry, although that doesn't always mean he won't do it again. But if I scold Grant, he takes it incredibly personally and gets very upset. With him I have to take a much more gently, gently approach and really take the time to explain things to him. That said, he then takes on board exactly what I've said and remembers it the next time. It's quite funny, because the other day I heard Grant trying to impart his received wisdom to his brother, telling him not to play with the plant pot because 'Mummy said no', which of course fell on completely deaf ears.

ACCEPT THAT BAD DAYS HAPPEN TO GOOD PEOPLE

We all have off days, and it is worth bearing this in mind when it comes to toddler discipline. Maybe it is you who is struggling to cope, and everything your toddler does is pushing your buttons, or perhaps it is your toddler who is careering from one crisis to another. Whatever the situation, try not to be too hard on your toddler or, indeed, yourself. As the old cliché goes: tomorrow is another day...

UNDERSTAND THAT CONSISTENCY IS THE KEY

Toddler discipline is all about teaching your toddler what is acceptable and what is not, so it is vital that if something is forbidden one day, it is not suddenly allowed the next. For example, if your toddler has been told that they are only allowed to eat at the table, don't then feed them in front of the television a couple of days later because you want an easy life. Inconsistency will confuse your toddler and make them less likely to stick to the behaviour you want to encourage. Also, by being consistent in disciplining your toddler you will help develop a bond of trust. Your toddler will come to understand that you do what you say. Another important factor to take into consideration when it comes to being consistent is making sure that other family members and caregivers are aware of the rules and know the discipline methods you have chosen to use with your toddler.

Insight

In my experience consistency is the first thing to go in the heat of the moment, which is why it really helps to have a pre-planned approach to discipline. Take the time to work out how you want to discipline your toddler and you'll be far more likely to stick with it.

DON'T OVERWHELM YOUR TODDLER WITH RULES

If you bombard your toddler with too many dos and don'ts, they will end up tuning out your commands. It is a similar scenario to the one discussed in Chapter 3, when constantly using the word 'no' results in it becoming less powerful. Only stipulate rules that you feel are really necessary, for example, your toddler must always say 'please' when asking for something and 'thank you' upon receiving it. Save other rules (for example, your toddler should take their shoes off when coming into the house) for when they are a little older and better able to understand. Instead, you can take your toddler's shoes off for them. In the early toddler years you could also look at prioritizing the rules you make, giving top priority to the safety of your toddler and others (for example, your toddler must hold your hand when walking down a busy road), then to correcting behaviour that harms property (for example your toddler must not throw balls in the house). Finally, you can move on to behaviours such as whining, interrupting, etc.

Top tip

When teaching your toddler rules you might find it easier to teach them one or two that pertain to a specific situation, such as mealtimes, than to try to train them a little in many different areas.

NEVER FORGET THAT DISCIPLINE IS ALL ABOUT RESPECT

Respect is a two-way street when it comes to disciplining your toddler. By showing your toddler respect even when they are misbehaving, for example never name-calling or humiliating them in front of people, your toddler is far more likely to respect your authority and abide by your wishes. In turn, this mutual respect between you and your toddler will help them learn to respect others, which is crucial if they are to function successfully in society.

Case study

Only once have I ever called Hannah 'stupid', and that was when we were in a restaurant garden on holiday and I'd told her not to feed a mangy old dog that was lurking around the tables. Despite specifically asking her not to, Hannah decided to offer the dog a morsel from her plate. The creature couldn't believe its luck and came bounding over. Hannah is actually quite nervous around dogs, so when it tried to take the food, she abruptly pulled back, and fell off her chair. I'm ashamed to admit it, but my first reaction was anger that she'd deliberately defied me, and I blurted out: 'You stupid girl'. Well of course this was the worst thing I could say, and Hannah immediately started screaming, 'not stupid, not stupid'. Everyone in the restaurant turned to see what was happening and I felt so awful – not because Hannah was shouting, but because I'd humiliated her in front of everyone. Okay, she had been wrong, but I had been worse, calling her stupid. I immediately told her I was very sorry and that I shouldn't have called her names, to which she replied, 'naughty Mummy'.

TELL YOUR TODDLER PRECISELY WHAT YOU WANT THEM TO DO

An instruction must be clear enough for your toddler to understand what is expected of them. So, for example, simply shouting 'Get off!' when they start jumping up and down on the couch does not signal clearly what you actually want your toddler to do. It is much better to say firmly and clearly, 'We sit on the couch but can jump on the floor'. Similarly, saying 'Stop that!' when your toddler is running around the house shouting gives them no indication of what part of the behaviour is the misbehaviour or how your toddler can change it into acceptable behaviour. Instead, you could try saying: 'Screaming and shouting is too loud for indoors. If you want to scream and shout, let's go outside'.

PATIENCE IS INDEED A VIRTUE...

... and never more so than in the field of toddler discipline. With very young toddlers, it can sometimes feel a bit like banging your head against a brick wall as you tell them for the twentieth time that day that they must not pull the cat's tail. But it is important to persevere. It might take some time – it is a scientific fact that toddlers under the age of two do have trouble remembering and understanding rules, and that they are usually not disobeying you on purpose – but the message will eventually sink in. Also, it is worth remembering that as your toddler grows and matures, you will eventually be able to reason with them much more quickly and successfully.

Play fair

Your toddler needs to see discipline as being fair. That is why it is so important that the consequences for misbehaviour are natural and logical, and are directly related to the infraction. For example, cancelling going to a birthday party because your toddler did not eat his breakfast is an unfair consequence. Letting him go hungry for a few hours is much more appropriate. Admittedly, it is hard to be fair when you are angry. If you can feel your temper rising, try to take a step back from the situation and then, with a clear head, make sure the misbehaviour and the consequence are somehow related.

Insight

Perhaps the biggest hindrance I've encountered to effective discipline is empty threats. If you ask your toddler to do something and they refuse, tell them what the consequence will be. Then, if the behaviour continues, you must act.

Top tip

There will undoubtedly be times when your toddler exhibits unacceptable behaviour and becomes out of control. When this happens, try not to think of them as being 'bad'. When you are unhappy with your toddler's behaviour, make it clear that it is the behaviour, not your toddler, that you do not like. For example, try starting a rebuke with 'I don't like it when...' as this will focus attention on the behaviour.

BE YOUR TODDLER'S ROLE MODEL

As with most aspects of toddler behaviour, you are your toddler's biggest role model, and it is from watching how you conduct yourself that your toddler will learn much of what is expected of them. Therefore it is important to ask yourself what sort of example you are setting your toddler. Are there discrepancies between what you say and what you do? When it comes to being your toddler's best role model, it is worth bearing in mind the following:

- ▶ *Your toddler wants to do everything you do, from eating the food that you eat, to doing the chores you do around the house, to the way you look after yourself.*
- ▶ *It is by imitating you that your toddler learns. If you find yourself raising your voice or shouting a lot, your toddler will start to do the same. If you say 'please' and 'thank you', your toddler will start to say them, too.*
- ▶ *If you respect and look after yourself, your toddler will again do the same. If your toddler learns the importance of healthy food, being physically active and taking the time to sleep and relax at an early age, they are more likely to continue these habits into adulthood.*
- ▶ *If you embrace the wider world, your toddler will too. It is easy to become insular when caring for young children, but it is worth remembering that it is by seeing you interact socially and being involved in your local community that your toddler will learn to do the same.*

Methods of toddler discipline

Having looked at the various factors that make up effective discipline, what of the actual act itself? As discussed earlier, for much of the toddler years, discipline will simply be an ongoing process – indeed, you probably won't even notice that you are doing it as it has become just another part of your everyday life. For example, say you are in a cafe with your toddler, who starts clambering over the chair. Almost subconsciously, you will try to engage your toddler, talking to them more animatedly in the hope that the chair climbing becomes a less attractive prospect. You will try to divert and distract their attention with crayons, toys, a story or whatever is to hand, so that they will temporarily forget about their desire to climb over the chair. When the urge becomes too great, and your toddler attempts to climb again, you will gently replace them on the chair, thus sending them the clear message that chair climbing is not okay. All of this will probably take place without you even thinking that you are disciplining your toddler, but that is, in fact, precisely what you have done. And yes, your toddler will probably try to climb the chair again when next in the cafe, but the attempts will gradually decrease. Slowly but surely, by setting a limit, you will have taught your toddler that climbing on chairs in cafes is not acceptable behaviour. Here are some common toddler discipline techniques.

THE POWER OF POSITIVE REINFORCEMENT

What is it?
Most toddlers want to do what you want them to do and they love to please you. That is why your love and attention are the strongest motivators in the world when it comes to getting the behaviour you want from your toddler, which is what makes positive reinforcement such a powerful tool. The basic concept of positive reinforcement is to accentuate the positive, to home in on and praise the things that your toddler is doing right, and take the emphasis off of the negative behaviour, i.e. what they are doing wrong.

How it works
It is a very simple, but very effective, strategy that can be encapsulated as follows:

1 *Your toddler wants your approval very much.*
2 *You notice and comment on specific positive behaviour and provide natural and logical rewards (sometimes just your words of praise can be reward enough).*
3 *Your toddler feels noticed and basks in your approval, leading to an increase in the good behaviour, while the misbehaviour stops or decreases.*

4 *Your toddler also begins to recognize the value of his own positive qualities and actions.*

Let's look at an example. Say you discover your toddler colouring on the wall. Tell your toddler that it makes you unhappy and then immediately hand them some paper. When your toddler starts colouring on the paper, lavish them with praise. The key to successful positive reinforcement is giving attention to the good behaviour and not giving attention to the bad. It sounds simple, but studies have shown that often the time a child gets the most attention from their parents is when they are misbehaving, and for some toddlers any attention, even if it is negative, is a lot better than no attention at all.

When to use this method
There really is no limit to the amount of positive reinforcement you should give your toddler – the more it happens the more effective it is. If, however, you are trying to encourage a new behaviour, such as toilet training, and are using a reward system (be it a sticker chart, a treat or a small toy) only give the reward if your toddler successfully achieves the desired behaviour. For more on reward charts, see below.

Top tip
When offering positive reinforcement, try to focus on what your toddler has done rather than on your toddler themselves. For example, instead of saying, 'What a good boy you are!', try saying 'What a good helper you are!'. This will enable your toddler to see the merit of the specific behaviour, and they will be much more likely to repeat it.

Reward charts
Reward charts, or sticker charts as they are sometimes called, are a good way of encouraging certain types of behaviour in your toddler. The principles for using one are as follows:

1 *You are trying to encourage a desirable behaviour and your toddler receives a reward when they achieve the said* behaviour. However, it does not matter if your toddler does not or cannot achieve the behaviour – there is no comeuppance.

2 The goals set need to be realistic and achievable – not too hard, but not too easy either. It might help to break things down into more manageable portions. For example, if the desirable behaviour you want is for your toddler to be toilet trained, in order to achieve that goal the first step might be getting your toddler just to sit on the potty, for which they receive a reward. You can then progress to them actually going to the toilet in the potty, and so on.

3 When your toddler can easily achieve a task, try upping the ante to make it a little harder. For example, if your toddler has learnt to lie in their own bed to sleep, now they can try and stay in their own bed all night. But make sure your toddler knows what the new goal is, and if possible, try to involve them in the goal-making process.

4 For young toddlers the reward is usually just letting them put the sticker on the chart, but for the older toddler, after say ten stickers, reward them with something they really enjoy, like a trip to the soft play park or a small treat.

Insight

I've often found that parents start off using reward charts enthusiastically, but then become bored and half-hearted about them a week or so down the line. It's important to keep motivated, if you want your toddler to respond similarly.

Top tip

You can buy a reward chart online, but you might want to consider making one yourself, which is also very easy. This way you can customize it for your toddler, perhaps incorporating their photograph to make it feel more special to them, and getting their favourite themed stickers to put on it.

I used to think reward charts were a bit daft – we certainly never had them in my day – but when someone suggested we try using one on Louis to help us wean him off his dummy, I was so at my wit's end that I was willing to try anything. We'd already had several false starts at ditching the dummy, at one point giving it away to the birds, and another time, burying it in the garden. Each time Louis would be fine at first, but come the tail end of the day he would start grizzling and moaning for his 'noo noo', as he likes to call it, and in the end I'd capitulate and dig out an emergency one we kept in the back of a drawer in the kitchen. This time though, I was determined to go through with it, and having bought a chart, I sat Louis down and explained how it worked. I decided that we'd start by gradually restricting the amount of time he could have the dummy and build up to eventually throwing it away. Louis was soon proudly notching up the stars, and after every fifth one he'd get a little treat and, of course, heaps of praise. He's now gone a full fortnight without his dummy, which is incredible. Occasionally, especially when he's tired, he might ask for his 'noo noo'. But then I simply explain that it's gone and let him stick a star on the chart for doing so well without it. Amazingly, this seems to completely appease him.

Did you know?

Studies have shown that while 20 per cent of life's success is dependent on a person's intelligence, the rest is determined by self-motivation, persistence, self-control and delaying gratification.

TIMEOUT

What is it?
Having briefly touched on Timeout in the previous chapter as a method of dealing with temper tantrums, here it is explored in the

wider context of discipline in general. For example, perhaps your toddler is throwing their food around when they are old enough to know better. After several requests to stop throwing the food, your toddler continues with the behaviour. After being warned that they will be put in Timeout if they persist, your toddler once again throws the food. You then proceed to remove your toddler from the table and take them to a designated area where they can spend a little bit of quiet time reflecting on what they did and why it was unacceptable.

How it works
Timeout works by giving your toddler a bit of time and space to cool down and think about what they are doing. But it is important to stick to the guidelines when using Timeout, which are as follows:

1 *Your toddler should only be put in Timeout for one minute for each year of their life, so for a three-year-old, that is three minutes.*
2 *The place you choose for Timeout – be it a stair, a chair or a specific corner of a room – should be safe, dull and uninteresting. Make sure your toddler cannot see the TV, has not got access to their toys and is not able to interact with other children. The aim is to remove your toddler to a space where not much is happening. In no way should this place frighten your toddler.*
3 *Give your toddler at least one prior warning that if the undesirable behaviour continues they will be placed in Timeout.*
4 *Then, if it does continue, it is important that you follow through with the Timeout, calmly taking your toddler to the Timeout area, either holding their hand or carrying them. While taking them there, explain to your toddler in a calm and loving manner why their behaviour was unacceptable. For example, 'You need to sit in Timeout because you hurt your sister by pulling her hair'.*
5 *Do not negotiate with your toddler once in Timeout. As hard as it is, it is important to ignore them, even if they are shouting, crying or apologizing.*
6 *If your toddler refuses to stay in Timeout, simply pick them up and put them back. You may have to do this several times, but*

try not to make a fuss about it otherwise your toddler might start to view Timeout as a game.

7 *When Timeout is over, it is over. Create a fresh start by offering a new activity. Do not discuss the unwanted behaviour, just move on.*

8 *If your toddler repeats the behaviour that led to the Timeout in the first place, repeat the whole process. If used properly, Timeout will work eventually.*

When to use this method

As previously stated, young toddlers simply won't understand the concept of Timeout, so it is worth waiting until your toddler is approaching their third birthday before introducing it. Even then, some toddlers may struggle with it, and in some cases it can exacerbate the situation – much depends on the temperament of your toddler.

Tempting as it sometimes is, it is really important not to use Timeout as a threat. Threatening Timeout without actually imposing it will only teach your toddler that they can continue to misbehave. If you have given the necessary warning, then use Timeout – do not keep giving your toddler just one more chance to stop the unwanted behaviour.

Did you know?

It is widely recognized among psychologists that there are three distinct patterns of parenting style – authoritarian, authoritative and permissive.

▶ *Authoritarian parents are generally defined as parents who have strict ideas about discipline and behaviour. They tend not to be open to discussion.*

▶ *Authoritative parents tend to have ideas about behaviour and discipline that they are willing to explain and discuss with their children. They tend to be more flexible and more open to adaptation.*

> ▶ *Permissive parents are parents who tend to have very relaxed ideas about behaviour and discipline.*

Numerous research studies conclude that children raised in the authoritative style are consistently more contented, have more confidence, better social skills and better developed emotional regulation than children raised by authoritarian or permissive parents.

The behaviours you cannot ignore

There are some types of toddler behaviour that, while annoying, you will probably let slip under your radar (again, it is the old adage of choosing your battles wisely), but others you simply cannot turn a blind eye to. These behaviours are usually aggressive and include hitting, head butting, pinching, biting and kicking. While these types of behaviour are perfectly normal in toddlers, especially those who express their feelings with high intensity and easily lose control, the aggression should be acted on immediately. A toddler who is being physically aggressive to another child should not be given warnings about their behaviour, they should know instantly that they have done something wrong. One of the best ways to achieve this is to promptly remove them from the situation, followed by a clear and concise explanation of what they have done wrong and that such behaviour is not acceptable. Timeout is considered to be one of the most effective tools for dealing with aggressive behaviour, but whether you choose to use it will obviously depend on the age and temperament of your toddler.

Other things you could consider when dealing with aggression in younger toddlers are:

1 **Teaching your toddler alternatives.** *Wait until your toddler has calmed down, then calmly and gently discuss what has*

happened. Ask them if they can explain what triggered the outburst. Tell them that it is perfectly natural to have angry feelings but it is not okay to show them by hitting, kicking, biting or whatever. Encourage your toddler to find a more effective way of responding to those feelings, for example coming to you or another adult for help.

2 **Try role playing with your toddler.** *Using dolls or puppets you could try acting out some of the situations that trigger your toddler's aggressive behaviour. You could explore good behaviour and aggressive behaviour and ask your toddler which is right. Or you could just stop in the middle of the story and ask your toddler what the dolly or puppet should do.*

3 **Always make your toddler apologize.** *Make sure your toddler understands that they need to say they are sorry after they lash out at someone. A young toddler may not understand the purpose of an apology at first, but the lesson will sink in.*

Case study

My sister Janice and I have always been really close and when we found out we were pregnant at the same time, we were both delighted. Our children were born just ten weeks apart, and right from the beginning the babies have spent a lot of time together, so much so that they're more like brother and sister than cousins. We'd always assumed that as they got older they'd get on really well, but just lately my little boy has taken to being quite aggressive towards his younger cousin. Last week we were sitting in the kitchen chatting when we suddenly heard a piercing scream coming from the front room. We rushed in to find Paige sobbing her little heart out, while Shane was acting like nothing had happened, playing conspicuously quietly on the floor with a toy car. Janice then noticed a red mark on Paige's little arm, and on closer inspection you could definitely see teeth marks. I immediately hauled the culprit into the hall where I informed him that biting his cousin simply wasn't on, to which Shane kept saying, 'my car, my car'. Despite my sister's reassurances that

Paige would be fine and that biting is just a phase, I felt absolutely dreadful. She then reminded me of the time I bit her on the cheek while fighting over a favourite doll, 'and you grew out of it', she laughed.

Your embarrassing toddler

Just as your toddler can get into mischief because of their inability to control certain urges and impulses, similarly they can cause you considerable embarrassment through their complete lack of inhibition and self-restraint. A typical embarrassing toddler trait is to loudly make observations that would be far better left unsaid. For example, perhaps your toddler sees a rather plump man, and asks within earshot whether he has a baby in his tummy. Your toddler is not being deliberately rude, they are simply being inquisitive and trying to make sense of their world, as well as demonstrating their improved powers of observation.

There is no point in getting angry with a toddler who makes such a social gaffe. They honestly won't know what they have done wrong. The best course of action is to steer your toddler in the right direction by following a few guidelines.

▶ *Don't respond by embarrassing your toddler. Loudly telling your toddler, in front of everyone, that what they have done is rude or impolite will give your toddler a mixed message – if you care so much about the feelings of other people, why don't you care about theirs?*
▶ *Remember that these embarrassing episodes are normal. Your toddler's ability to empathize and be sensitive to and aware of others' feelings is growing every day. All too soon these gaffes will be a thing of the past, and in years to come they will probably become part of your family's folklore – perfect for re-telling at twenty-first birthday parties and weddings.*

We were round at our friends' house for quite a formal Sunday lunch, and one set of their parents were also there. They're quite an elderly couple and rather proper, so everyone felt as if they had to be on their best behaviour. Everyone except my son Milo, that is, who was two and a half at the time. The house wasn't particularly child-friendly, so I kept having to break off conversations to keep a close eye on him. Every few minutes I seemed to be running over to avert one disaster or another and quite frankly I was getting a bit tired of it. When Milo started rummaging in my handbag, I thought: 'Oh well, at least it'll keep him out of mischief for a while', and decided to let him get on with it. But then, from the corner of my eye, I suddenly saw him fish out a bright yellow packet. It took a few moments for me to actually register what it was, and then it suddenly dawned on me – it was one of my tampons! I immediately tried to take it from him, hoping that no one would notice. But Milo started screaming at the top of his voice: 'My sweetie, my sweetie'. Of course, at that moment all eyes swivelled in our direction to see my son furiously tearing open the tampon. I could have died!

EMBARRASSING BEHAVIOUR: WHAT TO EXPECT AND WHEN

Each stage of toddlerhood brings its own unique embarrassments. Here are some of the possible pitfalls.

One to two years of age

▶ *Your toddler may start to find it difficult not being the centre of attention. For example, you might be in mid-conversation with someone else when your toddler decides they want to talk to you. At this age your toddler will find it nigh on impossible to wait their turn, and may even try grabbing your face and forcing you to break off your conversation to focus solely on them.*

▶ *Aggressive behaviours, as discussed earlier, are most likely to surface at this age, as your toddler's language skills are still very limited, along with an inability to exert self-control.*

▶ *Not sharing is another antisocial habit that is particularly prevalent in this age group. But try not to put an adult spin on it and see it as selfish. Your toddler is simply acting in accordance with their age and stage of development.*

Two to three years of age

▶ *Your toddler can now speak quite clearly, and very loudly should they so choose, but they still lack the skills to understand that certain things are best left unsaid. But remember that comments such as 'lady has funny hair' are said without malice. Your toddler has not yet learnt to respect other people's feelings, but in time they will.*

▶ *Comments and observations that are okay in the home can now be repeated by your toddler in public, in a way that doesn't always sound appropriate. For example, perhaps your toddler saw you naked in the bath that morning, and decides to relate this encounter to everyone at playgroup.*

▶ *Toilet training will usually begin around now, and not surprisingly some toddlers become rather fixated with their bodily functions. For example, your toddler may announce to an entire restaurant that they need a poo, and then talk loudly about it afterwards. The actual word itself can also become a source of much amusement, for example, your toddler thinks it is funny calling you a 'poo-poo head'.*

▶ *Similarly, genital curiosity can often begin at this age. Your toddler will be out of nappies for the first time and will have just discovered a whole new part of their body to explore. This is an innocent habit and the best thing you can do is not to make a fuss. If it is in a public place, gently remove your toddler's hand and divert their attention to something else. Try not to get angry or embarrassed as your toddler may get the idea that there is something shameful about that part of their body.*

Insight

Toddlers are honest, spontaneous and direct in a way that they will never be again, and although this can lead to difficult and awkward situations, I think it's important to remember it can also lead to some of the funniest and most touching moments that you will treasure forever.

Smacking: is it ever the answer?

While toddlers often respond well to physical action when you need to discipline them, for example, taking them firmly by the hand, picking them up, holding or restraining them, it is generally agreed that smacking does not teach toddlers how to behave appropriately. In fact, numerous studies suggest that quite the opposite is true and that smacking toddlers has the following negative effects:

▶ *It decreases self-discipline/self-control.*
▶ *It increases anxiety and aggression.*
▶ *It increases the likelihood of criminal and antisocial behaviour in later life.*
▶ *It undermines a positive relationship between parent and child.*

Despite all the strength of evidence against smacking, it is still a common practice, with one recent poll suggesting that as many as seven out of ten parents still smack their children. But there is a huge difference between slapping a toddler's hand as they reach towards a boiling hot pan and lashing out at your toddler in anger because you have reached the end of your tether and can no longer cope. As stated at the outset of this chapter, disciplining a toddler is not an easy task, but if your aim is to raise a considerate child who knows the difference between right and wrong from an early age, then it is worth putting in the effort – using reason, communication and love, rather than fear or force.

Did you know?

Legally, parents have the right to smack their children if it is deemed 'reasonable punishment' – but not if it causes injury such as 'grazes, scratches, minor bruising or reddening of the skin, which stays for hours or days'.

10 THINGS TO REMEMBER

1 *Discipline should not be confused with punishment. It is not about issuing threats and bribes to your child in a bid to make them behave. Discipline is about teaching your child right from wrong, and will ultimately make it easier for them to operate in the wider world.*

2 *Discipline can be an uphill struggle in the toddler years as it goes directly against your child's natural disposition of pushing boundaries and testing limits. But that is precisely why it is so important.*

3 *It's worth thinking about how you want to discipline your toddler, and considering such things as boundary setting, consistency, your child's personality and your position as a role model, before misbehaviour occurs. This way you won't be just reacting to your toddler's behaviour as it happens.*

4 *One of the most effective methods of discipline in the toddler years is positive reinforcement. Nothing is more likely to get the behaviour you want from your toddler than your praise and attention.*

5 *Timeout works best on the older toddler (aged two or above) who can understand the concept that they need some distance from their actions and some time to reflect on them. Its effectiveness will also depend on the personality of your child.*

6 *Don't be tempted to use Timeout as a threat. Once you have given the necessary warning and if the behaviour continues, then act. If you do not, your toddler will learn that their behaviour, however unacceptable, has no consequences.*

7 *Seriously unacceptable behaviours such as biting and hitting should be acted upon immediately, with your toddler being removed from the situation without warning and told instantly that what they have just done is wrong.*

8 *Your toddler's lack of inhibition and self-restraint not only results in misbehaviour, but also embarrassment, with social gaffes and antisocial behaviour very common among this age group.*

9 *It's important to remember your toddler isn't deliberately trying to embarrass you – it's just that their ability to empathize and be sensitive to and aware of others is still at a fledgling stage.*

10 *As a discipline method, smacking is proven to be one of the least effective, as it instils no sense of self-discipline or control.*

7

Encouraging toddler talk

In this chapter you will learn:
- *about the development of speech and language*
- *the difference between expressive and receptive language*
- *your toddler's language milestones*
- *techniques to get your toddler talking more*
- *tips on reading to your toddler*
- *songs to sing to your toddler*
- *how much television your toddler should be watching*
- *tips on ditching the dummy*
- *how to deal with common speech problems.*

How speech and language develop

Over the toddler years your child's ability to communicate develops at a breathtaking rate. From a few barely decipherable words at one year of age, your toddler's vocabulary will suddenly explode and by the time they are three they will probably be talking in clear sentences and having quite complex conversations with you.

Your toddler's growing verbal skill marks an exciting and significant step in their development. As they become increasingly adept at letting you know what they want and how they are feeling, you will be better able to meet their needs and manage their behaviour. You will also gain a greater insight into your toddler's character, as they are better able to express the quirks and preferences that make them so unique and individual. And of course, because your toddler is a one-off, try not to compare them with other children, even siblings, when it comes to speech and language. Some toddlers are naturally talkative, while others will need more encouragement to speak.

Case study

Ever since I can remember Rachel has been a proper little chatterbox. Language came very easily to her and from quite an early age she's been very vocal and quite capable of telling me her needs. Even when she's playing on her own in her bedroom, I can hear her chatting away to herself. Matthew, however, has been completely different. He's now nearly two and while he clearly understands everything I tell him and loves doing things for Mummy, he can sometimes go a whole day barely saying a word. If he wants something, he'll point at it. His hearing is fine (he's been fully tested), and there appears to be no physical reason why his speech is a bit delayed. I never knew that speech and language development could vary so enormously in two children in the same family, but I've been told that this is often the case. I also wonder if it's because his big sister has tended to do a lot of the talking for him. Rachel starts school soon, so I think when it's just me and Matthew in the house on our own, he'll naturally start to express himself more.

Did you know?

Girls are much quicker than boys at learning how to speak, with boys being three times more likely to have delayed speech development than girls. A recent study into gender differences in verbal ability between the ages of two and four found that boys learn to speak at a slower rate because of the genetic make-up of their brains. Another contributory factor that has been suggested by another study is that mothers tend to use more open-ended questions and longer sentences when they speak to toddler girls than when they speak to boys the same age. In addition, a mother's speech pattern changes according to what gender she is talking to. With girls a mother's speech pattern is more likely to be exaggerated when communicating, while with boys their conversations are likely to be more matter of fact, focusing on whatever the boy happens to be doing at the time. By around the age of four, however, boys' speech and language skills have usually caught up with girls. This early gender difference in language is not seen in any other areas of toddler development.

The difference between expressive and receptive language

Of course your child has been communicating with you from the moment they were born, initially through their crying, then through babbling and baby sounds and now through actual words. This is called expressive language, and describes the process of learning to speak and later the use of language through reading and writing.

At the same time as your child was getting to grips with expressive language, they were also mastering their receptive language skills by listening and learning the rules of language. You might not have realized it at the time, but the conversations you had with your baby, even in the womb and as a newborn, were forming the basis of their understanding of language.

Receptive language will always be more advanced than expressive language in the early years of your child's life because it is much easier to receive a message than send one.

A child's first word is more often dada rather than mama, but this isn't because they are showing a preference for one parent over the other. It is simply that 'd' is an easier sound to pronounce than 'm'. After dada, the next most common word usually spoken is 'mama', followed by 'gone' and 'more'.

Your toddler's language milestones

While most children will reach the standard milestones of smiling, sitting and walking at roughly the same time, give or take a month or two, the development of speech and language is harder to pinpoint and can vary by as much as a year. So, for example, some children will say their first intelligible word before they are a year old, while others may not speak until they are over two. This difference is all within the range of normal. The following chart will therefore only give you a rough idea of your toddler's language milestones. If, however, you become concerned about your toddler's speech and language development do speak to your health visitor or GP who can then make a referral for a speech and language assessment. A hearing test will be included in any assessment because a hearing problem can affect speech and language development. In the vast majority of cases there is nothing wrong with a late-talking toddler, but there is no harm in seeking advice even if it is just to give you peace of mind.

Age	Receptive	Expressive
1 year	Recognizes own name. Understands the word 'no'.	May say one or two words, usually 'dada' and 'mama'.

Age	Receptive	Expressive
18 months	Understands simple requests, e.g. 'Pick up your dolly.' Can point to familiar objects on request, e.g. 'Where is your cup?'	May say ten or more words. Tries to copy new words. Talks nonsense to self that sounds like speech.
2 years	Acts on simple commands, e.g. 'Throw the ball to me.' Will listen to stories with pictures.	Can use at least 20 words, and join two words together, e.g. 'Want cup.' Also asks questions, e.g. 'What's this?'
2½ years	Follows simple stories. Can understand contrasting concepts, e.g. hot and cold. Can also understand two-stage commands, e.g. 'Get your teddy and put it in the box.'	Can use three words together, but may omit certain words and have difficulty with some sounds, e.g. f, s, sh. Will talk to other children as well as adults, although family members are usually best at understanding.
3 years	Begins to understand simple 'Who?', 'What?' and 'Where?' questions. Also understands words such as 'in', 'on' and 'under' as well as some adjectives, e.g. 'big', 'wet'.	Sentences are becoming longer, usually four words or more. Speech is mainly intelligible. Talks about past events, but tenses may be confused, e.g. 'I goed to the park.'

Top tip

Sometimes a toddler can start off speaking well, only to lapse a couple of months down the line. Don't worry if this happens. When your toddler first began talking they were simply mimicking you. In other words, what went in their ears came out of their mouth. Now, however, they are starting to use their head to formulate and transmit their own thoughts, and because this takes a considerable effort, your toddler is bound to make more mistakes.

CASE STUDY

Ned does get his words muddled up sometimes, and I must admit I find it really endearing. When he was younger he used to call his fingernails 'finger snails'. In fact, the name has now stuck, and just the other day I found myself calling him over because I needed to cut his 'finger snails'. Then last week, he came running into the kitchen, saying: 'Mummy, Mummy, two head hurt.' For the life of me I couldn't think what he was talking about, but he then started pointing to his forehead and I suddenly realized that my brilliant little boy had obviously heard us use the word forehead, and knew that it started off with something that sounded like a number, but just couldn't remember which one!

It's funny because even now, nearly 40 years on, my mum still remembers the mispronunciations I used to make as a toddler. Evidently I struggled to pronounce 'f' which usually came out as a 'th', so when my two elder brothers teased me, which they did mercilessly with me being the only girl, I'd usually tell them 'not funny'. But of course because of my slight lisp 'funny' would come out sounding more like 'sunny' to which came back my brothers' standard reply: 'We know it's not, it's raining!'

Did you know?

A parent can understand 95 per cent of what their two-year-old is trying to say to them, while an outsider will probably understand only 25 per cent.

Ways to get your toddler talking more

You have been talking and listening to your child from the moment they were born and this has undoubtedly helped create the foundations for good language and communication skills. And now, as your baby moves into the toddler phase, there are lots of things you can do to encourage and motivate them to talk more and improve their language. Here are some simple techniques you can use to help turn your child into a talkative toddler.

GIVE YOUR TODDLER A CHOICE

This technique really is incredibly useful when it comes to managing toddler behaviour. Not only will it reduce power struggles and tantrums, as previously discussed, it will also help boost your toddler's vocabulary and encourage them to vocalize more. Young toddlers are very visual, so show them the choices you are offering and name them, for example, 'Would you like this yoghurt or this banana?' Then, when your toddler points to their choice of, say, the banana, name it for them over and over again, e.g. 'the banana, here's the banana, eat the banana'. This way they will come to associate the word with the object. As you offer more and more choices in everyday situations, for example when getting your toddler dressed, they will become increasingly familiar with the words and will then start requesting their choices verbally.

PRAISE, REPEAT AND EXPAND

When your toddler tries to name something, praise them, repeat it back and then expand on what they have said. So, for example, if your toddler says 'ball', you say 'clever girl, yes, ball, a red ball'. This expansion of what your child is saying not only enlarges the vocabulary but also teaches word combinations. It is a technique that can also be successfully used on an older toddler who is just starting to form sentences. Initially your toddler will rarely speak in full sentences. Instead they will use only the essential words and leave out everything they feel is unnecessary window dressing. So, for example, your toddler will say 'I go sleep' rather than 'I am going to sleep'. Interestingly, experts call this phase of toddler language development Telegraphic Speech, which comes from the days when people sent telegrams and because they were charged by the word they omitted everything that was not absolutely essential to convey meaning. To help your toddler move through this phase, respond by reiterating what they have just said in complete form. So, when your toddler says 'I go sleep', you respond with, 'yes, you are going to sleep now.'

MODEL WORDS

When your toddler says a word incorrectly, do not tell them they have got it wrong. Simply repeat the word back to them, slowly, clearly and correctly. For example, your toddler says 'gog' and you say, 'yes, it's a dog'.

TEACH YOUR TODDLER TO LISTEN

Having good attention and listening skills is crucial for the development of speech and language. You can boost your toddler's ability to listen by drawing their attention to the sounds around them. For example, if someone rings the doorbell, point in the direction of the door and say 'listen, it's the doorbell... ding, dong... can you hear it?'

ENCOURAGE YOUR TODDLER TO COPY SOUNDS

Once your toddler has heard a sound, see if you can get them to repeat it back to you. For example, perhaps your toddler is playing with a toy cow. You say, 'Look, you're holding the cow... the cow says moo, moo', and then encourage your toddler to repeat the sound.

PROVIDE A RUNNING COMMENTARY

Everything your toddler does is an opportunity to use words, and one of the most effective ways of encouraging them to do this is by providing your toddler with a running commentary, talking about what you and they are looking at or doing as it is happening. This will help your toddler develop their spoken language skills in a natural and relaxed way. For example, perhaps you are in the kitchen doing the washing-up. Talk to your toddler about the water, whether it is hot or cold, the bubbles, cups, plates, spoons, whether they are clean or dirty, the splashes, etc. Naming things that you and your toddler see is essential in building up their store of words. Like adults learning a second language, toddlers are learning a language when they learn to talk, and they need to hear the same words over and over again before they will be able to use them.

Insight

I've found that for some people, providing a running commentary for their toddler feels awkward and unnatural at first. Keep at it, and it will start to come more easily. In fact, in time, it will feel more like a conversation, albeit one in which you do most of the talking.

KNOW WHEN TO LIMIT YOUR TALKING AND TAKE THE TIME TO LISTEN

As adults we often feel compelled to fill silences with words, but if you do this with your toddler it will give them less opportunity to talk. During play sessions or bath time, for example, be aware of how much you are talking or leading the conversation. Also, when your toddler is talking, it is important to take the time to listen to what they are saying. Toddlers can sometimes take a while to find the words they want, and this can be frustrating. But try to refrain from jumping in and completing your toddler's sentences. By giving them the chance to use their budding vocabulary, you will affirm your faith in your toddler's abilities.

BECOME A PAIR OF BOOKWORMS

Try to put aside some special time each day when you and your toddler sit down together and read picture books and simple storybooks with lots of rhyme and repetition. Numerous studies have shown that reading is one of the most effective ways of exposing your toddler to language and boosting their communication skills.

Here are some tips for reading to your toddler:

▶ *Read whatever books your toddler asks for, even if it is the same book every night for week after week after week. Remember, your toddler learns through repetition.*

▶ *Read slowly enough for your toddler to understand.*

▶ *Read expressively, using different voices for different characters and raising or lowering your voice if appropriate. Also, if your toddler is sitting beside you rather than on your lap, you can use facial expressions to help convey different emotions.*

▶ *Use finger puppets or even your bare fingers, for example to create an Itsy Bitsy Spider, as this will bring the story to life.*

▶ *Encourage your toddler to clap or sing when you read rhythmic, singsong books.*

▶ *Talk about the pictures with your toddler. Point to items and name them. Then ask your toddler to name them with you and offer enthusiastic praise when they do so.*

▶ *Substitute your toddler's name for the character in the book.*

▶ *Ask open-ended questions: 'Why do you think the teddy is going into the woods? What do you think will happen next?' This encourages your toddler to think about the story and to ask questions.*

Insight

If you think your toddler's too young to join a library, I strongly suggest you think again. As well as lots of age and stage appropriate books, there are often activities your toddler can participate in, all designed to help build their speech and language skills.

ENJOY A SING-A-LONG

Singing is another excellent way to encourage your toddler's interest in speech and language – from learning to pay attention and developing an enjoyment of listening to understanding about rhythm and rhyme. Also, research shows that toddlers remember words more easily when they form part of a song. Even if you aren't at all musical, there is no reason singing cannot be a regular part of your toddler's everyday life. You can build a song around all sorts of activities; for example, while bathing your toddler you could sing to the tune of 'here we go round the mulberry bush', substituting 'this is the way we wash your face, wash your face, wash your face...'. As this becomes a predictable and enjoyable accompaniment to the washing process, your toddler will begin to understand the link between the action and the word as well as the part of the body you are referring to. Here is a table detailing the sort of songs that can best help your toddler's speech and language development at different ages.

Age	Type of songs that are appropriate	How singing helps
1 year +	Songs which your toddler can copy the actions from and which make them laugh, e.g. 'Round and round the garden', 'Row, row, row your boat' and 'This is the way the lady rides'.	Encourages enjoyment in communication. Helps link words with actions and develop vocabulary.
18 months–2 years	Songs which your toddler can copy words from, especially those that have an exciting end, e.g. 'Humpty Dumpty' and 'Ring a ring o' roses'.	Encourages the linking of words and awareness of rhythm and rhyme.
2–3 years	Slightly more complicated action songs, e.g. 'Wind the bobbin up', 'Once I caught a fish alive' and 'The wheels on the bus'.	Continues to develop an understanding of rhythm and rhyme. Can also help your toddler predict what is coming next and build vocabulary.

SWITCH OFF THAT TELEVISION

Limit the amount of time your toddler is exposed to television, as well as DVDs and computer games, as over-exposure can have damaging effects on their communication skills, particularly their attention and listening skills. Recent research suggests that in the toddler years, any more than two hours' viewing a day could cause problems, and that ideally your toddler should not be watching more than an hour a day. If possible, try to make the time to sit with your toddler whenever they are watching the television as this will give you the opportunity to provide the repetition and running commentary that your toddler needs to get any benefit from what they are watching. If your toddler is watching television on their own it becomes a 'one-way' communication that offers very little in the way of learning.

DITCH THE DUMMY

As your child enters the toddler years it can become difficult to separate them from their dummy, but it is important in terms of their speech and language development that you do so, because prolonged use of a dummy can have quite an adverse effect on your toddler's ability to communicate. Indeed, a recent study conducted by speech therapists has found that a high proportion of the toddlers that are referred to them for speech therapy are dummy users, for the following reasons:

▶ *A toddler who has had a dummy in their mouth since babyhood has had fewer opportunities to babble, which is the foundations of speech.*
▶ *Also, a dummy user's ability to swallow can be impaired, which can result in difficulties with speech.*
▶ *Once speaking, a dummy user is more prone to talking from the back of the mouth instead of the front, which results in the 't' sound coming out as 'k'.*
▶ *Persistent and long-term use of a dummy can sometimes contribute to future speech difficulties by causing incorrect positioning of the teeth, so that the bottom and top teeth do not meet properly at the front. As a result, a toddler may not learn to use the full range of tongue movements that are necessary for making all the speech sounds.*

Here are some tips to help your toddler kick the dummy habit:

1 *If you can bear it, it is probably best to let your toddler go cold turkey. They will only fret for two or three days, which, as long as you are prepared for it, is not that bad for a dummy-free future.*
2 *Of course the alternative to this is gradual reduction. For example, start limiting the dummy to use in the house and then only to bedtime. But while this approach may seem less harsh, it does prolong the agony – for both of you.*
3 *Make sure the timing is right for both your toddler and you. Do not choose a time of upheaval or disruption when your toddler is already likely to feel unsettled, and try and make sure you have the support you need.*
4 *Try to enlist the help of an older child who can convince your toddler that dummies are for babies and not for big boys and girls.*
5 *If your toddler's birthday is approaching, why not make it a double celebration and turn it into the day they also gave*

up their dummy? Perhaps they could give it to the birds,
bury it in the garden or simply throw it in the rubbish bin.
Your toddler is likely to be so distracted for much of their
big day that they will have little time to dwell on their
dummy's absence.

Insight

If your child is a thumb sucker, obviously getting them to
stop is a wholly different proposition. Most toddlers give up
thumb sucking of their own accord, but if yours persists, I've
found it helps to pay attention to the cues when they suck
their thumb and help them find an alternative (without them
knowing you're doing it).

TRY TO GET OUT AND SOCIALIZE WITH
YOUR TODDLER AS MUCH AS POSSIBLE

Sometimes a toddler's language is under-developed simply because
they have had limited opportunities to mix and communicate
with children their own age and in different social settings. This is
where local mother and toddler groups can really help, and who
knows – it might just kick-start your social life too.

Case study

Malachy started babbling away at around four months and I really
thought he was going to be an early talker, but up until a few
months ago – he's now two and a half – he mostly communicated
by grunting. When he did speak he would often get it wrong.
For example, he couldn't say 'mummy' and called me 'mimi',
while both my parents were 'grandad'. He also used to call a
bus a 'two' – I've no idea where that came from! But he clearly
understood everything. I remember asking my husband, Keith,
to pass me the remote control and Malachy was up like a shot
getting it for me. But just lately there's been a marked improvement
in Malachy's speech and I really put it down to getting him off
his dummy. I'd been putting it off as I was dreading the ensuing
tantrums. But honestly, once I'd made the decision it wasn't

half as bad as I thought, and within just a few days Malachy was a different child. Whereas before he would happily sit sucking away, suddenly he was filling the time chatting. Since then his speech has come on amazingly well and he's just started making short sentences like 'Where's daddy gone?' and 'Wee wee please mummy.' Maybe my little boy will turn into a chatterbox after all.

Did you know?

According to studies, 13 per cent of toddlers at two years of age are late talkers but nearly all of these will completely catch up with their more communicative peers by the age of seven. Research has also revealed that education, income and parenting style have no impact on a toddler's likelihood of being a late talker.

Common toddler speech problems

Because the toddler years are such an extraordinary time of speech growth, do not be surprised if your toddler experiences a few hiccups along the way. Here are some of the more common speech problems to look out for:

MISPRONUNCIATION

Many toddlers mispronounce words, which is what makes young toddlers particularly difficult to understand to anyone other than their nearest and dearest. Common mistakes include substituting an 'f' or 'd' sound for a 'th'. For example, your toddler will say: 'dat's mine', instead of 'that's mine'. Most mispronunciations will disappear over time by employing such simple techniques as modelling, as described earlier. Indeed, the majority of these mispronunciations will have been rectified by the time your toddler is three.

LISPING

Pronouncing a 's' as a 'th' is not unusual among toddlers. A normal 's' sound requires your toddler to put their tongue behind the top teeth. This, however, doesn't come naturally to some toddlers, who find it much easier to push their tongue out, thus creating the lisp. Again, as with mispronunciation in general, the problem is usually outgrown, without any need for intervention.

FLOW

Watch most toddlers trying to communicate and you will see them struggling with the flow of words coming out of their mouth. They are simply battling a bit with their new speech skills, and as such it is perfectly normal. It is also normal and healthy for your toddler to become frustrated when this happens. It means that they are really keen for you to understand them and to communicate with you.

STUTTERING

Your toddler's brainpower may sometimes outstrip their verbal ability and when this happens it may appear as if they are stuttering as they struggle to express themselves properly. In the majority of toddlers this isn't in fact a true stutter – they are hesitating, repeating whole words or repeating the first syllable of a word, usually because they are either excited, tired or upset. This occasional stumbling over words is called dysfluency. A true stutter is in fact quite rare and will only affect five per cent of toddlers. Signs of a true stutter are:

▸ *Your toddler holds out the first sound in a word, for example, 'c-c-c- cat'.*
▸ *They repeat the sound, for example, 'Sh-sh-sh-shut door'.*
▸ *Your toddler may also open their mouth to say something, but get stuck before any sound comes out.*

▶ *Your toddler may look tense when the stuttering occurs, for example they tighten their jaw or clench their fist.*

No one really knows what causes stuttering, but it can run in families and it is four times more common in boys than girls.

Since many toddlers go through a stuttering-like phase while learning to talk, most experts recommend waiting until your toddler is three before taking action. If, however, you are growing increasingly concerned about your toddler's stutter, talk to your GP or health visitor who can arrange an early referral to a speech and language therapist.

Fascinating talking facts

▶ *New research looking at how toddlers manage to build their vocabulary so quickly between the ages of one and two has discovered that it is because toddlers are exposed to lots of words all at once and that these words range in difficulty. If a toddler were to learn one word after the other, progressing in difficulty, then this typical language spurt would not be guaranteed.*
▶ *You probably thought long and hard when naming your child, giving much consideration to what their name would convey. But to your toddler, their name also forms the cornerstone of learning speech and language. Studies have shown that when a child starts breaking up sentences into smaller parts so they can learn individual words, they use their name as a sort of 'anchor' into the speech stream, which enables them to learn better the word that follows their name.*
▶ *New research has discovered that young toddlers only think in terms of a whole object and not the parts when learning language. For example, a young toddler simply sees a dog and not its constituent parts, so if you want them to recognize the dog's tail or listen to the dog's bark, then these aspects of the animal will need to be specifically pointed out to them.*

10 THINGS TO REMEMBER

1 *Before the age of four, girls tend to have more advanced speech and language skills than boys, but after that, boys quickly catch up.*

2 *Language can be divided into two types. Expressive is the speaking, reading and writing of a language, while receptive is the understanding of it through listening and learning. Toddlers' receptive language tends to be more advanced than their expressive.*

3 *Unlike other developmental milestones, speech and language is far more variable. More than a year's difference between toddlers is not unusual.*

4 *When it comes to understanding your toddler no one is better than you. An outsider will only pick up a quarter of what your child is saying, whereas you will understand 95 per cent.*

5 *When your toddler says a new word, praise them for saying it, then repeat it back to them, but slightly expand on it with more description. This will not only enlarge your child's vocabulary, but also help them start to form sentences.*

6 *If your toddler says a word incorrectly, don't tell them they've said it wrong. Simply repeat it back to them correctly – a technique that's known as modelling.*

7 *It might sound obvious, but it's through talking to your toddler that speech and language skills are best learnt. Therefore provide them with a running commentary on what you are doing, however mundane. You'll be amazed how much they're taking in.*

8 *Reading and singing to your toddler are excellent ways to encourage your toddler's interest in speech and language,*

teaching them to listen and pay attention and fostering an enjoyment and understanding of rhythm and rhyme.

9 *Rather than assisting your toddler's communication skills, television can actually have a detrimental effect, reducing their attention span and compromising their ability to listen. Try not to let your toddler watch TV for more than an hour a day.*

10 *If your toddler mispronounces certain words, don't worry. It's very common and will usually disappear by the time they're three.*

8

How to handle a fussy eater

In this chapter you will learn:
- *why food fussiness is so common*
- *how personality affects fussiness*
- *about the link between eating and independence*
- *tips on offering new foods*
- *how to monitor your toddler's intake*
- *ways to be a good role model*
- *what is a good toddler diet*
- *what is a toddler portion*
- *how to spot a food allergy*
- *tips on making mealtimes fun.*

Why most toddlers are fussy about their food

Rare is the parent of a toddler who has not experienced a fussy-eating episode with their child. Indeed, being picky about what they eat and reluctant to try new foods is a perfectly normal part of a toddler's development. There is even a special name for it – it is called neophobia, or fear of the new. Psychologists who have studied this extremely common toddler response believe it evolved many thousands of years ago as part of a young child's basic survival mechanism. By being suspicious of new foods and sticking to a tried and trusted, albeit rather limited, diet an increasingly mobile toddler is less likely to accidentally eat anything poisonous or harmful to them. Seen in this context, your toddler's fussiness makes perfect sense, but of course, when you are faced with their refusal and/or pickiness on a thrice-daily basis it is hard not to become anxious and, on occasion, very frustrated. But try to remember that this response is perfectly natural too, because feeding your toddler is not just about providing them with the right nutrients – it is also an expression of love and a way of showing the rest of the world your ability as a parent. So it is no wonder it feels so awful when your efforts are constantly rejected.

Did you know?

A recent survey found that 82 per cent of parents felt that food rejection in their toddler was a cause for concern and that their toddler's fussy eating ranked as the third most stressful parenting problem after financial worries and illness. So the next time your toddler turns up their nose at the meal you have just prepared from scratch and announces 'don't like it' without even trying a mouthful, try to take comfort in the fact that you are definitely not alone.

FOOD JAGS

A toddler's neophobic response to food can often result in what is known as a 'food jag'. A food jag can manifest itself in two ways:

1 *Your toddler gets stuck on certain foods and repeatedly requests them at every meal, for example they insist on eating yoghurt for breakfast, lunch and dinner.*
2 *Your toddler suddenly refuses a food that they liked in the past, for example scrambled egg may always have been a firm favourite, but now your toddler won't even allow it to pass their lips.*

Again, both of the above behaviours are a perfectly normal and temporary stage in your toddler's development.

Case study

When I weaned Edie she was a really adventurous little eater, happily tucking in to my vegetable purées and later enjoying finger food such as carrot sticks and hummus. But as she's got older she's become more and more fussy and at the moment she's stuck in what we call her 'white food' phase. Basically everything has to be milk-based, so she'll only eat pasta or potato if it has a cheese sauce on it. She's fine with yoghurts and fromage frais, but she won't touch fruit, except for bananas, and even refuses to drink juice, always opting for milk instead. I've tried disguising vegetables in her food, but there's no fooling Edie who can sniff out a niblet of sweetcorn at a hundred paces. The other day I tried to ring the changes by making her little ham pizzas, which she used to love. I even tried to involve her in the cooking process, getting her to help me roll out the dough and putting on the toppings. But while she thoroughly enjoyed making the things, she steadfastly refused to eat them. I try not to get stressed by it, but mealtimes with Edie aren't particularly enjoyable at the moment. Also, I do worry whether she's eating enough, but she certainly seems to be growing okay – in fact she's the tallest girl at her nursery.

Top tip

Rather than focusing too much on what your toddler does not eat, try looking at what they do eat – not meal by meal or even day by day, but over the course of an entire week. Keep a record of everything that your toddler consumes, including snacks and drinks, and the chances are you will be very pleasantly surprised by how balanced their diet really is.

EXTREME FUSSINESS

While neophobia about food is inherent in all toddlers, some will display a much stronger response than others. These toddlers may have extreme anxiety about trying new foods and can be very rigid about the food they will eat, which in severe cases may mean eating as little as five different foods. Some toddlers are also very sensory-sensitive to food and have an extreme reaction to the touch, taste and smell of certain foods. Such extreme responses are thankfully quite rare but interestingly they are far more common in boys. Indeed, in one clinical sample of extremely fussy toddlers, boys outnumbered girls by approximately ten to one. If you are concerned about your toddler's food fussiness, speak to your GP or health visitor, who may refer you to a specialist feeding clinic if one is available in your area, or a clinical psychologist who specializes in children's feeding problems.

Personality and fussiness

Experts have identified several temperament traits that tend to make a toddler more prone to fussiness. These are:

▶ *Your toddler has a high intensity level and is very emotionally responsive.*
▶ *Your toddler has a low adaptability level and finds it difficult to accept change.*
▶ *Your toddler's sensory threshold level is high and they become concerned about such things as loud noises, bright lights, clothing and food textures.*
▶ *Your toddler has a high rhythmicity level and is not very predictable in their daily routines.*

Delaying introducing lumpier foods until your baby is approaching toddlerhood can cause fussiness. According to research conducted by Bristol University, a baby who is not given lumpy food until they are ten months or older is more likely to be frightened by food that needs to be chewed or is wary of anything with a different texture. To help combat this, try gradually to introduce slightly more solid foods in small amounts so that your toddler can learn how the food feels in their mouth. Then start increasing the firmness of the foods offered as your toddler becomes used to them.

EATING AND INDEPENDENCE

Another factor that can make feeding a toddler such a challenge is the fact that mealtimes provide the perfect opportunity for them to exert their growing need for independence, as discussed in Chapter 3. In this instance your toddler is not refusing to eat their food because they are suspicious or uncertain about what you are offering them – their refusal here is a way of pushing the limits of your authority and asserting some control over their lives. And what is more, it is a battle your toddler knows they can win because no matter how much you may sometimes feel you want to, you should never force-feed your toddler.

Insight
In my experience, the issue of independence and eating can be largely overcome by involving your toddler as much as possible, from helping to decide what to eat to choosing what colour cutlery they want to eat with.

OTHER REASONS WHY YOUR TODDLER MAY BE RELUCTANT TO EAT

▶ *They are over-tired.*
▶ *They are distracted, perhaps by toys, games, television or a new environment.*
▶ *They are not hungry because they have eaten enough either at that meal or from eating too many snacks before it.*
▶ *They are not hungry because they have drunk too much milk, juice or squash.*
▶ *They are feeling unwell – a sore throat, a cold or a temperature can all affect a toddler's appetite.*

Top tip

If you want to help your toddler overcome their neophobia about food, it will really help to establish a good mealtime routine. If everything around them feels safe, secure and very familiar, your toddler will be better disposed to try new foods. For hints and tips on how best to establish a good mealtime routine, see pages 55 and 60.

Offering new foods

It is very tempting to stick to what you know your toddler likes, rather than constantly trying to expand their repertoire. But it really is worth persevering with new foods because studies have shown that a toddler may need to be offered something ten or more times before they overcome their neophobic rejection response. Yet a recent poll found that more than half of parents give up offering a new food after just two or three refusals, never giving their toddler enough of a chance to accept it. If, however, after repeated attempts your toddler is still rejecting a certain food, then it is important that you respect their taste and do not push them too hard. But by all means try it again a couple of months down the line.

THE DOS AND DON'TS OF OFFERING NEW FOODS

Here are a few things to consider when offering your toddler
something new to eat.

DO:	DON'T:
▶ Offer one new food at a time otherwise your toddler will feel overwhelmed.	▶ Make a big deal about giving your toddler something new to try. Simply place it on the dinner table along with everything else.
▶ Serve one favourite food with one new food as this will often help your toddler to try the new food.	▶ Present the new food in too large a quantity. Just give your toddler a taste and if they do like it, then they can always have some more.
▶ Give a new food to try when you know your toddler is hungry.	▶ Be tempted to mix the new food in with a favourite one as the chances are your toddler will reject it all.
▶ Praise your toddler when they try a new food, even if it is just a morsel. Toddlers respond positively to praise and will be more likely to try different foods in the future.	▶ Give up on a new food just because your toddler rejects it. As previously stated, many toddlers will not try a new food until they have been offered it ten or more times.

Insight

In my experience toddlers learn to like the foods they are
most familiar with, so put foods that you'd like them to eat
in full sight from an early age.

MAKE AN EXPLORING NEW FOODS CHART

To encourage your toddler to be more adventurous with food, why
not make an Exploring New Foods Chart. Simply draw nine columns

on a sheet of paper and in the first column write the name or draw a picture of the new food your toddler will be exploring. Above columns two to eight draw the senses that your toddler will use:

▶ *an eye (sight)*
▶ *a nose (smell)*
▶ *a hand (touch)*
▶ *an ear (to represent sounds that can be made with the food – the snap of a carrot, the crunch of an apple)*
▶ *a mouth (the feel of the food on the lips)*
▶ *a tongue (chewing the food)*
▶ *and finally an arrow pointing downwards to signal that your toddler has swallowed the food.*

You can tick each column with your toddler as they manage to explore each new food, and in the last column you can add a smiley face if your toddler liked it.

Did you know?

Because most toddlers learn to recognize the food they like through its visual appearance they would probably reject a favourite biscuit if it was broken as it wouldn't look the same as the whole ones they'd enjoyed so much previously.

Practise what you preach: how you affect your toddler's eating

Of course nothing influences how your toddler behaves towards food more than you. If you never eat vegetables and have a penchant for junk food, then how can you expect your toddler to be different? Similarly, avoid passing your own food hang-ups and dietary anxieties onto your toddler. For example, if your toddler sees you regularly skipping meals or avoiding certain food groups this will send out a very mixed message about what constitutes healthy eating. And remember that older siblings can have a considerable impact on your toddler's dietary likes and dislikes. Therefore it is important to try to encourage everyone in the family to be a good role model to your toddler when around food and especially at mealtimes. Here are some simple ways to be a good role model:

1 *Encourage family mealtimes whenever possible. As in so much of toddler behaviour, they will learn about eating properly, as well as picking up a few table manners, from watching and copying you. Also, by making mealtimes sociable and fun, your toddler will come to look forward to them and enjoy participating.*
2 *Make a conscious effort to eat the foods that you want your toddler to eat. Better still, make meals that all the family can eat together, rather than separate food for your toddler.*
3 *Try to avoid grabbing a bite on the run when in front of your toddler. For example, at breakfast time it is tempting to dash around the kitchen, unloading the dishwasher, etc. while munching on a slice of toast. But your toddler will think that this is the best way to eat breakfast, and other meals too, if you are not careful.*
4 *Another great way you can lead by example is by showing an appreciation of, and interest in, food preparation and cooking and encouraging your toddler to join in. For example, let your toddler help scrub the baked potatoes and sprinkle the cheese on top once they are cooked. If your toddler has been involved in preparing the meal it will become a source of pride and they will be much more likely to eat it.*

Did you know?

Research shows that of the 27 per cent of toddlers who are classified as fussy eaters, 22 per cent of them had parents who admitted to being fussy eaters themselves.

Case study

Up until recently I had quite a complex relationship with food. In my teenage years I suffered from bulimia and went down to 6½ stone (41 kg). Then at university I ballooned and put on loads of weight. Since then I've really grappled with my weight, cutting out certain foods, going on mad exercise regimes and even on occasion, starving myself completely. For a long time I really did see food as the enemy. But when I got pregnant I was determined to eat healthily for the sake of my unborn child. Then, when Sophia was born, I vowed not to pass on my own food and body issues to my daughter. My mum had always been a yo-yo dieter and one of my earliest childhood memories is of her grabbing her tummy and moaning about how fat she was. She'd often sit eating a Ryvita while the rest of us tucked into a Sunday roast. Now that Sophia's nearly two we usually have our meals together, and I'm determined for her to see her mummy eating a healthy, balanced diet. In fact, most of the time we eat the same thing, such as a bowl of pasta with pesto, and while she can sometimes be a bit of a fusspot, I hope that by setting a good example, she'll grow up having a much healthier attitude towards food and her body than I ever did.

Top tip

Be aware of how you talk about yourself and food in front of your toddler. Psychologists warn against being negative about your own body image and diet within earshot of your children, especially if you are a mum with a daughter. Studies have shown that young girls are more influenced by their mother's attitudes toward body image and food than any other factor.

What should a toddler eat?

Most toddlers have good and bad days when it comes to food. Perhaps yesterday they happily devoured everything you offered, whereas today they are pushing their food around their plate, showing very little interest in actually eating it. As mentioned previously, when this happens try to remember what your toddler has eaten over the last week, rather than what they are not eating today. Also, sometimes our expectations of what a toddler should be eating are unrealistic, as we pile up their plate with a portion that is nearly that of an adult. It is worth knowing that a toddler's stomach is only one-third of the size of yours. However, your toddler's relative daily energy requirement is around three times that of an adult (95 kilocalories per kg of body weight, compared with 30–35 kilocalories per kg of body weight). Therefore it is essential that your toddler's diet is well balanced and highly nutritious, and unlike that of adults and older children, it should contain some foods that are high in fat and low in fibre.

WHAT IS A GOOD, BALANCED TODDLER DIET?

Providing a good balanced diet for your toddler simply involves combining foods from the following five food groups and serving them in the correct amount.

1. Bread, cereals and potatoes
Includes: rice, couscous, pasta, noodles, sweet potatoes and yam

Amount: serve at each meal and also offer as snacks. A serving size is ½ slice bread, 2 oz pasta, potato, cereal, etc.

2. Fruits and vegetables
Includes: apple, banana, orange, kiwi, broccoli, green beans, canned sweetcorn, frozen peas, raisins

Amount: serve at each meal and aim for five small servings a day. A serving size is approximately 1 to 2 tablespoons.

3. Milk, cheese and yoghurt
Includes: fromage frais, cheese sauce, custard

Amount: serve three times a day. A serving size of milk (whole milk if your toddler is under two) is approximately 4 fl oz, cheese between ½ and ¾ oz, while for yoghurt and fromage frais it is around a 4 oz pot.

4. Meat, fish and vegetarian alternatives
Includes: eggs, nuts (not whole, due to choking hazard), peanut butter, kidney beans, chickpeas, hummus, lentils

Amount: serve one to two times a day if your toddler is eating meat and fish, or two to three times a day for vegetarian toddlers. Serving size is ½ egg, 2 tablespoons of pulses, 1 tablespoon of peanut butter, 1 oz fish or meat.

5. Foods high in fat and sugar
Includes: olive oil, butter, margarine, crisps, cakes, biscuits, ice cream, sweets, sweetened drinks

Amount: use a mixture of different oils, butter and margarine when required. Offer other high-calorie and sugary foods occasionally, and only as an addition to foods from the other four groups, never instead of.

THE IMPORTANCE OF SNACKS

When your toddler is being a picky eater it is tempting to cut out the snacks in the hope that they will eat more at mealtimes. However, this will probably have the reverse effect because your toddler will be over-hungry and in no mood to sit down and eat a meal. The best way to view snacking in the toddler years is as a sort of insurance policy. Because your toddler's eating habits are erratic and their tummies are too small to take in everything they need in three sittings, a healthy, well-timed snack will help balance out their uneven diet, and provide further opportunity to boost their nutrient intake.

Here are a few healthy snack suggestions:

▶ *fresh fruit slices*
▶ *vegetable sticks*
▶ *cheese cubes*
▶ *crackers/toast*
▶ *small sandwiches*
▶ *yoghurt/fromage frais.*

Try to avoid the following:

▶ *Letting your toddler drink more than 16 to 24 fl oz of milk a day.*
▶ *Allowing them to drink more than 4 to 6 oz of undiluted juice a day.*
▶ *Letting your toddler fill up on sweets and crisps.*
▶ *Providing snacks too close to mealtimes.*
▶ *Giving portions that are too big. As a rough rule of thumb, a toddler portion is approximately a ½ of an adult's portion size.*

Insight

I'd recommend keeping a careful eye on your toddler's milk intake. If they drink too much they are more at risk of becoming fussy eaters. Such toddlers tend to avoid lumpy or chewy foods, preferring to fill up on milk.

Foods to be careful about

Salt

This should be kept to an absolute minimum. Many foodstuffs, for example certain breakfast cereals, already contain salt and processed foods, even those specifically aimed at children, can have a very high salt content. Check labels and go for lower salt options. As a result of the salt already present in much food, you do not need to add salt to your toddler's food – children aged one to three years should have just two grams a day. If you want to add flavour to a dish, try using mild herbs and spices instead.

Additives and sweeteners

Although all food is tested for safety, it is a good habit to read the labels of the food and drink you are giving your toddler and avoid a product that contains large amounts of additives and/or sweeteners. Studies have shown that these can have an adverse effect on your toddler's behaviour.

Raw eggs
The risk of salmonella, which causes food poisoning, increases if your toddler consumes raw eggs and food that contains raw or partially cooked eggs. If you give eggs to your toddler, make sure that they are cooked until both the white and yolk are solid.

Other foods to avoid
Shellfish – similarly to eggs, all shellfish should be well cooked to reduce the risk of food poisoning.

Whole nuts – to prevent choking always crush or flake nuts when giving them to a toddler.

Large fish – shark, swordfish and marlin should be avoided because these fish contain relatively high levels of mercury, which might affect a toddler's developing nervous system.

FOOD ALLERGIES

It is estimated that between two and four per cent of toddlers have allergic reactions to foods. Symptoms can include:

- *eczema*
- *reflux*
- *vomiting*
- *diarrhoea*
- *wheezing.*

The most common food allergens in toddlers' diets are:

- *cows' milk*
- *eggs*
- *wheat*
- *peanuts*
- *soya.*

If you suspect that your toddler has a food allergy it is important that you get it properly diagnosed either by a paediatrician or at an allergy clinic. Eliminating an important food item from your toddler's diet, for example wheat or milk, without proper consultation can greatly reduce the nutrients your toddler is receiving. If a food allergy is discovered, your toddler's diet will need careful management by a professional to make sure suitable nutritional replacements are incorporated.

Toddler drinks

Giving your toddler too many calories from drinks such as milk and juice is one of the most common toddler feeding mistakes. You should offer your toddler between six and eight drinks a day – one with each meal and each snack. Your toddler may, however, need more fluids in very hot weather or if they are being particularly active as this is when they can become dehydrated quite quickly. Milk and water are the best drinks to offer between meals. Squashes and fruit juice drinks should always be given well diluted, and only give pure juice drinks at mealtimes as the acid they contain can damage milk teeth when given without food.

Did you know?

While oily fish such as mackerel, salmon and sardines are an excellent source of omega-3 fats, they should not be served too regularly because of the traces of toxins that are found in them. The Food Standards Agency recommends that boys eat such fish a maximum of four times a week, while girls should not exceed twice a week. The reason why girls should eat oily fish less is to prevent them accumulating toxins and carrying them through into their childbearing years.

Keeping mealtimes calm and relaxed

When it comes to feeding a fussy toddler, it is really important to try to keep things calm and relaxed at mealtimes. If you become stressed and visibly anxious about your toddler's food intake, trying to cajole them into eating, then food becomes a power struggle, with mealtimes quickly descending into a battleground that is unpleasant for everyone concerned.

One way to help your toddler eat well and help you worry less is to accept what food experts call the 'division of responsibility', which effectively defines what your and your toddler's roles are when it comes to eating, thus leaving little room for power struggles and bribery.

Here are your job descriptions:

▶ *Your job is to provide nutritious food choices at meals and snack times. In other words, you decide the what, where and when of eating.*
▶ *Your toddler's job is to choose how much they will eat of the foods you serve. In other words, your toddler decides how much or even whether to eat.*

If you adhere to your job description, your toddler will realize that they are allowed to eat as little or as much as they want at each meal and at snack time and as a result they will learn to listen to their bodies and trust their internal hunger gauge.

Here are a few other things to consider when trying to maintain mealtime peace:

▶ *Try to remember that a toddler will never voluntarily starve themselves. They are actually extremely good at judging their hunger and what their little body needs. In fact, children can regulate their appetite to meet their growth requirements* from as little as a few weeks old and as such, your toddler is better than you at knowing how much they need to eat.

▶ Keep calm and don't make a fuss when your toddler refuses to eat. By giving your toddler more attention when they don't eat you could be unwittingly encouraging them to refuse food in order to get your attention. Remember, even negative attention is better than no attention at all.

▶ Try to keep meals simple. If you put a lot of effort into making your toddler's food you are bound to feel resentful when they refuse to eat. For example, a pan-fried piece of salmon with some boiled potatoes is equally as nutritious as a home-made fishcake and an awful lot less hassle to make.

▶ Don't threaten, nag or shout at your toddler in the hope it will make them eat. If you create a non-threatening atmosphere at mealtimes, it will make your toddler feel safe and secure and much more likely to try their food. Besides, how would you feel if someone stood next to you at dinner, shouting at you to clear the plate – it is a sure-fire way of killing off even the healthiest appetite.

▶ Avoid force-feeding. Your toddler will become anxious and frightened around food if you force-feed them at mealtimes. Also, if you give your toddler control over their food intake they will learn to eat to their appetite.

▶ Don't use food as a reward. Studies show that if you reward your toddler for eating one food with another, for example, only giving dessert if all the dinner is eaten, then the reward food becomes more desirable than the food they are rewarded for eating.

Knowing when your toddler has had enough

As mentioned previously, you should never try to force your toddler to eat, so it is important to recognize the signs your toddler gives when they have had enough food. Here are eight typical signs that should be heeded:

1 *Your toddler says no.*
2 *They keep their mouth shut when food is offered.*
3 *Your toddler turns their head away from the food that is being offered.*
4 *They push away the spoon, bowl or plate with the food.*
5 *Your toddler holds the food in their mouth and refuses to swallow it.*
6 *They repeatedly spit out the food.*
7 *Your toddler starts to cry, shout or scream.*
8 *They gag or retch.*

Insight

I've often seen parents bribing their toddler with the promise of dessert if they'll just eat one more spoonful of their dinner. Always give the pudding whether the savoury course is eaten or not otherwise you'll reinforce the idea that sweet things are more desirable.

The vegetarian toddler

There is no reason why you should not give your toddler a vegetarian diet, if you so choose, but obviously it is important to make sure it is balanced and contains all the necessary nutrients. It is also worth being conscious of the amount of iron your toddler is consuming as toddlers are prone to iron deficiency anaemia and it is more difficult to absorb iron from vegetable sources than from meat. The following suggestions should help combat the problem:

▶ *Give your toddler iron-rich foods every single day.*
▶ *Also try to give food high in vitamin C, such as fruit and vegetables and diluted fruit juices, at mealtimes because these will make it easier for your toddler to absorb the iron.*
▶ *Do not give your toddler tea or coffee as the caffeine in these drinks will reduce the amount of iron your toddler absorbs.*

Did you know?

How we feed our toddlers varies greatly throughout the world. In the West it is largely assumed that a toddler will only eat bland food, such as macaroni cheese and fish pie. Yet in Japan, some of the best-selling baby foods include rice with chopped burdock root, sardines ground up in white radish sauce, cod roe spaghetti, mugwort casserole and flounder and spinach stew.

Case study

Last Sunday we went out for lunch together as a family and it was an absolute joy. Sitting there with the twins as they tucked into their spaghetti bolognese, sauce smeared all around their mouths as they slurped up the pasta, I finally felt that we'd come out of a long tunnel. At one point, a year or so back, I honestly thought we'd never be able to eat out in a restaurant again – mealtimes had become such a nightmare. The boys were really picky eaters, often refusing to touch anything. My stomach used to sink as they pushed the food around their plates, occasionally toying with the idea of putting something in their mouths, only to change their minds at the last minute. Also, keeping them sitting at a table was practically impossible, if it wasn't Adam then it would be Euan playing up. Mealtimes would invariably descend into chaos, and I'm not proud to admit it, but on several occasions I completely lost my rag, shouting at the boys to sit down and eat their food. Yet looking at them now, it's amazing how things have changed. They have started to take a real enjoyment in their food, even asking me when's breakfast or what's for dinner.

10 THINGS TO REMEMBER

1 *Most toddlers go through a fussy eating phase of refusing to try new foods and/or sticking to a very limited diet. This is known as neophobia (fear of the new) and is believed to be a self-survival mechanism, designed to prevent young children from accidentally eating anything poisonous or harmful.*

2 *Feeding is a fundamental part of nurturing, which is why it can be so upsetting when your child rejects food you have lovingly prepared for them. But try not to get too anxious at mealtimes, as this will make your toddler anxious and less likely to eat.*

3 *Rather than focus on what your toddler hasn't eaten at a given sitting, try to look at the bigger picture. Spread out over a week, the chances are they've eaten a far more balanced and nutritious diet than you thought.*

4 *When offering your toddler new foods, don't give up after one or two rejections. It will often take more than ten attempts before a child can overcome their neophobic reaction.*

5 *How you eat has a massive impact on what your toddler eats. Seeing you tucking into lots of fruit and vegetables will make them far more willing to try them themselves as they can see that there is nothing to be suspicious about.*

6 *A toddler's stomach is only a third of the size of yours while their daily energy requirement is around three times more. It's therefore very important that every meal and snack is highly nutritious.*

7 *View your toddler's snacks as a sort of insurance policy. It is through them you can help balance out an uneven diet and provide further opportunity to boost their nutrient intake.*

8   *Giving your toddler too many calories through drinks such as milk and juice is one of the most common toddler feeding mistakes. Your toddler should be drinking six to eight drinks, evenly spaced throughout the day, and always make sure juice and squashes are well diluted.*

9   *Don't be tempted to threaten, nag, shout or bribe your toddler to eat. Mealtimes need to be non-threatening because only when a toddler feels safe and secure are they likely to eat.*

10 *Accept when your toddler has had enough and don't insist on just one last spoonful. Your toddler knows their appetite far better than you and you must learn to trust them.*

9

Getting your toddler to sleep better

In this chapter you will learn:
- *why toddlers struggle with sleep*
- *why a baby who sleeps soundly can become a wakeful toddler*
- *the different stages of sleep*
- *the amount of sleep a toddler needs*
- *ways to help your toddler sleep better*
- *why naps matter*
- *how to deal with nightmares and night terrors*
- *tips on moving from cot to bed*
- *ways to keep your toddler in their bed.*

Why toddlers often struggle with sleep

Getting your toddler to go to sleep without fuss, to stay asleep through the night, and preferably to remain in their own bed until a reasonable time in the morning is undoubtedly the holy grail of toddler sleeping. But is it a realistic one? The fact is, a lot of toddlers do struggle with one, or often several, aspects of sleep. For example, the child who happily goes to bed after a quick story and a kiss and a cuddle might sleep soundly until the small hours, but then gets an irresistible urge to creep into mummy and daddy's bed. Similarly, the toddler who gets upset or angry several times before finally settling may then sleep through, but is up at the crack of dawn, raring to go.

It is all too easy to see your toddler's challenging sleeping habits as somehow indicative of your poor parenting skills, and while there will always be ways you can help your toddler to sleep better, here are some other factors to consider:

▶ *How your toddler sleeps can be attributed partly to their temperament. Some toddlers are more demanding at night, and studies have shown that this is especially the case for those with lower sensory thresholds and less adaptivity.*
▶ *Other parents often exaggerate how long their children sleep for. Indeed, recent research found that between 20 and 30 per cent of toddlers are poor sleepers, regularly have difficulty settling and frequently awaken during the night.*

Why a baby who sleeps well can become a wakeful toddler

Another factor that can throw many parents off guard about their toddler's poor sleeping is that their child probably slept very well as a baby. In fact, it is estimated that half of toddlers who struggle to stay asleep were sleeping through prior to entering the toddler years. So why does this occur? Here are two factors to consider:

1 *Your child is now at a stage of massive growth and change. They are leaping from one developmental milestone to another and the excitement and stimulation this creates can make it very difficult for a younger toddler to switch off, and indeed remain switched off.*
2 *In addition, your toddler is much more aware of their surroundings and they are learning how to make things happen. As your toddler's independence grows, so does their will and if your toddler doesn't want to go to bed then they are now quite capable of letting you know. Similarly, now if*

your toddler wakes in the night they are more likely to create a fuss because they have learnt that if they do you will come and attend to them, and they will receive all the attention that entails.

Did you know?

It might not feel like it judging from the bags under your eyes, but by the age of two your toddler will have spent more time asleep than awake and overall they will spend 40 per cent of their childhood asleep.

Understanding your toddler's sleep

A final factor worth considering when evaluating how well your toddler sleeps is that a toddler sleeps differently from an adult, and that your expectations should be adjusted accordingly. Whereas an adult can enjoy seven to eight hours of deep uninterrupted sleep, for a toddler this is impossible. Your toddler has a shorter sleep cycle than you do and will surface from a deep sleep into a lighter sleep approximately five times a night. It is during these periods of lighter sleep that your toddler is more susceptible to waking.

WHAT IS HAPPENING WHEN YOUR TODDLER'S SLEEPING?

Sleep plays a crucial role in your toddler's health and well-being. It is while your toddler is sleeping that important developments occur not only to their body, but also to their brain. Sleep can be divided into two broad types, each serving a different purpose for your toddler:

▶ **Non-Rapid Eye Movement (NREM)** – *during this type of sleep blood supply to your toddler's muscles is increased, tissue* *growth and repair occurs, energy is restored and important hormones are released that assist your toddler's development and protect their immune system. NREM is usually a deep sleep.*

▶ **Rapid Eye Movement (REM)** – *this is the stage of sleep when your toddler's muscles go into a state of rest and their body becomes totally relaxed, yet at the same time their eyes move back and forth very quickly beneath their eyelids. Your toddler is now dreaming, and scientists believe that this is the brain's way of trying to make sense of what has happened during the day, processing all those new experiences and storing important ones for future reference. REM is a lighter sleep than NREM and infants and toddlers experience it more frequently than adults. It is while in this stage that your toddler is more likely to wake up.*

Did you know?

A chemical called acetylcholine is released during REM sleep and it is this that triggers a switch in your toddler's brain to make them start dreaming. Acetylcholine is so powerful it can even induce dreaming when it is artificially administered.

How much sleep should your toddler have?

Just like adults, every toddler's sleep requirement is different, so there are no hard and fast rules. But here is a rough guide:

Age	Number of naps	Nap hours	Night hours	Average total
9 months	2	2½ to 4	11 to 12	14
12 months	1 to 2	2 to 3	11½ to 12	13 to 14
2 years	1	1 to 2	11 to 12	13
3 years	1	1 to 1½	11	12

Are you worried that your toddler isn't getting enough sleep? Then ask yourself the following questions:

▶ *Is your toddler always falling asleep in the car or in their pushchair even when it is not naptime?*
▶ *Do you have to wake your toddler up almost every morning?*
▶ *Does your toddler seem over-tired, cranky, irritable, aggressive, over-emotional or hyperactive?*
▶ *On some nights does your toddler doze off much earlier than their usual bedtime?*

If you answered yes to two or more of these questions, your toddler may not be getting enough sleep.

Ways you can help your toddler to sleep better

Here are some simple strategies that should help ensure that everyone gets a better night's sleep:

ESTABLISH A GOOD BEDTIME ROUTINE

This really should be your first port of call if you are struggling with your toddler's poor sleeping. Various studies have shown that toddlers settle easier and sleep better if their bedtime follows a regular, predictable pattern. For more on establishing a good bedtime routine see page 61.

TEACH YOUR TODDLER TO SETTLE THEMSELVES

Your toddler's ability to settle themselves when going to sleep, and subsequently if they wake up in the night, is essential to a good night's rest for your toddler and indeed you. Yet some children find this a difficult skill to master, often because they have never been taught it. Perhaps you have allowed your toddler to doze off on the settee or in your arms before putting them to bed for the night. Or maybe they have become reliant on the comfort of a bottle or dummy to get to sleep. As a result they do not know how to fall asleep by themselves, and have become dependent on certain external factors to lull them into a state of slumber. When, however, your toddler wakes in the night to find that they are no longer on the settee or in your arms or that their bottle or dummy has gone, it is hardly surprising that they become confused and upset and then cry out for you. There is no right way to teach your toddler to settle themselves, but the following three sleep training methods are all effective – it just depends on what you feel you can cope with, because once embarking on a sleep training programme, it is important to be firm and consistent.

1 **Cold turkey.** *This involves ignoring your toddler so they learn that you don't respond to their cries at night. It can however be very traumatic for all concerned and is not recommended for very young toddlers. The benefit is that it can work very quickly – in as little as four days.*

2 **Controlled crying.** *This involves popping in and out of your toddler's room to settle them with reassuring pats or hushes. There are two ways to do it:*
    a *Go in every five minutes the first night, every ten minutes the second night, 15 minutes the third night, etc. until your toddler goes to sleep.*
    b *Go in after five minutes, then ten minutes, followed by 15 minutes, and so on, extending the length of time throughout the course of a single evening, and do the same on subsequent nights.*
   Controlled crying takes approximately a week to work.

3 **Staying with your toddler.** *This entails sitting by your toddler's cot or bed while they fall asleep. You have to be very calm and boring to reinforce the idea that night-time is for sleeping, but your presence should be reassuring enough for them to fall asleep. Every night move just a little bit further towards the*

*door. This gradual withdrawal method is the gentlest and, as
such, can take up to two weeks to work.*

Insight

When you settle your toddler to bed at night, I think it's
worth considering exactly what you are doing, and asking
yourself whether you'd be happy to be doing it again at
2 a.m. If the answer's no, then you might want to reconsider
your bedtime routine.

Case study

Probably one of the hardest things I have ever done was sleep
training Jasper. I think it goes against every instinct to leave your
child crying, even just for a short while. I remember sitting on the
stairs, outside his bedroom, waiting for the allotted ten minutes to
be up, my head in my hands and tears streaming down my face. It
took all my willpower not to go rushing in and scoop him up, but
after a few days the crying really did start to subside. Now, a few
months down the line, I'm so glad I stuck with it because finally
Jasper will go to bed on his own, without me having to sit beside
him for half an hour, waiting for him to go to sleep. I'd honestly say
to anyone out there about to embark on sleep training their toddler,
be prepared to feel absolutely wretched while you're going through
it, but the benefits will far outweigh that brief period of agony.

Top tip

Most parents are unaware of how much attention they give a
toddler who wakes in the night. It is very easy to unwittingly
find yourself engaged in a conversation, telling your toddler
how everyone else is asleep or reasoning with them to stay
in their bed. Coupled with the extra kisses and cuddles you
probably give, you can see how waking in the night can
become an attractive prospect to an attention-seeking toddler.
It will therefore help to develop a 'last phrase' to say to

(Contd)

your toddler as you exit their room, and to repeat, should you have to re-enter. This can be anything from 'sleep time' or 'snuggle down' to 'shhh now', and will send your toddler a very clear message that it is time for sleep and that there will be no further interaction or communication – in other words, you mean business!

Typical toddler sleep problems

Here are three common toddler sleep problems and ways to deal with them:

BEDTIME BLUES

What is happening
My toddler has started being difficult at bedtime.

Why it is happening
Assuming you have got a good bedtime routine in place and that your toddler knows how to settle themselves, then it could be that your toddler is using bedtime as a way of exerting their independence.

What you can do about it
It is worth avoiding bedtime power struggles whenever possible, and one of the most effective ways of doing this is offering your toddler a choice during their bedtime routine. For example, let them choose which bedtime story they would like you to read or allow them to select the pyjamas they want to wear. Do not, however, ask them whether they want to go to bed because the chances are they will say no. It is much better to offer them the choice of going to bed now or in five minutes' time, and either way you are happy with the outcome.

Most toddlers soon develop delaying tactics at bedtime, the most common being a string of different requests. Try anticipating your toddler's and make them part of the bedtime routine. For example, place a beaker of water on the bedside table, remind them to use the potty/toilet one last time, give them lots of extra kisses and cuddles to last them through the night. Then allow your toddler one extra request – but make it clear that there will be no more after that.

Then, if your toddler continues to refuse to settle, remain calm and consistent. Avoid making a fuss and give minimal attention. If your toddler attempts to get out of bed, simply put them back again without engaging in conversation. Your toddler will soon learn that they must remain in their bed until they fall asleep.

Case study

In some respects I think it is easier to get a baby to sleep than a toddler. When Manon was little, she'd go to bed with minimum fuss and I just assumed that was the way it would always be. But just lately she's picked up on the power of the 'just one mores', which we've started calling her endless list of things she needs or wants before she could possibly even contemplate closing her eyes. Sometimes I've found myself going up and down the stairs a dozen times before she finally settles, by which time I'm so shattered I've barely got the energy to eat, let alone anything else. It's made me realize that I've got to be firmer with her, so the other day I told her that mummy was going downstairs now and that if she shouted out for anything else I wouldn't come. All was silent for a while and I remember thinking, 'Gosh that was easy'. But then I heard the pitter-patter of tiny feet. Manon had obviously decided that if I wasn't coming to her, then she'd come to me!

Insight

If your toddler is developing ever more elaborate delaying tactics, I suggest you set some time aside to sit down with them and write a fun checklist of everything they need before going to sleep. Once the checklist is ticked off at night, they are allowed one last request and then it's time for bed.

NIGHT-TIME WAKING

What is happening
My toddler keeps waking up in the night.

Why it is happening
If you know your toddler can sleep through the night and is
capable of self-settling, it could be that they are going through
a developmental phase. For example, your toddler has suddenly
discovered the power of their imagination, conjuring up monsters
under the bed and strange noises. Or maybe they are suffering
separation anxiety and need to know that you are there.

What you can do about it
Reassure your toddler that they are safe and okay and that you are
nearby, but try not to take them out of their cot/bed or strike up a
conversation. You need to be gentle but firm. Also let your toddler
bring toys and comfort objects to bed, as their familiarity will help
ease fears and separation anxiety in the middle of the night. If you
haven't done so already, it might also be worth installing a nightlight
in your toddler's room so that when they wake up in the small hours
they will be able to see that nothing has changed, everything is safe
and secure and they will then be more likely to re-settle.

EARLY RISER

What is happening
My toddler wakes up far too early.

Why it is happening
The fact is that most toddlers are notoriously early risers and their
interpretation of what is 'morning' is likely to be a good few hours
shy of yours. The chances are that your toddler has had all the sleep
they need and, unlike you, they are bright eyed and raring to go!

What you can do about it
There is not much you can do to keep a lively toddler asleep once
they have had their sleep quotient, but you could look at changing
the hours at which they are sleeping. For example, if your toddler

is still having two naps during the day, you could try stopping one, while if they're having one long nap try reducing its length. Similarly you could try putting your toddler to bed a little later.

Also, especially if it is the summer, it could be the early morning light that is waking your toddler and if so, try using thick, dark-coloured curtains or a blackout blind to help keep their room darker for longer.

Another thing you could consider for an older toddler is a special alarm clock, which gives a visual cue that it is morning. For example, the clock may be in the shape of an animal's face and at the set hour its ears pop up. Your toddler won't necessarily stay asleep to the desired time, but you can teach them to stay in their bed until then.

Insight

Older toddlers who continue to be up with the lark can, I've found, be encouraged to occupy themselves with a book or a toy for 20 minutes or so upon waking. Keep a box of distractions under their bed, along with a bedside lamp they can turn on by themselves.

Top tip

Sometimes when you are sleep deprived yourself, it is hard to work out exactly what is happening with your toddler's sleep, or lack of it. This is when keeping a sleep diary over a period of time can come in very useful. Looking at this information may help you find some patterns. Once you see patterns, you may be able to find a solution. Here is what you should keep track of:

▶ *what time they woke up in the morning*
▶ *times and lengths of naps during the day*
▶ *what time they went to bed in the evening*
▶ *what time they settled in bed in the evening*
▶ *issues in settling, what you did, and how it worked*
▶ *times and lengths of waking at night*
▶ *what you did about night waking and how it worked.*

Why naps matter

As your child enters the toddler years they will probably be having two naps a day, usually one in the morning and a longer one in the afternoon. Around the age of two, however, most toddlers can get through the day on just a single afternoon nap and this will probably continue until they are three or perhaps even four years old.

The reason toddlers still need naps is that they cannot yet get all the sleep they need during the night. However, when your toddler isn't sleeping well at night it is tempting to cut the naps, but without a daytime rest they will be more tired and have even more trouble falling asleep and sleeping through the night. The following chart gives a rough guide to the number and length of naps your toddler should be having according to their age:

Age	Number of naps	Length of naps
12 months	1 to 2	2 to 3 hours
2 years	1	1 to 2 hours
3 years	1	1 to 1½ hours

If your toddler has difficulty staying asleep for long enough during the day, you might want to try the following to increase the length of their nap:

▶ *Give your toddler a healthy snack or their lunch half an hour before their nap.*
▶ *Put your toddler to nap in their bedroom and make sure the room is dark.*
▶ *Make sure your toddler takes their nap in comfortable clothing. You could consider changing them into their pyjamas first.*
▶ *If your toddler does wake early, don't assume they have had enough sleep and immediately get them up. Wait and see if they will re-settle.*

I never realized the importance of naps until I had a child of my own. When friends with children used to say, 'Oh we can't meet you then, so and so will be having their nap', I used to roll my eyes and think how indulgent. But now that Kirsten's a toddler, tearing around and into everything, without that afternoon nap she becomes tired and grumpy and completely impossible to manage. Quite frankly, I'd rather miss out on a shopping trip or lunch out with friends than have to deal with Kirsten when she's not had her nap. Besides, I've really grown to love those brief couple of hours in the afternoon when Kirsten is down. Quite often I'll have a lie down myself either reading a book or watching telly. The other day I must have drifted off because I awoke to the sound of Kirsten shouting for me. She was standing in her cot, wide awake, and from the cross look on her face she obviously had been for a while.

The difference between nightmares and night terrors

Many toddlers have nightmares, but few actually have night terrors, yet often people confuse the two. Night terrors are in fact an inherited disorder in which a toddler dreams during deep sleep from which they find it difficult to awaken. It is estimated that only two per cent of toddlers experience night terrors. The following chart explains the ways in which they differ from nightmares:

	Night terrors	Nightmares
Time of night	Early, usually within four hours of going to bed	Later in the night
How toddler acts	Confused and disoriented	Scared and upset

(Contd)

	Night terrors	Nightmares
Response to you	Doesn't know you are there and can't be comforted	Can be comforted
Memory of event	Usually none	Can remember their dream
Return to sleep	Usually quick, unless fully awakened	Often delayed because scared
Sleep stage	Deep non-REM sleep	Light REM sleep

WHAT TO DO IF YOUR TODDLER HAS A NIGHTMARE

If your toddler wakes up with a nightmare, you could try the following:

▶ *Gently lay your toddler back down.*
▶ *Try not to talk much about the nightmare as it will prolong the memory.*
▶ *Soothe your toddler in whatever manner they are used to, for example gently stroking their hair or rubbing their back.*
▶ *Wait until your toddler is relaxed and calm enough to go back to sleep.*
▶ *Tell them, 'Go to sleep now', or whatever last phrase you usually use, and exit the room.*

WHAT TO DO IF YOUR TODDLER EXPERIENCES NIGHT TERRORS

If your toddler has night terrors, you will not be able to comfort them. Your toddler is actually still asleep, just like a sleepwalker or someone who talks in their sleep. In this instance you should:

▶ *Try not to disturb your toddler, but stay near them and make sure they don't hurt themselves.*
▶ *Try to make sure your toddler is getting enough sleep, because over-tiredness can cause night terrors.*

The move from cot to bed

When to move your toddler from a cot into a bed is entirely up to you, although most toddlers make the transition sometime between the ages of 18 months and three years. There are several factors that can precipitate this move:

▶ *The arrival of another baby will often mean that your toddler needs to free up the cot.*
▶ *Your toddler may have outgrown their cot and/or have started to climb and jump out of it.*
▶ *You may be potty training your toddler and therefore want them to have easy access to the toilet.*

HOW TO EASE THE TRANSITION

Whatever has prompted the move, here are a few things you can do to ease the transition for your toddler:

▶ *Prepare your toddler for the move, explaining that it is because they are now so grown up. Talk up the change in status.*
▶ *Let your toddler help you choose their bed.*
▶ *If possible, place the bed in exactly the same position as the cot.*
▶ *Initially use the old cot bedding, even if it is too small, as your toddler will find its familiarity comforting.*
▶ *Give your toddler lots of praise when they stay in their bed.*
▶ *If at first your toddler finds the freedom of a bed a bit too much and keeps getting out, be calm but firm and simply keep putting them back.*

If you are moving your toddler to a big bed because you are expecting a baby it will help if you make the change a month or two before the new arrival. This will give your toddler plenty of time to get used to their new bed and they will be less likely to feel that the baby has somehow usurped them by taking over their cot.

SAFE SLEEPING

With your toddler spending between 11 and 13 hours a day sleeping it is essential to ensure that their bed and its surrounding environs are safe and secure. Here are some tips to help keep your toddler safe:

▶ *When choosing your toddler's first bed, go for one that is low and close to the ground.*

▶ *You might want to consider buying some adjustable guard rails until your toddler gets used to their new bed.*

▶ *When positioning the bed, be aware of temperature and make sure it is away from windows, doors or radiators.*

▶ *Also be aware of strangling hazards such as blind cords.*

▶ *If against a wall, make sure the bed is as close to it as possible so that your toddler cannot become trapped between the side of the bed and the wall.*

▶ *A baby sleeping bag is one of the safest options for a young toddler who is still in a cot, but once they have moved to a bed it is better to use a toddler-size duvet and pillow.*

Did you know?

The reason many toddlers find it difficult staying in their beds is that they lack impulse control. A toddler's ability to not immediately act on their desire doesn't usually start kicking in until around the age of three.

There were three in the bed: how to encourage your toddler to remain in their bed and out of yours

In many homes up and down the country the marital bed has become the family bed, with a toddler peacefully ensconced between mum and dad. Some parents are perfectly happy with this arrangement because they enjoy the intimacy and they feel that everyone gets a better night's sleep. But for others, their toddler is an uninvited guest whose constant fidgeting and ability to sleep in the shape of a starfish means a disturbed and uncomfortable night. If you are one of these, and would like your toddler to remain in their own bed, try the following:

1 *Explain to your toddler exactly what you expect of them, for example that starting from tonight you want them to stay in their bed.*
2 *Do not threaten your toddler or bribe them to remain in their own bed.*
3 *If your toddler then sneaks into your bed during the night, which they probably will, simply take them back to their own bed.*
4 *Don't cuddle, kiss or fuss over your toddler once back in their bed; just say whatever it is you usually say to them before exiting the room.*
5 *You may have to repeat this process several times in one night and over the course of several days, but eventually your toddler will get the message that sleeping in their own bed is what is expected.*
6 *The key is to be firm and consistent. It won't be easy at first – after the fourth visit of the night you might be tempted to give in for a quiet life – but your persistence will eventually pay off.*

If, however, the above sounds a little too harsh, then you could, as an interim measure, consider placing a futon or mattress next to your bed and allowing your toddler to sleep there.

Did you know?

The practice of solitary sleeping for babies and toddlers is only about 100 years old. For hundreds of thousands of years, all children slept next to their parents and siblings. And in many cultures today, this is still considered normal practice.

10 THINGS TO REMEMBER

1   *A sleeping baby can transform into a wakeful toddler through no fault of your own. Your child is undergoing massive growth and change and the excitement and stimulation that this brings can make it hard for them to switch off.*

2   *Bedtime can also become a battle of wills as your toddler starts to exert their independence about when they go to bed and whether they stay there.*

3   *Sleep is crucial to your toddler's health and well-being, with important developments both mentally and physically only occurring when your child is asleep. A typical two-year-old needs around 13 hours sleep over a 24-hour period, with one or two of those hours taken as a nap.*

4   *To help your toddler get a better night's sleep, establish a good bedtime routine. Not only will it result in fewer power struggles, but it has also been proven to help toddlers to settle easier and to sleep longer.*

5   *Your toddler's ability to settle themselves is also crucial to a good night's rest. Make sure your toddler doesn't become reliant on a particular object or place (other than their bed) to fall asleep.*

6   *If you decide to sleep train your toddler, choose a method that you are happy with and feel confident you can sustain, as consistency is very much the key to success.*

7   *If your toddler has developed delaying tactics at bedtime, the most common being a string of different requests, write a checklist with the help of your toddler and then incorporate them into the bedtime routine, making it clear that they're allowed one extra, and after that there will be no more.*

8   *If your toddler is going through a particularly bad sleeping phase, don't be tempted to cut their lunchtime nap in the hope*

that they'll then sleep better at night. Without a daytime nap they will become over-tired and have even more difficulty sleeping.

9   *When moving your toddler from a cot to a bed, involve them as much as possible in the process, explaining why they are being moved in terms of how grown up they are and letting them help choose the bed. Give your toddler plenty of time to settle, especially if you're expecting a new arrival.*

10 *If your toddler has become a regular visitor to your bed at night and your attempts to discourage them have thus far failed, you could consider putting a temporary mattress on the floor next to you and allowing your toddler to sleep there.*

10

Tricks to successful toilet training

In this chapter you will learn:
- *the signs that your toddler is ready for toilet training*
- *when is the best time to start*
- *which is best, potty or toilet*
- *tips on preparing your toddler*
- *how to get started*
- *ways to minimize accidents*
- *what to do when out and about*
- *common problems and how to deal with them*
- *how boys and girls differ*
- *tips for dry nights.*

Waving goodbye to nappies

Learning to use the potty or the toilet is a rite of passage for your toddler. Nothing better symbolizes your child's move away from babyhood than doing away with their daytime nappies. But getting to this stage can take time, understanding and patience on your part, while for your toddler the process can be scary, confusing and inconvenient. Yet toilet training needn't be something to dread. If you approach it with the right attitude – making it fun and relaxed – your toddler will enjoy showing you how grown up they can be and they will delight in the attention and praise they will receive for their efforts. Often, in as little as a few months, a toddler will have toilet training cracked. Of course, that doesn't mean there won't still be the occasional accident, but with regular reminders and gentle encouragement your toddler will soon be trotting off to the toilet of their own accord and you will be left wondering why you ever thought toilet training was so daunting.

> **Insight**
>
> If you're feeling particularly anxious about starting toilet training, I'd recommend speaking to an experienced mum who's been through the process several times over. She'll no doubt tell you it isn't anywhere near as bad as most first-timers think it's going to be.

Is your toddler ready?

One of the keys to successful toilet training is getting the timing right. Your toddler needs to be ready and, in order to ascertain whether they are, you need to look out for certain signs and clues. Most toddlers will reach this stage of readiness at some time between their second and third birthdays, but like many aspects of your toddler's development, it can vary quite considerably. For example, some toddlers will be ready to get to grips with toilet training at just 18 months, while some three-year-olds will still be showing very little interest.

Here are 12 typical signs that a toddler is ready to begin toilet training:

1 *Your toddler does a poo at about the same time every day.*
2 *Your toddler can stay dry for a few hours or wakes up dry from their afternoon nap.*
3 *Your toddler knows when they want to go to the toilet.*
4 *Your toddler understands the association between being dry and using the toilet.*
5 *Your toddler can undress themselves and pull elastic-waist trousers up and down.*

6 *Your toddler lets you know when they have a wet or soiled nappy.*
7 *Your toddler can follow simple directions, like 'Let's go to the bathroom'.*
8 *Your toddler understands toilet training terms such as wet, dry, wee, poo, dirty and potty.*
9 *Your toddler tells you when they need to go to the toilet.*
10 *Your toddler imitates other family members going to the toilet.*
11 *Your toddler shows interest and asks questions about going to the toilet.*
12 *Your toddler wants to do things 'by myself'.*

WHAT'S IN A NAME?

To help your toddler with toilet training it is important that they know the words for their body parts and their actions. But make sure they are the same words used by the rest of the family and that you feel comfortable with them, as your toddler will undoubtedly be sharing them with a wider audience! Whether you choose to give your toddler the proper names, for example penis or vagina, or something less medical, for example willy or pee-pee, is entirely up to you. Just make sure they are words that your toddler can say and understand, for example wee and poo are more toddler-friendly than urination and defecation.

Insight
Giving your toddler's private parts a specific name is something I know that many parents find embarrassing and try to avoid. Even if you are uncomfortable, I'd recommend going ahead. Remember, you're setting the stage for open, honest discussions in the years to come.

Top tip
To help your toddler to start to associate the signs of needing a wee or poo with actually doing one, try to notice when they are going red in the face or pushing (the usual signs that they are filling their nappies) and say to them, 'Are you doing a poo?'.

TODDLER TOILET TRAINING QUIZ

Ultimately you are the best judge of your toddler's readiness, but to help you decide, why not do the following fun quiz.

1 *How old is your toddler?*
   a *Under 18 months.*
   b *Between 18 months and two years.*
   c *Over two.*
2 *What does your toddler do if they need to wee or poo?*
   a *I only know if my toddler's been by their facial expression or if I have checked their nappy.*
   b *My toddler usually tells me after the event.*
   c *My toddler lets me know before doing it in their nappy.*
3 *How does your toddler react to a dirty nappy?*
   a *It doesn't bother them.*
   b *My toddler is aware that it is dirty but doesn't really get upset.*
   c *My toddler will insist on being changed as soon as their nappy is wet or soiled.*
4 *Does your toddler show any interest in the toilet or potty?*
   a *Not really – my toddler won't even sit on it.*
   b *My toddler will sit on it, but they have never actually used it.*
   c *My toddler loves sitting on the potty/toilet and is keen to learn how to use it.*
5 *After your toddler's nap their nappy is:*
   a *always wet.*
   b *sometimes wet, sometimes dry.*
   c *usually dry.*

If your toddler scored mostly 'a'
Your toddler is still some way off being ready for toilet training. You need to wait until they are capable of letting you know when they want to go to the toilet and they also show more interest in the whole process of going to the toilet. It is important not to feel pressurized into starting toilet training until your toddler is

ready. If you wait until your toddler is physically, mentally and emotionally more developed the process will be much smoother.

If your toddler scored mostly 'b'
Your toddler is almost ready to start the toilet training process, but you might find it easier if you wait another couple of months. By then your toddler will probably be dry after their nap and will also be able to tell you that they need to go to the toilet before they actually go – both of which will greatly facilitate toilet training.

If your toddler scored mostly 'c'
Your toddler is now ready to begin toilet training. They can stay dry for a good couple of hours and they let you know that they want to go to the toilet before the event. Your toddler is also taking a keen interest in the whole process of going to the toilet and is eager to learn how to do it for themselves.

Did you know?

As with many aspects of child rearing, toilet training has changed considerably over the years. Today the average age a toddler is toilet trained in Europe and North America is 28 months, but in the 1950s the vast majority of toddlers were toilet trained by 18 months, using methods that have since been discredited for being too harsh. Yet it is estimated that 50 per cent of the world's children, the majority of whom live in developing countries, are toilet trained by the time they turn one, through a method known as Communication Elimination. This process involves the main caregiver using timing, signals, cues and intuition to anticipate their baby's toileting needs, thus avoiding the need for nappies. Interestingly it is a method that has recently been gaining in popularity among environmentally aware parents in the West.

Are you ready?

As well as your toddler being ready to start toilet training, it is
important that you are too. Here are a few things you might like
to consider.

THE TIME OF YEAR

Summer is often deemed the best time to start toilet training as
your toddler won't be wearing layers of bulky clothing and may
even be able to run around bare-bottomed. Also, if an accident
does occur, it is more likely to take place outside. However,
warm sunny days are not essential for toilet training. There is
an argument that if your toddler has to wear their grown-up
underwear from the outset, they will get used to it more quickly.

WHAT IS HAPPENING IN YOUR LIFE

It is important that you feel calm and relaxed when you commence
toilet training your toddler, so try to avoid starting it when anything
big or new is happening. Even good events such as holidays or the
arrival of a new baby will make toilet training more stressful than it
need be, so wait until life is back on a more even keel.

Potty versus toilet

Before you begin toilet training you need to decide whether you want your toddler to use a potty before graduating to the big toilet or to encourage use of the big toilet from the outset by introducing a toilet trainer seat and a step stool. The choice is a completely personal one, but whatever you do decide, try to be consistent and make sure that anyone else who cares for your toddler, for example a childminder or nursery, knows what you prefer your toddler to use. Here are a few things to consider when making your choice.

The case for a potty
▶ *A potty is small, easy for your toddler to use and is non-threatening. You can buy fun, brightly designed ones that are more appealing to a toddler than a trainer seat.*
▶ *A toilet trainer seat can't be moved from room to room like a potty – although it is always best if your toddler uses the potty in the bathroom.*
▶ *A potty promotes independence because your toddler will be able to use it on their own. If using the toilet your toddler will initially need to be supervised throughout.*

The case for the toilet
▶ *A toilet can simply be flushed, whereas a potty will need to be cleaned after each use.*
▶ *If your toddler starts off using a potty they will eventually have to make the transition to the toilet.*
▶ *Taking a potty with you on outings, even a portable one, can be a pain, and using one in a confined space, such as a cafe or restaurant, isn't really an option.*

Case study

With Jack we didn't even think about using the toilet, we just assumed that a potty was what everybody used. After all, most people still refer to toilet training as potty training. We bought two potties and had one positioned upstairs in the bathroom and the other downstairs in the front room because the downstairs toilet was too small to fit it in. I can't tell you the number of times that potty was accidentally knocked over! So when it came to training Lexie we decided to bypass the potty stage completely and encourage her to use the regular toilet with an insert seat. I think it's probably taken her a little longer to get the hang of it – at first she was nervous of climbing up on the stool and insisted that I lift her on – but it's such a relief not to have to keep cleaning out the potty or tripping over it!

On your marks: preparing your toddler

Once you have established that both your toddler and you are ready to begin toilet training and you have chosen to either use a potty or the toilet, it is time to get started. Here's how:

▶ **Talk to your toddler.** *Explain to them how commonplace going to the toilet is, how everyone does it and that it is a normal part of life. Tell them how wees and poos go down the toilet. Let them try to use the flush. Get your toddler excited about the prospect of wearing grown-up underwear and ditching the nappies. Use this time to read books to your toddler or watch DVDs with them about using the toilet/potty.*
▶ **Involve your toddler.** *Arrange a trip to the shops with your toddler where they can choose their grown-up underwear (ones with favourite characters on are always a big hit), their potty or insert seat and stool. Make your toddler feel involved in the decision-making process.*

Get set: getting your toddler familiarized

Before fully embarking on toilet training, allow your toddler time to get familiar with the new equipment. Here's how:

- ▶ **Let your toddler play.** *At first your toddler might treat the potty or trainer seat as if it is a toy. Don't discourage this – it is just your toddler's way of learning about something that is new and unusual.*
- ▶ **Let your toddler sit.** *Once your toddler is more familiar with the potty or trainer seat, let them practise just sitting on it without any pressure to do anything. First they could sit on it fully clothed and later try it bare-bottomed.*

Insight

I've found that books and DVDs are excellent ways to prepare your toddler for toilet training, but rather than spend money on something that's going to have a rather limited use, why not check out what's available at your local library.

Go: the start of toilet training proper

Once toilet training begins in earnest, try to establish the following:

- ▶ **Regular toilet breaks.** *Now that your toddler is happy to sit on the potty or toilet, encourage them to do so at regular times throughout the day, for example when they first wake up, after meals, before getting in the car and before bed. Don't worry if your toddler doesn't always do something, but do praise them for trying.*
- ▶ **A swift reaction.** *Look for signs that your toddler needs to go, for example squirming, squatting or holding the genital area, and respond quickly. Tell your toddler it is time to go to the potty or toilet – don't ask them if they want to go!*
- ▶ **A relaxed atmosphere.** *It is important that your toddler feels calm and relaxed when going to the toilet. If you hover over them, anxious about whether they have been, they will start to feel anxious too and will then be unable to go. Try making your toddler's trips to the toilet light-hearted and fun by reading a book together, telling a story, singing or talking about the day – all will help keep the tension down.*

▶ **Good hygiene.** *Make hand-washing part of the routine. Keep a stool by the sink so that your toddler can reach easily, and have fun, child-friendly soap to hand.*

Accidents and underwear

REDUCING ACCIDENTS

As your toddler starts to get to grips with toilet training there is a greater scope for accidents and near misses. To minimize these and lessen the impact, try the following:

▶ **Stay calm.** *Your toddler hasn't had an accident to irritate you. Avoid embarrassing your toddler further by telling them off or disciplining them. Keep your tone even and matter-of-fact, for example tell them: 'You forgot this time. Next time you'll get to the bathroom sooner'.*
▶ **Teach your toddler to slow down.** *Toddlers are often in such a rush to get on with the next activity that they don't completely empty their bladder when going to the toilet. Remind your toddler to relax and take it slowly.*
▶ **Gently prompt your toddler.** *An accident will often happen when a toddler is completely absorbed in something, for example, building a tower becomes much more interesting than going to the toilet. Suggest to your toddler a trip to the toilet on a regular basis.*
▶ **Be prepared.** *If your toddler is prone to frequent accidents, keep a change of clothing handy, especially for nursery or at the childminder's.*

Did you know?

In the UK, 15 per cent of children are not toilet trained at
three, and four per cent are still not trained at the age of
four. However, studies have shown that a toddler's toilet
training age is not linked to their intellect and that it has no
correlation with other stages of development. For example,
if your toddler was an early talker, it doesn't mean they will
be toilet trained earlier.

TRAINER PANTS OR ORDINARY UNDERWEAR?

Many people favour training pants in the early stages of toilet
training as they can be pulled up and down like ordinary
underwear but avoid the risk of accidents and are also disposable.
Yet, as with the potty versus the toilet debate, your ultimate goal is
eventually to get your toddler into ordinary underwear and using
training pants can, in some instances, prolong the transition. Again,
it is a personal choice whether you bypass the training pants and go
straight for the underwear. The important thing is to be consistent.

Rewards and incentives

In Chapter 6, the use of rewards and incentives was discussed in
some detail. During toilet training these can be an effective way

of keeping your toddler interested and motivated. Whether it is stickers, a reward chart or a little treat for making such a good effort, these can all work well providing, of course, that your toddler is ready to be toilet trained in the first place.

Case study

I'd just started toilet training Gabriel and things weren't going brilliantly. I was talking to a friend about it and she told me that with her little boy she gave him a Smartie every time he used the potty. I'd never really given chocolate to Gabe, but I thought, what the heck, if it gets him on the potty I'll give it a go. So the next day after he eventually used the potty, I told him what a brilliant boy he'd been and that as a special treat for being so good, mummy would give a sweetie. The look on his little face when he tasted that chocolate was one of pure ecstasy and of course he was very keen to repeat the experience. For a while things seemed to be going fine, with Gabe getting his little treat after each successful trip to the loo. But then he started running to the potty every ten minutes, sitting on it for a few seconds doing nothing and then expecting another Smartie afterwards! It is amazing how cunning a two-and-a-half-year-old can be.

Top tip

As your toddler becomes more adept at using the potty or toilet, you will probably need to reconsider your reward system. For example, stop offering them a small treat for sitting on the potty, and instead start placing a star on a chart for each time they use it. Progress to a big sticker for an accident-free day and then, after seven accident-free days, they could get a special treat.

Toilet training away from home

One common misconception about toilet training is that you have to remain completely housebound in the early weeks. While staying at home as much as possible does make things easier – and holidays and long journeys are probably best avoided – shopping and visiting family and friends will be necessary at some point. At these times you might be tempted to put a nappy back on your toddler to avoid accidents, especially if they are wearing just ordinary underwear. But nappies will be confusing to your toddler and could lead to regression. Similarly, even if your toddler is in training pants, avoid letting your toddler use them like a nappy when out and about, as they will start to think this is perfectly acceptable.

Here are some tips to help get you through those first few outings:

1   *Explain to your toddler what will happen when you are out, how it will be different from home and any concerns you may have.*
2   *Get them to go, or at least try to go, to the toilet before you leave the house.*
3   *Find out where the toilets are as soon as you get to wherever you are going and go straight away. It is much easier doing this calmly before your toddler really needs it than in a mad rush.*
4   *Remember to keep watching your toddler for those telltale signs that they need to go.*
5   *If you do not have a portable potty or a toilet training seat with you, try crouching beside your toddler while they are sitting on the big toilet and hold their hand or their body if they seem scared about slipping in.*
6   *Another thing you could try is sitting as far back as possible on the toilet yourself and then put your toddler in front of you.*
7   *Take some spare clothing, a couple of plastic bags, and some baby wipes and paper towels with you in case of accidents.*
8   *If your toddler has an accident in a shop or restaurant, let the staff know so they can clean it up. It might be embarrassing but rest assured you won't be the first. Apologize immediately and leave a big tip.*

9 *If your toddler has an accident at a friend's house then it is your responsibility to clean it up.*

10 *As well as accidents, there may be several false alarms, with your toddler wanting to find out what happens when they say the magic word. If you find this is happening, try not to get cross with your toddler. They will soon become bored with the non-stop trips to the loo.*

COPING ON CAR JOURNEYS

If you do have to undertake a long car journey during the early stages of toilet training, you might want to check out your route so that you know where the petrol stations and services are. You might also want to consider buying an inflatable potty – they are compact and inexpensive and can be stashed easily in the back of the car in case of sudden emergencies. Another thing worth investing in is a car seat/buggy protector. These absorbent, machine-washable pads are not costly and will protect your toddler's car seat from little accidents.

Insight

Rather than packing spare clothes for each outing, I've found that always keeping a small bag of old clothes in the car, and/or at the bottom of the buggy, means that you're never caught out when accidents happen.

Did you know?

Just like so many other areas of toddler behaviour, much of toilet training comes down to temperament. One study found that toddlers who struggle adjusting to new situations are likely to take longer to toilet train than those with an easy, flexible temperament.

Common toilet training problems

There are several problems you might encounter when toilet training your toddler. Some might be evident from the outset, while others only surface when toilet training is underway. Here are some of the most common.

TOTAL REFUSAL

What is happening
My toddler simply refuses to use the potty/toilet.

Why it is happening
Provided that your toddler is ready for toilet training, one of several other factors might be at play. First, check that your toddler is not constipated as nothing will put your toddler off of using the potty or toilet more quickly than the prospect of passing a painful poo. If that is not the case, then maybe your toddler is afraid of something, for example, falling into the potty/toilet, the sound of the flush or maybe the lack of light in the bathroom.

What you can do about it
You need to find out what is scaring your toddler through a process of elimination and once you are confident that their fears have been addressed, calmly try to encourage potty/toilet use again.

SUDDEN REGRESSION

What is happening
My toddler seemed to have toilet training cracked, but has suddenly started having accidents again.

Why it is happening
Again your first port of call should be checking for constipation. If this is not the problem then consider if there have been any changes in your toddler's environment that could account for the

regression, for example, illness, a new sibling, changes in childcare, an absent parent or any other event that might have disrupted your toddler's daily routine.

What you can do about it
Try to keep things as normal as you possibly can, and offer your toddler lots of extra reassurance. Despite the setback, it is important to keep the toilet training going and resist the temptation to go back to nappies.

STUBBORN RESISTANCE

What is happening
Whenever I suggest to my toddler that they use the potty/toilet, they become defiant and say 'no'.

Why it is happening
Your toddler wants sitting on the potty or toilet to be their idea and will resist if they think otherwise. This is because toilet training has become another way for your toddler to exert their independence and, if you are not careful, it could turn into a battleground.

What you can do about it
There are a couple of ways you can address this problem. The first is to stop asking or telling your toddler when to use the potty or toilet and let them take the lead. The second is to make your toddler think that using the potty or toilet is their idea. For example, try telling your toddler that you need to use the bathroom for a few minutes but will let them know when you are done just in case they need to go too. Never try to force your toddler to go and sit on the potty or toilet as this will only create tension and is likely to lead to even more resistance.

Did you know?

Your toddler will not be able to wipe their own bottom until at least four years old. It is around this age that they will develop the necessary dexterity and also their arms will have grown in length, making it easier for them to reach their bottom.

AFRAID OF POOING

What is happening
My toddler will happily wee on the potty/toilet, but refuses to do a poo in it.

Why it is happening
Again, provided that constipation is not a problem, it is likely that your toddler is simply scared. Doing a poo in a nappy is a very different feeling from doing one in the relatively open expanse of a potty or toilet, and that sensation of almost losing part of themselves can make a toddler very fearful. As a result, many toddlers will request a nappy when they need to poo, or will disappear from sight and do it in some hiding place.

What you can do
If your toddler demands a nappy before pooing, still encourage them to sit on the potty or toilet while doing it. Once this has been accomplished, you could then make a hole in the back of the nappy so that the poo can drop through. When this is achieved heap lots of praise on your toddler and let them wave goodbye to their efforts as it is flushed down the toilet. Or, if your toddler is going off to poo in secret, watch them closely for signs beforehand and then quickly take them to the potty or toilet. Often a toddler will overcome their fear after just one or two poos have landed in the potty or toilet and they realize that nothing untoward will happen.

....
Top tip
Don't be tempted to skimp on the liquids when toilet training your toddler in the hope that this will lessen the number of accidents. Toddlers can easily become dehydrated, especially
(Contd)

during warm weather, and should be drinking at least six water-based drinks spread throughout the day. Also, if your toddler is drinking a lot, the more they will wee, which will give them plenty of practice in mastering using the potty or toilet.

When to call a halt

It is not unusual to have false starts when toilet training, and it is important that neither your toddler nor you perceive this as failing in any way. Sometimes it is simply better to call a temporary halt to training, especially if your toddler or you display any of the following behaviours:

1 *Your toddler persistently refuses to use the potty or toilet.*
2 *Your toddler simply cannot understand the concept of toilet training.*
3 *Your toddler becomes upset or angry over toilet training.*
4 *You find yourself shouting or becoming increasingly angry or resentful about your toddler's slow toilet training progress.*

Case study

I did feel under quite a bit of pressure to start toilet training Alice, even though in my heart of hearts I knew she wasn't ready. And to be honest, having only recently had another baby, I wasn't really feeling up to the task either. But after several well-meaning relatives had enquired as to why Alice was still in nappies while remarking how in their day a child was expected to be clean long before their second birthday, I thought I'd better bite the bullet and just get on with it. Of course, from day one it was a disaster. Alice didn't want to even sit on the potty, let alone do anything in it, and the more I tried to encourage and remind her, the more obstinate she got about it. I also tried keeping her nappy off with the result that I was constantly clearing up after yet another little accident. By day four I was at the end of my tether, while Alice was no nearer to understanding the process. It was then that I decided to stop for both our sakes, and I'm so glad I did, because when I did resume toilet training about four months later, Alice was absolutely ready and willing. Being that little bit older, she could understand my instructions and in less than a fortnight she was happily using the potty with hardly any prompting.

Top tip

Try to remember that all toddlers are different and as such they all develop at different rates. Avoid comparing your toddler's toilet training with anyone else, and don't be pressurized by family and friends. Your toddler will master toilet training when they, and indeed you, are good and ready.

WHEN TO SEEK HELP

Although most toilet training difficulties can be resolved with patience and understanding, in a few cases there may be an underlying medical condition, such as a urinary tract infection or constipation. If you are at all concerned about your toddler's toilet training, contact your GP or health visitor for advice.

How boys and girls differ

Research shows that girls tend to show an interest in toilet training a couple of months ahead of boys, and that they usually grasp the concept more quickly. Yet no one knows exactly why this should be the case. Obviously a major difference between the sexes is that a boy will eventually urinate standing up, but usually begins by weeing in the sitting position. Some experts have suggested that it is this extra step in the toilet training process that goes some way to explaining why it can be lengthier for boys.

So when should you teach your son to wee standing up? Well the general consensus is not until after they have fully mastered toilet training, which usually means approaching the age of three. Here are a few things to consider:

▶ *Boys need role models to help them learn to wee standing up, so arrange for your son to follow their dad, an uncle or family friend to the bathroom to watch them in the act.*
▶ *When your son seems to understand how to do it, let him give it a go. If he is still using a potty, place this next to the toilet and let him try in that.*
▶ *If your son seems reluctant, turn it into a fun game by floating a small flushable object in the toilet bowl. He can then have fun practising his aim.*
▶ *Be prepared for regular clean-ups as learning to aim accurately will take time.*

Achieving dry nights

Just as toilet training shouldn't be rushed, the same goes for keeping your toddler dry at night. Indeed, there is much greater variety in the age a child is dry at night than there is regarding daytime dryness – the norm ranges from two to six years, with the average being between the ages of three and four. Again, it is important not to feel pressurized into getting your toddler out of night-time nappies. Often your toddler will lead the way, presenting you with a dry nappy most mornings and showing an eagerness to leave the nappy off altogether when suggested. When you do decide to give it a go, here are a few things to consider:

▶ *It is important not to limit your toddler's fluid intake, but do try to give them their last drink at least an hour before bedtime.*
▶ *For the first few weeks at least, protect the mattress with a plastic sheet.*
▶ *Make sure your toddler has a last wee before you tuck them into bed.*
▶ *Leave a nightlight or landing light on and make sure that the potty or toilet is in easy reach.*

▶ As with daytime training, accidents are inevitable. Don't make a big fuss when one does occur and remember to celebrate and praise your toddler's successes rather than honing in on the occasional failure.

▶ It is not uncommon for children to still be wetting the bed beyond four years old, sometimes up to junior school age and beyond. If you are at all concerned by your child's bed wetting, contact your GP or health visitor for advice.

Insight

Some parents choose to lift their toddler before they go to bed themselves of an evening in a bid to pre-empt any need for a night-time wee. I'd suggest that if practising this method, make sure your child is sufficiently awake to realize they are emptying their bladder on the toilet.

Did you know?

For a toddler to stay dry at night their brain must be able to keep a full bladder from emptying, their bladder needs to be big enough to hold the urine and the signal from the bladder must be strong enough to wake them up to use the potty or toilet when they really need to – all of which is known as the bladder control mechanism. Development of this is in fact an inherited trait and research shows that if both parents were late to stay dry throughout the night, then their child has a three out of four chance of being late too.

10 THINGS TO REMEMBER

1 *Don't begin to attempt toilet training until you are sure that your toddler is completely ready. Starting too soon will only result in frustration and probable failure.*

2 *You also need to be calm, relaxed and prepared for the task in hand, so avoid times of upheaval and stress.*

3 *It's entirely up to you whether you opt for a potty and then progress to a trainer seat and toilet or bypass the potty altogether. Just make sure any other caregivers know of your choice and adhere to it.*

4 *Having established that you're ready to begin, involve your toddler as much as possible, explaining what's going to happen and letting them help choose their new, grown-up underwear and toilet training equipment. Then let them familiarize themselves with it.*

5 *In the beginning you will need to encourage your toddler to take regular toilet breaks, but don't hound them if they refuse and don't worry if they do go and do nothing. Keep things calm and relaxed and learn to recognize the signs that they need the toilet so you can then act swiftly.*

6 *Accidents will inevitably happen, but avoid telling your toddler off. Deal with the situation calmly and matter-of-factly and encourage them to get to the potty/toilet sooner next time.*

7 *Rewards and incentives have proven very effective in keeping your toddler interested and motivated in toilet training.*

8 *Don't be tempted, for the sake of convenience, to put a nappy back on your toddler when out and about. This will only lead to confusion and possible regression.*

9   *Boys tend to get to grips with toilet training slower than girls, perhaps because they have the extra step of learning to wee standing up. To help your son along, let him see a male family member in action.*

10 *Getting your toddler dry through the night usually precedes toilet training by several months to several years, depending on the child. Let your child lead the way and don't feel pressurized by others' expectations.*

11

Fun and games with your toddler

In this chapter you will learn:
* *how play benefits development*
* *why free play is better than structured play*
* *tips on playing with your toddler*
* *the different types of play*
* *how toddlers play with other children*
* *what toys are best for toddlers*
* *how gender affects toy choice*
* *about toy safety*
* *the everyday objects that make great toys*
* *fun games to play with your toddler.*

Why your toddler's play is so important

As adults it is all too easy to dismiss toddler play as pointless and unproductive. Just consider the expression 'child's play' meaning something very easy or a trivial matter. Yet your playing toddler is embroiled in anything but 'child's play' in this sense. They are in fact very hard at work, engaged in an essential activity that is vital for all aspects of their development – not for nothing has play been called the 'occupation of childhood'.

It is through play that your toddler begins to learn about their body and the world around them, to understand how and why things work the way they do. Indeed, playing and learning are so completely enmeshed for toddlers that it is impossible at this age to separate one from the other. Play is your toddler's first step on the long journey of acquiring the necessary knowledge and skills that will see them into adulthood, and as such its importance should never be underestimated.

How play helps your toddler's development

Play helps your toddler's development in all areas – physically, mentally, socially and emotionally. Here's how:

PLAY AND PHYSICAL DEVELOPMENT

Through play your toddler continues to fine-tune their physical skills. Look at a toddler running around a playground, playing in the sandpit or clambering up a slide – they are in fact honing the power and agility of their little bodies, developing their gross motor and fine motor control as well as their overall balance and co-ordination. Even the toddler engaged in a relatively sedentary activity, such as building a tower from blocks or daubing paint on to paper, is learning to better use the small muscles in their fingers and how to co-ordinate their hand and eye. Also through play your toddler is learning to love their body and all the incredible things it can do.

PLAY AND MENTAL DEVELOPMENT

Play enables your toddler to engage their senses through taste, smell, sight, touch and sound. Psychologists believe that it is through using their senses that the intellectual abilities of infants and young toddlers start to evolve. An early understanding of size, colour, texture and weight are all learnt through play, and later on comes the rudiments of counting. Play also allows your toddler to experiment, for example discovering what floats and what sinks when playing in the bath tub, and enables them to practise problem solving, for example where a puzzle piece goes or how to dress and undress a doll. In time your toddler will begin to understand logic and make logical connections in their play, for example pretending to swim across the room and then needing a towel to dry off. Play also develops your toddler's symbolic thinking, so that they can let one thing represent another, for example an old blanket becomes a tent or a cardboard box becomes a house.

PLAY AND SOCIAL DEVELOPMENT

Your child's social development will evolve considerably over the toddler years and nowhere is this better demonstrated than in the area of play. Whereas a young toddler enjoys playing alone and will often barely acknowledge a child of a similar age, let alone play with them, by the time they are approaching their third birthday most toddlers are happily playing alongside their peers – something known as parallel play – and enjoy being around other children. And while they may still sometimes struggle with the concepts of sharing and taking turns, they are slowly beginning to understand their relevance. Also, it is through play that your toddler attempts to make sense of the social structure they see around them, for example who is who in the family and the various roles that we play.

PLAY AND EMOTIONAL DEVELOPMENT

Much of your toddler's play is about self-expression. For example, drawing a colourful scribble with crayons, making 'music' by banging on an upturned saucepan or serving up a tea party for their toys all demonstrate your toddler's personal, unique response to their environment and help build up their confidence and self-esteem. In addition, your toddler's play often enables them to work through their emotions, as they express their feelings through the games they are playing. For example, perhaps your toddler is pretending that their dolly is crying because its mummy has gone, in which case they are probably trying to understand their own feelings of separation anxiety.

Case study

Harriet has this doll which my mum bought for her when she was still a baby, and it is called Closed Eyes, as it is meant to look like it is sleeping. Harriet absolutely loves this doll above and beyond any of the others she's got, and when she was smaller she would drag Closed Eyes around by its hair, like a little caveman. Now that she's a bit older, she's become much more caring about Closed Eyes' welfare and will spend ages fussing over her, pretending to feed her and tucking her up in bed. The other week Harriet was off from nursery because she'd been running a fever when I noticed Closed Eyes lying on a cushion on the couch with a wet wipe over her head. When I asked Harriet why, she told me that Closed Eyes was poorly and I realized that she was trying to cool her doll, just like I'd been doing to her with a cold, wet flannel earlier in the day. It did make me smile.

Top tip

The next time your toddler is playing, take the time to watch and listen to them. As their cognitive skills grow, you will begin to see their pretend play becoming increasingly complex. They begin to make more and more observations and logical connections between ideas. For example, now after your toddler feeds their doll they may put it to sleep. You can further encourage your toddler's logical thinking by asking questions about what they are doing, for example: 'Is dolly cold? Should we get her jumper?'.

Free play versus structured play

Free play takes place when your toddler is leading the play experience, in other words they have decided on the activity, and they have set out the rules and boundaries. For example, perhaps your toddler has built a birthday cake out of sand for their teddy bear and is collecting twigs to use as candles. Structured play, however, is adult-led and is guided and planned. For example, perhaps you have enrolled your toddler at a local music and movement class that they attend once a week. Experts agree that while structured play has its place in a toddler's life, free play is far more beneficial to their early development as it enables them to use their imagination, find out what they really like, be less inhibited and ultimately more resilient. A toddler cannot really have too much free playtime, whereas structured play should be limited. Studies have shown that if a toddler is overloaded with supposedly educational activities and organized classes their stress and anxiety levels increase and what is supposed to be doing them good could end up having the opposite effect.

The benefits of free play can be summed up as follows:

▶ *It enables your toddler to use their creativity and develop their imagination, dexterity and other strengths.*
▶ *It encourages your toddler to interact with the world around them.*
▶ *It will help your toddler conquer their fears and build their confidence.*
▶ *As your toddler gets older, it will teach them to work in groups, so they learn to share and resolve conflicts.*
▶ *It enables your toddler to practise their decision-making skills.*
▶ *It is great fun.*

Insight

I understand the allure of structuring your toddler's play – it enables you to feel more in control and to encourage them in a specific direction. But in the early years, it will help to focus on just a few activities. Once they start school the classes and clubs will build up thick and fast.

Did you know?

It is recommended that a toddler has approximately 30 minutes of structured active play a day, such as playgroups, swimming and dance classes, and up to several hours of planned active free play, such as trips to the park or playground, or time spent in the garden. In addition, a toddler should spend no more than an hour sitting or lying still at any one time, unless of course they are sleeping.

Tips on playing with your toddler

Having established that unstructured free play is the best sort of play for a toddler, it would be wrong to assume that your or another adult's presence and involvement is not required. First, toddlers need supervision when playing to keep them out of harm's way and also out of mischief. Second, and equally importantly, your toddler will benefit greatly from having you as a regular playmate. Not only is playing with your toddler a wonderfully bonding experience – you will be giving your toddler their favourite thing, your time and attention – but also, through gentle suggestion and encouragement, you will be able to enhance your toddler's play, making it even more enjoyable! Here are some dos and don'ts on playing with your toddler:

DO:	*DON'T:*
▶ Let your toddler be the play leader while you adopt the more subordinate role of follower.	▶ Tell your toddler what to do when they are playing. They need to explore, discover and experiment for themselves.
▶ Offer your partnership when required, for example when playing chase or rolling and receiving a ball.	▶ Wade in when your help is not necessarily needed. By all means help your toddler out if they are too small or not strong enough to do something, but then back off when the immediate problem is solved.
▶ Offer gentle suggestions and casual demonstrations on how your toddler could make a game more fun or interesting, for example, they could try rolling their ball down the slide. But it is up to your toddler to decide whether they take up the suggestion or not.	▶ Always set limits on the amount of time you play with your toddler. Remember that your toddler is learning through continuous repetition and this can be time-consuming.

(Contd)

DO:	DON'T:
▶ Help your toddler to concentrate on a difficult game, for example a jigsaw puzzle or a sorting toy, by offering encouragement and support. Your presence will help them stick at it for longer and who knows, they might even complete it.	▶ Sit back and expect your toddler to play nicely when other toddlers are around. You will need to help your toddler to manage, especially with children they don't know very well. At this age playing together needs to be supervised so that toddlers can play alongside each other and enjoy each other's presence.

Insight

In today's busy world I know it's tempting to relegate playing with your toddler as a luxury that's often usurped by other, more pressing chores and commitments. Try to prioritize your toddler's play. Not only will it benefit them, it will also benefit you.

Top tip

As with other areas of growth and development, all toddlers are different and you may find they enjoy different toys and play experiences. Respect your toddler's preferences and try not to push them into doing something they do not want to do.

DOES WATCHING TELEVISION COUNT AS PLAY?

Watching television and DVDs is a passive activity that, unlike play, doesn't actually teach your toddler anything. Studies have shown that while a toddler learns through play, watching the same games and exercises on a television screen has no educational merit whatsoever. Similarly, computer games and so-called educational toys are also deemed to be no substitution for actual play as they have a limited scope, do not encourage imagination or creative thought processes and generally involve your toddler responding to a scenario constructed by someone else. For more on television and how much your toddler should be watching, see page 150.

The different types of play

Your toddler's play can be broadly divided into four different categories. No one type of play is more valid than another and sometimes they may well merge into each other. Also, your toddler may show a particular preference for one type of play over another and that preference may well change over time. The important thing is that your toddler has access to and is encouraged in all types of play and they can then pursue what they enjoy.

CREATIVE PLAY

This covers a range of activities including drawing and painting, modelling with clay, cutting and sticking, as well as building, dancing, making music and cooking. Creative play gives toddlers a great sense of satisfaction as they create from their imaginations and express themselves through their endeavours. It also helps your toddler develop their fine motor skills such as holding a crayon, becoming more adept at making marks on paper and eventually being able to draw recognizable objects.

It is also through creative play that your toddler can experiment with and learn about different textures.

Insight
I'm a big fan of art and craft boxes, whereby you pop all manner of interesting bits and bobs (ribbons, scraps of material, wallpaper samples, pom poms, feathers, etc.) into a box and bring it out the next time your toddler feels like being creative.

ACTIVE PLAY

This covers many different indoor and outdoor activities that require your toddler to move and be physical. It can involve equipment, for example a soft play area, a climbing frame or a tricycle, or nothing at all other than your toddler's boisterousness and unbridled energy. Active play, in all its different forms, is important to your toddler's general health and well-being as it encourages good eating and sleeping patterns and sets the foundation for healthy living habits in later life. Active play will also help develop your toddler's self-confidence and physical competence by improving both their fine and gross motor skills, as well as their muscle control.

Did you know?

Scientists in Finland have discovered that active outdoor play helps a toddler's brain develop. If a child has access to outdoor space and the freedom to play out their fantasies, their brain is more stimulated which makes them better at developing ideas and understanding the world around them.

PRETEND PLAY

This is when your toddler make-believes and role-plays using their imagination. It can take many different guises and will change and evolve considerably over the toddler years. For example, young toddlers often need a little guidance and most enjoy copying everyday activities such as sweeping up or cooking, while older toddlers are usually capable of all sorts of complex scenarios from playing shops and dressing up as different characters to building secret dens in the garden. Whatever form it takes, pretend play helps your toddler learn to use their imagination, develops their language through the speech they use while playing and also teaches them to express their emotions and work through their worries or concerns.

Insight

Similarly to an art and craft box, I think a dressing-up box is a must too. You don't have to spend a fortune on ready-made costumes. Wigs, colourful scarves and clothing in interesting fabric will all help stimulate your toddler's imagination.

Case study

Sid has a box full of toy animals in his bedroom which he loves playing pretend games with. Sometimes he'll build a zoo for them out of his wooden blocks and other times he'll make a hospital or nursery. I often hear him chatting away to himself while he's playing, putting on all these different voices – quite gruff ones for the authority figures such as the teachers or the doctors, and squeaky, high ones for the children and little babies. The other day I was in the bathroom when I heard Sid calling out 'Mummy, Mummy', and thinking that he must need me, I rushed in to see what he wanted. As I entered the room, he spun round and looked really shocked, as if I'd just caught him doing something naughty. It was then that I realized he hadn't been calling me after all, and that he'd been playing make-believe with his animals in which one of them wanted its mummy. He'd been in such a little world of his own that my bursting in had taken him completely by surprise, and to be honest, I also think he was a bit embarrassed that I had seen him so deeply engrossed in his game.

According to studies, as many as 65 per cent of children will at some point invent an imaginary friend, usually in the toddler years, and most commonly among firstborns. Psychologists conclude that these invisible pals offer companionship and emotional support, aid creativity, boost self-esteem and create a 'sense of self'. Indeed, parents should not worry even if their child dreams up multiple companions. Interestingly, boys tend to have imaginary friends who are more competent than they are, while girls' imaginary friends are usually less competent.

DEVELOPMENTAL PLAY

This is provided by such items as puzzles, board games, jigsaws, memory games, card games, flashcards, etc. and while these things can be fun for your toddler, it worth remembering that all play is in fact educational at this stage. For example, your toddler will learn just as much from pouring water from one container into another as they will from trying to do a jigsaw. That said, however, books also fall into the developmental play category and there is no doubt that toddlers really benefit from having plenty of books around and having someone read to them. Not only will reading boost your toddler's mental development, helping them learn letters, numbers and colours, it will also help a lot with their language skills. In addition, books will give your toddler's social and emotional development a boost too, as they learn through stories about the world around them and how to empathize with others. For more on reading to your toddler, see page 147.

Playing with other children

The following chart shows how your toddler's play with other children will evolve over the coming years:

0 to 2 years	Your child tends to play alone and there is little interaction with other children.
2 to 2½ years	Your toddler is a spectator around other children and will happily watch them playing, but won't join in.
2½ to 3 years	Your toddler now enjoys playing alongside other children in what is known as parallel play, but doesn't want to play with them.
3 to 4 years	Your child is now starting to interact with other children in what is known as associative play. They are also starting to develop friendships and show a preference for playing with certain other children.
4 years +	Your child now happily plays with other children in what is known as co-operative play, creating rules together and sharing goals.

Top tip

Just because your toddler doesn't play with other children just yet, that doesn't mean they don't like having them around and watching what they are doing. Organize a one-to-one playdate for your toddler, but just remember to keep it short – an hour is more than enough. Don't expect too much at this age and be on hand to mediate when they start grabbing and snatching each other's toys. To minimize such tussles you could organize play so that two versions of a toy or activity are available, as research shows that under these circumstances toddlers don't snatch, they simply take up the matching toy or activity and copy what the other child is doing. Remember that by encouraging your toddler's sociability you are laying the foundations for their future friendships.

Insight

If you'd like your toddler to get together with a friend, but don't particularly want to host a playdate, I suggest you arrange to meet at a park or playground. That way no guests overstay their welcome, all the equipment is shared, and nothing gets messed up – it's the ultimate low-maintenance playdate.

Top ten toddler toys

You really don't need to spend a fortune on expensive, supposedly
educational toys for your toddler. The following basics will see
your child all the way through the toddler years, and in certain
instances, even beyond. Interestingly, how your toddler plays with
these toys will change over time as they learn to use them in fun
and increasingly interesting and new ways.

1 *A doll or a teddy bear*
2 *Wooden blocks or bricks*
3 *A push-along toy, such as a toy pushchair or wheelbarrow*
4 *A ride-on toy*
5 *Lots of books*
6 *A toy tea set*
7 *Modelling clay, such as playdough*
8 *A box of dressing-up clothes*
9 *A train set or cars and a garage*
10 *Plenty of crayons, paints, felt-tipped pens, etc.*

Top tip

Instead of forking out on shop-bought playdough, why not
make your own? Here's a very simple recipe for it:

450 g/1 lb flour
110 g/4 oz or 8 tbsps salt
½ small packet of cream of tartar
½ tablespoon oil
475 ml/16 fl oz water
food colouring if required

Mix the flour, salt and cream of tartar together in a saucepan.
Add the oil and water, stirring all the time. Cook slowly over
a low heat, but remember to keep stirring, until it thickens.
When the dough comes together in one lump, remove from
the saucepan, allow to cool and then knead until smooth.
This can be stored for three months in an airtight tin.

Gender and toy choice

Young toddlers don't really distinguish between boys' and girls' toys. For example, an 18-month-old boy will happily play with a doll, while a girl of that age may be fascinated with toy cars. Research shows that it is around the age of two that toddlers start to become aware of the gender difference between certain toys, and as they approach their third birthday they will become increasingly conscious of their choice of toys. Interestingly, studies have shown that children apparently ask for more gender stereotyped toys than the ones parents spontaneously choose, which tend to be suitable for either gender. One study went as far as examining the types of toys typically found in a toddler's bedroom and how they differed according to gender. It found that while boys and girls had the same number of books, musical items, stuffed animals and the same amount of furniture, boys had a greater variety of toys, and they tended to have more toys overall. In summary, the following differences were reported in the types of toys boys and girls possessed:

BOYS

Boys tend to have more vehicles, for example toy cars, lorries and trucks, and more educational and arts materials. They also have more 'spatial–temporal' toys, such as shape-sorting toys, magnets and puzzles, as well as toys with an outer-space theme. Boys also have more sports-related toys, for example balls, kites and skittles.

GIRLS

Generally girls have more dolls, especially female and baby ones, as well as dolls' houses and Wendy houses. They also have many more domestic items, for example toy cookers, sinks, washing machines, tea sets, shopping baskets, etc.

Case study

Linus went through a real pink phase when he was little, when all his favourite toys tended to be in this colour. I was quite happy to go along with it as I knew it was something he'd probably grow out of, although my husband would raise an eyebrow when Linus once again reached for the pinkest thing in the toy shop. His bestest, bestest toy around this time was a powder pink teddy bear which he christened Bambie, and which went with us everywhere. I lost count of the number of times we had to make a frantic dash back to a cafe or playground to look for Bambie after Linus had misplaced it. Anyhow, as I predicted, Linus grew out of his pink phase with a vengeance and almost overnight everything of that colour was banished from his bedroom, having been dismissed as being 'for girls', and of course that included the previously adored Bambie. But unfortunately for Linus, evidence of his pink phase can't be erased that easily. The other day I was on the computer, organizing some photos, when I realized that Linus was holding Bambie in practically every shot we'd taken over a six-month period – outings, family visits, holidays – you name it, Bambie is there. It did make me laugh, although my little lad is going to be mortified when he sees them.

Toy safety

Accidents involving toys are quite common, especially among toddlers, with 40,000 happening each year in the United Kingdom alone. Therefore it is important to consider the safety of your toddler's toys by taking the following factors into account:

The toy's age and stage suitability
Check the recommended age range of the toy, as most toys nowadays have guidelines. Yet remember, these are not set in stone, so if you consider your toddler to be mature enough and physically ready you might want to go for something aimed slightly older, or vice versa.

Its size
Consider the size of the toy. Until your toddler turns three, toy parts should be bigger than their mouth to avoid the risk of choking. Also check the size and weight of the toy in relation to

your toddler. Is there a danger that it could topple onto them or will they drop it due to its weight?

How the toy has been put together
Is the toy well made? Are its various parts secure? Check that buttons, eyes, tails, beads, ribbons, etc. are all properly attached and cannot be snapped or bitten off. Make sure the toy doesn't have sharp or rough edges and can't cause splinters. Also, if the toy has moving parts, make sure they are not a potential trap for little fingers. In addition, make sure that a toy does not have strings or cords that could cause strangulation. Dressing-up clothes should also be checked for cords that could become lodged in a door or a piece of machinery.

Its condition
Many toys are passed down from older relatives and siblings or are bought in jumble sales or charity shops. If this is the case, make sure it is in good working order and that all parts are secure and intact. If in doubt, throw it out.

> **Top tip**
> If you are unsure whether a toy poses a choking hazard, get hold of an empty toilet paper roll. If the toy or part of the toy can fit through the cylinder, then it is not safe for your toddler.

Eight everyday objects that make great toys

As previously stated, you really don't need to spend a fortune on your toddler's toys. In fact, some of the best playthings can be found among everyday household items.

1 **Empty water bottle.** *Just fill with dried beans or cereal and put the top back on for the perfect toddler musical instrument.*
2 **Empty toilet paper or kitchen paper roll.** *A trumpet? A loud-speaker? The beginnings of a robot? Let your toddler decide.*

3 **Pots and pans.** *Let your toddler try their skills as a percussionist with some upturned pots and pans and a wooden spoon.*
4 **Cardboard box.** *Not for nothing has the humble cardboard box become the toddler toy of choice (usually it is preferred to the fancy toy that came in it), as its uses are only as limited as your toddler's imagination.*
5 **Laundry basket.** *Put on its side, this becomes a great toddler den. Alternatively, put your toddler inside and take them for a ride.*
6 **Washing-up bowl.** *Fill it with water and place it on the floor, or even better, in the garden, along with a few empty plastic containers and your toddler will play happily for ages.*
7 **Old socks.** *Who needs a shop-bought puppet when you have an old sock and your toddler's wonderful imagination to hand?*
8 **Empty squeezy bottle.** *Great for squirting in the bath.*

Did you know?

In honour of the cardboard box's reputation as such a great toddler plaything, in 2005 it was added to the National Toy Hall of Fame, one of very few non-brand-specific toys to be included.

Great games you can play with your toddler

There really is an infinite number of games you can play with your toddler, many that you might have played yourself as a child, and many more that you and your toddler can make up together. Here are a few suggestions suitable to your toddler's age.

One year to 18 months

▶ *Pretend that your toddler's favourite doll or teddy bear has come to life. Give it a voice and make it walk. Arrange a tea party or a jungle adventure in the garden.*

▶ *Now that your toddler's a little older, you can start evolving their favourite game of peek-a-boo to become more akin to hide and seek. For example, if your toddler gets into bed with you in the morning, take it in turns to hide under the bed sheets. Another great game is creating a 'bag' out of the towel at bath time and carrying your toddler into another room.*

18 months to 2 years

▶ *Your toddler loves to be chased, so pretend you are a big bear or a cheeky monkey and try to catch your toddler. When you catch them, reward them with a bear hug or some monkey tickles, then let them chase after you.*

▶ *Crank up the CD player and dance with your toddler. You could try doing different actions to the music, for example pretending to play different instruments or marching like a soldier.*

2 to 3 years

▶ *Hide a small treat in a room or somewhere in the garden and encourage your toddler to try to find it. When they get close to it, tell them they are warm, getting hotter and finally burning hot when they are right next to it. The further away they get, the colder they become until they are finally a frozen block of ice.*

▶ *Make a game out of deliberately getting things wrong, so your toddler can have the fun and satisfaction of correcting you. For example, point to a tomato and say 'that looks like a scrummy apple'; your toddler can then delight in telling you that you are wrong. Then let them make a deliberate mistake and you can do the response.*

Ways to turn everyday activities into a game

With a little bit of thought and some imagination, many everyday chores and activities can be turned into a fun game for your toddler. Here are a few examples:

1 *Turn dressing your toddler into a game of peek-a-boo, for example pausing as the jumper goes over their head and wondering out loud where they have gone before pulling it down with an exclamation of surprise and delight.*
2 *Make picking up toys into a counting game, for example, 'let's each pick up ten toys each', or into a colour sorting game, for example, 'you pick up all the red blocks, I'll pick up the blue'.*
3 *If you are working in the garden, give your toddler a bucket and see how fast they can fill it with the leaves that have fallen on the lawn.*
4 *When you are sorting through the washing, get your toddler involved by seeing if they can match the socks.*
5 *At the shops, engage your toddler in a game of 'find the...', asking them to hunt down a specific item with you, for example a pineapple in the fruit and vegetable section.*

10 THINGS TO REMEMBER

1   *Play is an incredibly important part of your toddler's development, helping them to learn about their body, the world around them and how and why things work the way they do.*

2   *Free play, where your toddler decides on the activity and sets the rules and boundaries, is generally considered more beneficial to development than structured play, which is adult-led and planned and guided.*

3   *When playing with your toddler try not to dominate the proceedings. Much better to sit back and let your toddler lead the way, offering your help and suggestions as and when required.*

4   *Television, DVDs, computer games and supposedly educational toys are no substitution for actual play as they do not encourage your toddler to use their imagination or be creative.*

5   *Of the different kinds of play – creative, active, pretend and developmental – no one type is better than another. Indeed, often they will merge into each other.*

6   *Your toddler may prefer one type of play over another, but this preference may change with time. Encourage and give your child access to all types of play.*

7   *A young toddler tends to be a spectator around other children, enjoying watching them play but not joining in. It is usually around the age of three that children start playing alongside each other in what is known as parallel play.*

8   *Parallel play will give way to what we recognize as playing together only around your child's fourth birthday. This is also the time they start developing friendships.*

9 *Young toddlers don't really distinguish between boys' and girls' toys. It is only around the age of two that they start to become aware that certain toys are aimed at different genders, and by the age of three they will become conscious of their toy choice relating to gender.*

10 *Make sure your toddler's toys are suitable for their age and stage and that they don't present a choking hazard, especially if they are under three years of age. Shockingly, more than 40,000 accidents involving toys happen each year in the UK.*

12

Helping your toddler cope with change

In this chapter you will learn:
- *how change affects your toddler*
- *ways to prepare your toddler for a new sibling*
- *what to do when the baby arrives*
- *ways to prepare your toddler for moving house*
- *how to help them to settle*
- *how to choose the best childcare*
- *tips on preparing your toddler for childcare*
- *the signs that your toddler is unhappy*
- *how to help your toddler through a family break-up*
- *ways in which you can ease their upset.*

Why change cannot be avoided

If most of us adults find change hard, just imagine how difficult it is for your toddler, who relies on familiarity and predictability to make sense of their world. But change cannot be avoided and a certain amount is almost inevitable in the toddler years. For example, if you are planning to add to your family, the likelihood is that this will happen when your firstborn is still a toddler. Then, with your expanding brood, you may have to reconsider your living conditions, moving to a bigger home, or one located in a more family-friendly environment. Childcare is another factor that may need to be considered at this stage. Perhaps you are planning to put your toddler into childcare for the first time or maybe you are reviewing your options now that your child is no longer a baby. Finally, although by no means inevitable, relationship break-ups are all too common these days, and this can have a big impact on a toddler, as well as, of course, the rest of the family. Yet while these aforementioned changes will undoubtedly cause a certain amount of upheaval and unsettledness, they need not be too distressing to your toddler. In each case there are a few simple strategies that you can put in place to minimize the negative impact, and ensure that life goes on as smoothly and as routinely as possible for your toddler, who is, after all, such a creature of habit.

What change means to your toddler

Some toddlers are naturally more amenable to change than others – for them transition is both exciting and fun, and these toddlers tend to be very flexible and adaptable. Meanwhile, those who are highly sensitive need more time with transitions, and those who get upset when their routine is disrupted will probably be a little anxious and clingy and need extra reassurance to help them cope with change. Whatever your toddler's personality type, however, it is important not to assume that just because everyone else knows what is going on, your toddler does too. Your toddler is still getting to grips with language and communication, and there is much that they still do not understand. Therefore any change will need to be explained to your toddler in the absolute simplest of terms, and reiterated over a period of time. For example, telling your toddler that they are 'moving house' is an expression that is open to misinterpretation – how do you move a house? Similarly, what is a 'new arrival'? Help your toddler understand through the use of toys and drawings and also seek out toddler books on the subject. All of this will better prepare your toddler for the imminent disruption that the change entails. In addition, it is important that whatever change is occurring, you do not project your own stress and insecurities onto the situation. With toddlers, the key is to make the change seem as normal as possible and focus on the positive things that will come out of it.

Helping your toddler adjust to a new sibling

For all of their little lives your toddler, especially if firstborn, has been at the very centre of your universe, but with the arrival of a new baby all that is about to change. Even if your toddler appears excited about the prospect of having a sibling, it is important to prepare them for the inevitable adjustment that will need to occur, and this process can begin as soon as the pregnancy becomes public knowledge.

Did you know?

In the UK, most mums leave two to three years between births, although medical studies have concluded that the safest gap is actually 18 to 24 months.

EIGHT WAYS TO INVOLVE YOUR TODDLER IN THE PREGNANCY

1 *Start pointing out to your toddler other families with babies so that they can see that a family with more than one child is perfectly normal.*
2 *Let your toddler come along to the doctor's and/or hospital appointments.*
3 *Show your toddler the scans and explain that it is their little brother or sister.*
4 *Let your toddler feel the baby move.*
5 *Let your toddler help you prepare the layette and arrange the nursery.*
6 *Let your toddler join in the name-choosing process. Their favourites will probably not be yours – Tinkerbell, anyone? – but it will make them feel more involved.*
7 *Forewarn your toddler that the baby will need help and might do lots of crying. This will make your toddler feel more grown up and hopefully more tolerant of the needs of a new baby.*

8 *If the new baby's arrival necessitates other changes in your toddler's life, for example them moving out of the cot or nursery, then implement these changes slowly and in advance so that they have had time to get used to them and do not blame them on the baby.*

Top tip

If your toddler has not got one already, get them a baby doll so they can play families or pretend to be big brother or sister to it. Show them how to take care of the doll, just as you will be doing when the baby arrives. Through play, your toddler can explore some of the emotions they are likely to experience when the new baby arrives and also see some of the practicalities of caring for a newborn.

Insight

If your toddler is likely to need looking after when you go into labour, I would make sure they're familiar with the person who'll be taking care of them. If it's a friend or neighbour, prepare your toddler and let them spend some time in their company beforehand.

INTRODUCING YOUR TODDLER TO THE NEW BABY

Here are a few things worth considering when your toddler first meets the new arrival:

▶ *Wherever you are, home or hospital, keep things as quiet as possible. Having an audience of relatives looking on will in all probability totally overwhelm your toddler.*
▶ *Have a present ready for your toddler that you can say is from the baby. This will immediately put the new arrival in a favourable light as far as your toddler is concerned.*
▶ *Make a fuss of your toddler first and then show them the baby.*
▶ *Help your toddler feel more attached to the baby by calling it your toddler's baby brother or sister.*

▶ *Let your toddler do as much or as little with the baby as they feel comfortable with. Maybe they just want to look and then go off and play, or perhaps they will want to gently stroke the baby's hand or even have the baby placed on their lap with you supporting the head. Allow your toddler to set the pace.*

Top tip

If you are in hospital, tell a nurse on the ward your toddler's name, so they can be greeted not just as the baby's sibling, but by their name and then as the baby's sibling. This will help your toddler to feel extra special.

HELPING YOUR TODDLER ACCEPT THEIR NEW SIBLING

In all likelihood your toddler will want to lavish their new sibling with affection; indeed, you might find yourself having to gently fend them off. But even after an apparently successful introduction period, your toddler may suddenly develop the wobbles when they realize that the demanding little creature that is disrupting everyone's life is there for keeps. Here are a few tips on how to help your toddler to accept and even enjoy the new baby.

Expect some resentment

Don't be disappointed or upset if your toddler does start to show resentment towards the new baby. This is a perfectly natural response – the reality of having to vie for your attention is just sinking in. Let your toddler know that you understand their feelings and that it is normal to feel this way.

Typical signs of jealousy or resentment include:

▶ *bad behaviour and naughtiness*
▶ *attention-seeking behaviour, especially when you are busy with the baby*
▶ *regression, for example wanting to go back to a bottle, refusing to use the potty or waking up several times in the night.*

Offer constant reassurance

Keep telling your toddler how much you love them, and try to focus on what they are doing right rather than wrong. Your toddler needs lots of praise and positive reinforcement to make them feel safe and secure.

Make time for your toddler

Set aside some time each day when it is just you and your toddler. If you have the energy, you could try staggering naptimes so that you have that one-to-one time while the baby sleeps. However, even if you can only manage a few minutes together, drawing, playing or reading a book, this will still make your toddler feel special. Try to ensure that your toddler has quality time with other family members, too. Special outings with partners and grandparents will all help keep the green-eyed monster at bay.

Get your toddler involved

Your toddler loves to feel useful, so let them help out with the new baby by giving them special jobs. For example, let your toddler fetch the nappies, or perhaps at bath time they can help wash the baby's hands. Also let your toddler help choose the baby's clothes, for example: 'Do you think the baby would like to wear the green or the yellow babygrow?'.

Insight

I've found that the arrival of a new baby often creates a far more intimate bond between toddler and father. Rather than feel jealous, try to encourage this as it will greatly help your child to adjust to the change in circumstance.

Case study

It's funny how you imagine a scenario in your head, but then the reality is so different. Lying in the hospital bed with my newborn baby snuggled up to my breast, I couldn't wait for my husband to arrive with Esme. I was so excited to see her reaction to her little sister, who we'd decided to call Beth. When I was pregnant,

Esme had announced to anyone who'd listen that mummy was making a baby sister, especially for her. Even though we didn't know, Esme was absolutely convinced I was having a girl. So when she turned out to be right, I thought she'd be over the moon. But from the moment Esme walked into the ward, instead of running over to greet me and meet the little bundle in my arms, she hung back, shyly clinging to her daddy's legs. After much coaxing, she eventually came over for a hug, but showed no interest whatsoever in even looking at the baby. For the rest of the visit Esme acted as if Beth wasn't there – I would never have predicted that reaction in a million years. It's only now that we've been home a couple of weeks that she's started to become curious about the baby and wants to watch me change her nappy and has started asking questions, like 'Why baby crying Mummy?'. I guess Esme just needs some time to adjust to her new role as big sister, just as it's taking me time to adjust to being a mum of two!

Top tip

Once the baby has arrived, continue to let your toddler set the pace. If they don't want to be involved with the baby, don't force the issue. Some toddlers cope with the arrival of a new sibling by ignoring it, but given time, they will eventually come to accept and indeed love the latest addition to the family.

Moving house with your toddler

Moving house is often cited as being the second most stressful life event after the death of a relative and before divorce. But don't despair, because with some advanced planning and good organization, it needn't impact on your toddler too much. For adults, most house-moving concerns are usually practical. For example, how to get all the packing done, will all the furniture fit into the van, is the telephone going to be reconnected on time? For your toddler, however, their worries are likely to be more internalized and less fathomable, but generally associated with feelings of loss, which is why it is important to include your toddler in what is going on as soon as possible, letting them know that their world isn't about to fall apart and that what is happening is in fact exciting and positive.

FIVE WAYS TO PREPARE YOUR TODDLER FOR THE MOVE

1 *As soon as the move is definite, start talking to your toddler about the new house, playing up such toddler-attractive aspects as the big garden, its proximity to the park, the size of their room, etc. Make them feel excited about the prospect of moving there.*
2 *As well as talking about what will be different, remember to tell your toddler all the things that will be the same, for example your toddler's slide in the garden, the goldfish tank in the kitchen, etc.*
3 *If possible, take your toddler to visit the new place a couple of times before moving. Let them have a look around and see their new bedroom, garden, etc.*
4 *Explain the moving process to your toddler a few weeks in advance, using simple, reassuring language that leaves the door open for questions and the opportunity for a follow-up talk.*
5 *Let your toddler help in the packing process, by handing you unbreakable objects or having a box that they can fill up for themselves, for example with their soft toys. Helping you out will make your toddler feel that they have some control over the situation, which has in reality been totally instigated by you.*

Insight

Depending on how long it is until you move, I'd advise you begin by packing up some of the toys that your toddler isn't playing with much at the moment. That way in another month or so when you do move they will seem like new to your toddler when they are unpacked.

Top tip

If your toddler has a favourite toy or blanket, make sure it is put somewhere safe and easily accessible during the move, as they may suddenly want to turn to it for comfort and security. The last thing you need after an exhausting day moving is to be ripping open boxes with a crying toddler in tow.

HOW TO EASE THINGS FOR YOUR TODDLER ON MOVE DAY

After all those months of planning, the big day finally arrives. Here are some things you might want to consider to ease the transition for your toddler:

▶ *Rather than have your toddler around during the moving process, it might be better that they stay with a close relative or go to their usual childcare. This will give them a secure base during all the activity and will enable them to stick to their routine as much as possible.*

▶ *Before leaving the house, allow your toddler to say goodbye to it. Take them round each room to wave their farewells, taking extra time to say a special bye bye to their bedroom. This will help your toddler understand that it is the end of an era, and that another is just beginning.*

▶ *Once at your new home, make your toddler's bedroom number one priority, unpacking their favourite toys and familiar objects so that they immediately feel at ease in their new room. Now isn't the time to invest in a new bed and bedding. Stick to what your toddler had previously until they have grown accustomed to their new surroundings.*

▶ *Continue as much as possible to stick to your toddler's usual eating and sleeping schedule throughout the move as this will help them to settle more quickly.*

Studies show that toddlers cope better with moving house than older children. This is because their sense of security depends primarily on their parents and they usually feel safe provided their parents are around.

HELPING YOUR TODDLER SETTLE INTO THEIR NEW HOME

Your toddler will need a little time to get used to their new surroundings. In fact, it is estimated to take between six weeks and two months for a child to adapt to a new home and its environs. During this settling-in period, you might want to consider the following suggestions:

Take your toddler back to the old house
You might think this would upset them, but in fact the opposite is true. Seeing where they used to live will help them come to terms with the move and accept that things have changed. If everyone pretends that the old house doesn't exist, your toddler is likely to feel an even greater sense of loss.

Expect some regression
As with the arrival of a new sibling, your toddler's unsettledness may manifest itself through regression. Here are some of the typical signs:

- *thumb sucking*
- *wetting themselves when previously dry*
- *returning to baby babbling, having talked properly*
- *becoming more clingy.*

Don't make a big deal of it if regression happens – it is a perfectly natural response that will disappear in time.

Get your toddler involved in setting up the new home
If you are redecorating their bedroom, let your toddler help choose the colours; also consult them on where to place their toy box, where to hang their pictures and paintings, the best place for their bookcase, etc.

Be there for your toddler
In the aftermath of a move, it is all too easy to throw yourself into getting the new house organized to the detriment of time spent with your toddler. But it is important during this period of transition that you do spend some quality time with your toddler, even if it is a half hour's stroll together around the new neighbourhood after a hard day's unpacking.

Be patient
Don't worry if your toddler is taking longer to settle than you had hoped. As previously stated, new adjustments take time, and each child will handle things differently. Some toddlers will ease slowly into a new situation while others are happy to jump straight in. Allow for your toddler's individual personality.

Case study

We moved house two months ago and I was very conscious of the impact the move might have on Rajan, so I tried to prepare him for the disruption as best I could. Our first few days in the new house were fine, with Rajan tearing around, exploring every nook and cranny, in a heightened state of excitement. I was delighted he seemed so happy and thought that was it – job well done. But then, about a week later, Rajan's behaviour really began to deteriorate. It started at nursery, with biting and kicking other children, and then progressed to the home. At his worst, Rajan was throwing half a dozen tantrums a day, and even started banging his head, something he had never done before. I was beside myself, and didn't know what to do, but my husband was adamant that we shouldn't condone our son's behaviour just because of the move and that we should treat the tantrums and hitting as we would have done at any other time, i.e. with Timeout. I found this difficult at first, but now think it was the right call because slowly but surely Rajan's behaviour started to improve, and now I can safely say our son is back to his usual, happy-go-lucky self. Just the other week we had friends over and he couldn't wait to show them the new garden. It seems that he has finally made the change, in his own time. Now all we have to sort out is the cat...

Top tip

Be patient and supportive with your toddler during times of upheaval, but do not fall into the trap of tolerating bad behaviour, using the house move or whatever as an excuse. Just as it is important to keep routines, so it is important to maintain expected limits of behaviour. This will reinforce for your toddler that while other things in their life may be different, their relationship with you and what is expected of them have not changed.

Choosing the best childcare

The toddler years may see your child's first foray into childcare. Perhaps you have decided to return to work or maybe you feel that your toddler needs greater stimulation and to mix more with children of their own age. Also, around this time, many parents whose children have been in childcare since they were babies may start to reconsider their choices as their toddler's needs are now considerably different. Whatever your situation, starting or changing childcare represents a considerable step for you and your toddler and you want to be sure that you have made the best choice for everyone concerned – although of course your toddler's happiness and well-being will be paramount.

WHAT ARE YOUR CHILDCARE OPTIONS?

What childcare you choose for your toddler is a personal decision and will depend on various factors. Certain types of childcare may suit your toddler's needs and personality better than others, while your situation and circumstances will also have to be taken into account. Your childcare options can be put into four common categories (nursery, childminder, kinship care and nannies), each with their pros and cons, as discussed below.

NURSERY

Nurseries are an increasingly popular choice among many parents, with more than 700,000 children in the UK now attending a nursery for more than four hours a day.

Advantages
- *It is very reliable – unlike most other options, a nursery will never call in sick.*
- *A good nursery offers plenty of stimulation and provides your toddler with the opportunity to mix and socialize with other children and help build confidence.*
- *There is lots of play equipment and there are many toys to fire your toddler's curiosity and imagination.*
- *There is usually a wide variety of activities to teach different skills, for example, singing, dancing, listening to stories.*
- *It is a structured environment with trained staff, regular inspections and a manager who oversees the whole operation.*

Disadvantages
- *Depending on your toddler's personality and age, they may feel overwhelmed by a nursery setting and be happier with one-to-one care.*
- *Nurseries can be very expensive. The average cost for a full-time place for a toddler in the UK is £141 a week, based on a ten-hour day.*
- *There is little flexibility with a nursery – you have to conform to the opening and closing times (some nurseries impose financial penalties for late pick-ups) and will need to find back-up when your child is sick (for which you will still pay) or when the nursery is closed.*

So is it the right choice?

If you answer yes to most of the following questions, then you might want to consider a nursery for your toddler:

Do you want your toddler to be around plenty of other children and involved in lots of activities?

Do you want your toddler to have access to different toys, equipment and stimulation?

Do you think your toddler's personality is such that they will enjoy the group setting?

Do you want your toddler to be in a place where there are qualified staff?

Do you need childcare that is available for most of the year?

Do you need to know that there will always be someone to look after your toddler?

Six points to consider when choosing a nursery

1 *Visit the nursery several times and at different times of the day.*
2 *Check that all facilities, equipment and toys are in good condition, safe and clean.*
3 *Is it a warm and welcoming environment?*
4 *Watch the interaction between staff and children. Are the staff nurturing the children? Are they chatting among themselves?*
5 *Do the children seem happy?*
6 *What kind of meals does it serve? Is the food fresh and healthy? Are menus changed regularly?*

Insight

When visiting nurseries, try to keep a clear head and focus on what your toddler really needs. French and Spanish lessons may sound wonderful, but in my opinion, they're not that vital for the average two-year-old.

CHILDMINDER

A childminder is a registered childcare worker who works from their home, looking after a set number of children (no more than three children under five). It is the second most common form of childcare in the UK, the first being kinship care (see later).

Advantages
- *Your toddler is being looked after in a home environment, by someone they will grow to trust and possibly love.*
- *Your toddler will receive plenty of individual attention.*
- *Your toddler will spend time with other children, but on a more intimate level than in a nursery setting.*
- *A childminder is usually more affordable than a nursery. You can expect to pay anywhere between £3 and £6 an hour in the UK.*
- *A childminder can usually be more flexible about pick-up and drop-off times.*
- *A childminder is usually a parent themselves and is therefore likely to be attuned to the needs of your toddler.*

Disadvantages
- *Although trained, registered and checked, a childminder is not supervised on a day-to-day basis.*
- *Your toddler will be fitting in to the childminder's daily routine, rather than a routine specifically tailored to them.*
- *You will need to have a back-up plan in place, should the childminder fall ill.*

So is it the right choice?
If you answer yes to most of the following questions then you might want to consider a childminder for your toddler:

Do you prefer your toddler to be cared for in a home environment?

Does your toddler need a lot of individual attention?

Will your toddler cope better with just a small number of children?

Do you need a certain amount of flexibility in your childcare arrangements?

Six points to consider when choosing a childminder
1 *Look around the childminder's home and garden and ask to see all areas your toddler will have access to.*
2 *Is the level of hygiene and safety what you would expect?*
3 *Is there a suitable range of toys, books and equipment and are they in good condition?*
4 *How does the childminder organize their day? What activities and outings are provided?*
5 *Do the other children in the childminder's care seem happy and well occupied?*
6 *Check the childminder's registration certificate and latest inspection report.*

Insight
It's easy to slip into an informal relationship with a childminder, especially if you get on well with them. But while it's good to be friendly, in my opinion I think it's important to keep things on an organized and professional footing.

KINSHIP CARE

Keeping your toddler's care in the family, otherwise known as kinship care, is reckoned to be the most popular choice of childcare in the UK, although because the arrangement is usually an informal one, no figures exist to substantiate this. A recent study, however, estimated that as many as two in three families now rely on their relatives to do some childminding.

Advantages
▶ *You know and trust the person.*
▶ *A family member, especially a grandparent, is likely to love your toddler almost as much as you do.*
▶ *Your toddler will develop a particularly close bond with that relative, something that can be a benefit to both.*

- ▶ *The kinship carer is probably already a parent and so has direct experience with children.*
- ▶ *Kinship care is cheap and sometimes even free.*
- ▶ *There is likely to be a lot more flexibility about hours.*
- ▶ *Your toddler will probably still be looked after when sick.*
- ▶ *Your toddler will be cared for in a familiar environment.*

Disadvantages
- ▶ *A relative, particularly an elderly one, may find the demands of a toddler exhausting, no matter how willing they are to help out.*
- ▶ *Their ideas about parenting may be very different from yours, but because of the nature of your relationship it can be difficult to insist things are done your way.*
- ▶ *They probably won't have all the toys, books and play equipment necessary to keep your toddler occupied.*
- ▶ *The kinship carer's home may not be as toddler-proof as yours.*
- ▶ *Your toddler may not have as much contact with other children as you would like.*
- ▶ *If things go wrong, you run the risk of falling out with a family member.*

So is it the right choice?
If you answer yes to most of the following questions then you might want to consider kinship care for your toddler:

Do you have a good, honest and open relationship with the relative involved?

Do you feel confident that they are physically able to do the job?

Are you prepared for there to be a bit of give and take in the way your toddler is cared for?

Are you confident that your toddler will be safe and stimulated enough in the kinship carer's home?

Many of the parents I know like to mix their childcare, with their toddler perhaps spending two days in nursery or at the childminder's, and one with their grandparents. If workable, this arrangement is often the perfect solution.

NANNIES

Once the privilege of the rich and famous, a nanny is becoming an increasingly common childcare option among ordinary working parents, and it is estimated that there are now more than 100,000 nannies working in the UK. Assisting this trend is the growing popularity of nanny sharing, which can substantially bring down the cost.

Advantages
- *Your toddler will be receiving good one-to-one care, with all the attention and stimulation that entails.*
- *Your toddler will be cared for in their own home, enjoying its familiarity and security even though you are not there.*
- *Your toddler can adhere to their usual routine.*
- *You can have a big say in how your toddler is cared for, from what they eat to the sort of activities you would like them to do.*
- *A qualified nanny is usually a committed professional, trained in many aspects of childcare.*
- *A nanny can become a much-loved member of the family.*
- *A nanny is usually very flexible, and will cover for the unexpected and look after your child when they are sick.*

Disadvantages
- *A nanny can be prohibitively expensive, between £200 and £500 a week in the UK, depending on location, and even sharing may be too expensive for some.*
- *Like a childminder, a nanny will be unsupervised throughout the day.*
- *How much time your toddler spends with other children will depend on the nanny.*

- You will become a nanny's employer and as such you will be responsible for their tax, national insurance and paid holidays.
- Although a nanny may have various qualifications, they are not registered and inspected like other forms of formal childcare.

So is it the right choice?

If you answer yes to most of the following questions then you might want to consider a nanny for your toddler:

Do you want to be able to stipulate how your toddler is cared for?

Do you want someone who will fit around your toddler's existing routine?

Do you think your toddler's personality is such that they would be happier being cared for in their own home?

Are you willing to take the legal and financial responsibility of an employer?

If your nanny is to live in, have you thought through all the practicalities and do you definitely have enough space?

Six points to consider when choosing a nanny

1 Check that they have a recognized qualification in childcare.
2 Ask for references and phone each one individually. It is advisable not to rely on pre-written testimonials.
3 Don't be afraid to ask their referees probing questions and don't be fobbed off with vague answers.
4 Look for a nanny with extensive experience and who has worked with children of a similar age to yours.
5 Before hiring a nanny, let them spend some time with your toddler. Watch how they interact with them. Do they pick them up, speak to them, want to play with them?
6 Trust your gut instinct.

WHY NOT AN AU PAIR?

There can be little doubt that an au pair is far cheaper than a qualified nanny, costing as little as £60 a week, but as in all areas of life, you get what you pay for. An au pair is usually very young, doesn't speak the language very well and has little to no hands-on experience of looking after children. As such, au pairs are generally not considered suitable as a full-time carer for a toddler when you are not there. That said, if you work from home, want some help around the house and someone who will play with your toddler and to do the odd bit of babysitting, then you might want to consider this option.

SEVEN WAYS TO PREPARE YOUR TODDLER FOR CHILDCARE

1 *Talk with your toddler about what is happening. You can ease a lot of your toddler's fears by telling them what they can expect, and that always, at the end of the day, you will be there for them.*
2 *Be positive about childcare around your toddler. If you are unsure or feel guilty your toddler will pick up on this.*
3 *Tell them about all the toys, activities and other children they will be meeting and let them know that as well as being necessary, childcare will be fun.*

4   Point out any friends or cousins who have recently started childcare and talk about the fun they are having.
5   Visit your childcare provider several times with your toddler before they actually start. Familiarize them with the new environment and the people or person who will be caring for them.
6   Help your toddler get used to playing in larger groups of children by taking them to a local toddler group. You could also arrange a playdate beforehand with other children who will be in their class or who are cared for by the same person.
7   If your toddler has never been away from you before, it may help to get them used to the separation by leaving them with family or friends for short periods in the run-up to starting childcare.

EASING YOUR TODDLER INTO CHILDCARE

Whether starting childcare for the first time or changing your childcare provider, here are some things you can do to make the transition easier for your toddler:

▶   Whatever your childcare choice, ease your toddler into it very slowly. For example, any reputable nursery will have a settling-in period for your toddler, when you will initially stay with them, then leave them for a short period and build up over a few weeks until finally they can be left for the full duration. It is advisable to proceed similarly with a child-minder and nanny, as this will allow your toddler gradually to get used to the change in routine.
▶   When you do get to the stage of leaving your toddler, make sure you say goodbye to them properly with a kiss and a cuddle and tell them that you will be back to pick them up later. Avoid sneaking out to prevent a scene as this can cause confusion and even more upset.
▶   If your toddler starts crying, try to resist going back for just one more kiss and cuddle. Most toddlers will stop crying within a few minutes of their parent's departure. If you feel concerned, phone up and check 15 minutes later.

▶ *Let your toddler take a memento with them. This could be a favourite toy, or perhaps something that reminds them of you, for example your handkerchief that they can look after until you return.*

ENSURING THAT YOUR TODDLER IS HAPPY IN CHILDCARE

Toddlers do take time to adjust to childcare or being in a new childcare arrangement, although most are usually comfortable within a month of first starting. To ensure that your toddler is happy and is settling in okay, you might want to consider the following:

▶ **Keep an eye on your toddler's behaviour at home.** *Is your toddler eating, sleeping and generally behaving normally? If not, then they might be having difficulty adjusting.*
▶ **Factor in your toddler's personality.** *If you know that your toddler has difficulty adapting to new situations, accept that their settling-in period could be more lengthy. If you are confident about your childcare choice, stick with it. Changing it now will only mean your toddler has to start the process of adjusting all over again.*
▶ **Talk to your childcare provider.** *It is vital that there is a good level of communication between you and your toddler's carer. Voice any concerns you might have and ask them to report back on your toddler's activities and behaviour during the day.*
▶ **Pay a surprise visit.** *If you suspect that your toddler is having trouble adjusting, try making an unscheduled visit. This will enable you to see your toddler as they really are during the day, and not just at stressful times like drop-off and pick-up. You will be able to assess much better whether the childcare is a good fit for your toddler.*
▶ **Know when to call it quits.** *If your toddler seems to be very unhappy in childcare, despite the best efforts of the carer, then it may be that the childcare you have chosen does not fit your toddler's needs at this time. In this case, it may be best to reassess the situation.*

I went back to work part time when Daisy was six months old, and I found a lovely little nursery just over the road from us, where all the staff were warm and friendly. The baby room was beautiful, with all these cots lined against the wall and lots of soft play areas and toys to keep the children stimulated. Daisy's key worker was a big, jovial lady who obviously doted on her babies, and I remember once feeling a pang of jealousy when I arrived to pick Daisy up, only to find her happily snuggled up in this woman's ample bosom, sound asleep. But soon after Daisy started walking I realized there was a problem. The nursery didn't have any outdoor space to speak of, apart from a tiny roof terrace the size of a postage stamp, which they'd tried to make into a mini playground, but only a handful of kids could use it at any one time. The children were cooped up inside even on lovely sunny days and while it hadn't bothered me when Daisy was a baby, now that she was mobile and active it definitely did. Luckily a place became available at another nursery, slightly further afield. It's a 20-minute walk away, but that's a small price to pay for the gorgeous huge garden and watching Daisy tearing around like a mad thing!

Top tip

Don't be afraid to regularly review your childcare options. What suited your child when they were a baby may not be quite so appropriate now that they are a playful toddler with boundless energy.

Helping your toddler through a family break-up

In the UK, nearly 150,000 children a year are affected by divorce and, of these, it is estimated that around 20 per cent are under five years old. Add to this the many separations and relationship breakdowns that are not officially documented, then you can see that it is not an uncommon occurrence. Family break-ups are never easy on children, and for a toddler with limited understanding of what is going on, it can feel like their world has been turned upside down by all the changes a break-up usually brings. The good news is that you can make your toddler's adjustment to these changes much easier, minimizing the trauma and the negative impact.

FIVE WAYS TO PREPARE YOUR TODDLER FOR THE BREAK-UP

1 *Talk to your toddler about what is happening before any changes in the living arrangements occur. But do not do this months in advance – just a week to ten days beforehand will give your toddler less time to fret.*

2 *It is best if you and your partner tell your toddler about the split together. Make sure that your toddler understands that you both still love them and will take care of them.*

3 *Talk honestly and simply to your toddler. Avoid criticizing your partner and overwhelming your toddler with details.*

4 *Reassure your toddler that your decision to split is nothing to do with them and that it is because the two of you have not been getting along.*

5 *Acknowledge your toddler's feelings of sadness and be there to comfort them. Do not try and pretend that everything is fine. Your toddler is likely to be experiencing a sense of loss.*

HELPING YOUR TODDLER COPE WITH THE BREAK-UP

Break-ups come about for all sorts of reasons, but whatever has instigated yours there are a few golden rules which should be adhered to when a toddler is involved:

▶ *How your toddler copes with the split is largely dependent on how you and your ex-partner behave towards each other. If you can work together and be polite to each other you will substantially reduce the trauma to your toddler. Remember, you may no longer love each other, but your toddler loves you both very much.*

- With the break-up there will be change, but for your toddler's sake try to make arrangements that disrupt their routine as little as possible. Even if things must alter fairly drastically, establish new routines quickly and then stick to them.
- Do not spoil your toddler or try to overcompensate for what has happened. Treat your toddler exactly the same as you did previously and do not allow behaviour that you would not normally tolerate. Your toddler needs firm boundaries, however much they may test them, to make them feel secure during this time of upheaval.
- If your toddler is going to share time between two homes, make sure that the rules are similar in each place.
- Send your toddler's favourite toys or blanket with them when they go to the other house and allow them to have a photograph of their other parent and to make phone calls to them. This reminds them that their other parent is still there and still loves them.

Insight

If you find yourself constantly locked in battle with your ex, I'd suggest stepping back and remembering the bigger picture. Your toddler needs to have a good relationship with both of you throughout their lives. If you can keep that long-term goal in mind, you may be able to avoid the everyday disagreements.

MAKING SURE YOUR TODDLER IS COPING OKAY

Even when life is back on a relatively even keel, your toddler may still need help in coping with the changes that have been wrought by the split. During this time of adjustment, you might want to consider the following:

- **Don't focus on feelings of guilt and failure.** *This will do neither your toddler nor yourself any good. Instead, try to focus on all the positives in your family, even though it may no longer be the one you expected.*
- **Look after yourself.** *Your toddler will look to you to see how you are coping, so make sure you look after yourself*

and remember that a lone-parent family can be happy, successful and complete.

▶ **Enlist additional support.** *Don't brush off offers of help and support from family and friends. Their presence can be very reassuring to your toddler, providing familiarity and security, as well as being an excellent sounding board for you.*

▶ **Do what is best for your toddler.** *Although you might not want your toddler to visit your ex's relatives, it may help to honestly question whether that decision is in the best interest of your toddler.*

▶ **Communicate with others who care for your toddler.** *Be sure to keep everyone involved in your toddler's care informed about family changes. They need to know what is going on in order to understand and help your toddler.*

▶ **Encourage your toddler to express their feelings.** *Give your toddler plenty of opportunities and encouragement to express their feelings through play. Also use books to help your toddler understand some of the emotions they are experiencing.*

▶ **Give them time.** *Divorce is complex for toddlers, who may have difficulty understanding why their world has changed. Take some time to help them cope.*

▶ **Keep a close eye on your toddler.** *Look out for signs that your toddler is not coping. These may include:*
  ▷ *sleep disturbances*
  ▷ *tantrums*
  ▷ *regression*
  ▷ *sadness*
  ▷ *relentless and new types of limit testing.*

While these types of behaviour are all normal in the circumstances, if you are at all concerned about your toddler seek the advice of your health visitor or GP.

Case study

Lily was just over two years old when Joe and I split. At the time I was livid with him. I won't go into detail – it's all water under the bridge now – but suffice to say that I hadn't seen it coming and I was left reeling in shock. My first instinct was to never see him again. He'd hurt me so much, so why shouldn't I hurt him by denying him the one thing closest to his heart – our daughter? But of course, once my anger had died down, I knew this wasn't really an option. Lily adored her daddy and whatever he'd done to me, he'd always been a brilliant father. So for the sake of our daughter, I decided to keep things civil. My gosh, it was hard at first. Every time he came round to pick Lily up I'd have to quite literally bite my tongue, and then after he'd left with her, I'd be beside myself with nobody to distract me from my grief. But the old clichés are true, time really is a great healer, and now some six years down the line I am so glad for Lily's sake that we did manage to keep a lid on our animosity. She has a very loving and open relationship with us both and as we both have new partners her family is now quite large and complex. But she seems very happy – I have recently had a son with my new partner, while her dad has two stepdaughters and another baby on the way. The other day I actually heard Lily boasting to her friend how she has two mummies and two daddies and lots of brothers and sisters, and to be honest, I actually felt quite proud.

10 THINGS TO REMEMBER

1 *While your toddler may struggle to cope with change, relying heavily on the predictability of a routine for their sense of security, obviously a certain amount can't be avoided. However, with planning, understanding and careful management such changes needn't be too stressful.*

2 *Remember not to assume that your toddler knows what's going on just because it's being discussed freely around them. They are still getting to grips with language and communication and will need what's happening explained to them in the simplest of terms.*

3 *To help your toddler adjust to a new sibling involve them from the very outset, showing them the hospital scans, letting them feel the baby move in your tummy and helping with the name-choosing process.*

4 *Continue the involvement once the baby's born, letting your toddler help out, while offering constant praise and reassurance that you love them very much. When possible, make special time just for them.*

5 *If you're preparing to move house, make the time to talk to your toddler and explain exactly what is happening, while playing up all the toddler-attractive aspects. If possible, take them for a viewing.*

6 *Once in the new house, make setting up your toddler's room a priority. If possible, stick with old furnishings and bedding for the time being as this will help your toddler to feel at ease.*

7 *Whether choosing childcare for the first time or changing childcare because your toddler's needs have changed, it can be an emotional rollercoaster for all concerned. Be prepared to do the research and don't be afraid to trust your instinct.*

8   Whatever childcare you are considering – nursery, childminder, kinship care or nanny – take the time to talk to other parents in your area. Not only are they mines of local information, they can also tell you the pros and cons from personal experience.

9   When settling your toddler into new childcare, take things slowly at first. Begin with just a couple of hours, gradually building up over the space of a few weeks. This will give your toddler time to get used to the change in their routine.

10   Separation and divorce causes untold changes in the lives of all concerned, and is undoubtedly an unsettling and upsetting time. But how your toddler copes with the split largely depends on whether you and your ex can remain civil to each other. Your toddler loves and needs you both, and that should be paramount.

13

Toddler troubleshooting

In this chapter you will learn the answers to some of the questions you may still have.

20 of the most frequently asked questions answered

▶ **Cleaning my toddler's teeth has become a twice-daily nightmare. Why does she hate it so much?**
This is very typical toddler behaviour. Your little girl probably doesn't hate it, but is just exerting her independence. She can't understand why her teeth must be cleaned and resents being made to do it. She is too young to know about tooth decay, so your best bet is to turn the whole teeth-cleaning process into a fun game. Invest in a colourful toothbrush – there are even some musical ones on the market – and try to make teeth cleaning a happy and relaxed time.

▶ **My little boy always eats a huge breakfast, but only ever eats a tiny lunch, and a fairly small dinner. Is this something I should be worried about?**
As long as your son is growing well, then trust him to know how much he wants to eat at each mealtime. Many toddlers do wake up ravenous after a good night's sleep. After all, they have usually not eaten for around 13 hours. Try not to focus too much on each individual meal and instead look at the broader picture. Over the course of the day and indeed the week, he is likely to be getting all the nutrients his little body needs.

▶ **My daughter is very fussy, but one of the few things she will eat is eggs. Should I be limiting them?**
Eggs are very healthy, providing lots of protein, vitamins and fat, but you should make sure that they are cooked thoroughly before giving them to your toddler, as this will kill any dangerous bacteria. An egg a day is fine, but any more and your toddler is in danger of filling up on eggs to the detriment of other types of food. This is what is known as a food jag – when a toddler becomes fixated on one particular food. If this is the case, then do limit the number of eggs you give her. A hungry toddler is more likely to try different foods.

▶ **According to her nursery, my toddler has a very healthy appetite and tucks into everything she's given. So why is she so fussy at home?**
Toddlers are very influenced by their peers, and in the nursery setting your daughter is in all probability sitting down with a group of children to eat her lunch. Seeing the other children eating their food makes your daughter want to do the same. To encourage her to eat better at home, why not invite one of her nursery friends over for tea?

▶ **My 18-month-old son has suddenly started waking in the middle of the night. He'll eventually re-settle with a bottle of milk, but what can I do to get his sleep routine back on track?**
When a child suddenly becomes wakeful, everyone suffers. You are exhausted, while your toddler is probably a lot grouchier during the day. Resist putting your toddler down much later than usual in the hope that he will sleep through the night, as this will simply throw his whole routine off kilter. Put your son to bed before he becomes over-tired, and stop the milk as this is giving him a reason to wake at night. If he is thirsty, water will suffice.

▶ **My toddler, who's nearly three, is refusing to take her lunchtime nap. What age is it usually dropped?**
Some children do go on napping until around five years old, only stopping when they start school, but for the vast majority the third birthday usually marks the beginning of the end of the lunchtime nap. The first few weeks of stopping the nap can be tricky as your toddler may become tired and grumpy in the

late afternoon. During this transition phase, try setting aside some quiet time, when you can snuggle up on the sofa reading a book or listening to music together. Try not to let your toddler fall asleep after 4.00 p.m. as this will impact on their night-time sleeping.

▶ **I'm dreading moving my toddler from his cot to a bed. Doesn't this mean he'll be wandering around at all hours of the night?**

Many toddlers make the move to a big bed without any changes in their sleeping habits. Just because they can now get out of bed, doesn't mean they necessarily will. If, however, your toddler does take to night-time wandering, be firm and consistent. Keep placing your toddler back into his bed, with minimum fuss, until he gets the message.

▶ **I seem to be having constant battles with my toddler and I'm finding it so exhausting. Any suggestions?**

Life with a strong-willed toddler can feel like living in a war zone, but you can sometimes choose to retreat, and it doesn't mean you have capitulated. You have simply decided that some things aren't worth fighting over and you are saving your energy for the bigger battles. In doing this, your toddler will feel that they have more control over their life and will be less likely to be difficult when you do lay down the law.

▶ **My son is going through a terrible tantrum stage. We're due to visit my partner's parents soon and I'm tempted to cancel as they're bound to think I'm a dreadful mother.**

Honesty is the best policy in this situation. Phone your mother-in-law in advance and explain what is happening and how you have chosen to handle your toddler when he has a tantrum. Enlist her support. She has been a mum herself and is unlikely to judge you harshly. In fact she will probably be flattered that you have confided in her.

▶ **Sometimes, immediately after my toddler has thrown a tantrum, I feel that I don't like her very much. It doesn't last long, but is my reaction normal?**

It is normal. Your toddler has behaved in a manner that has stressed and vexed you and it is natural to feel a bit miffed

*with her. But of course you still love her and it is important
that she knows this. Don't rehash the tantrum or lecture
your child about it. As the adult, you need to get over your
annoyance and reassure your toddler that everything is okay.*

▶ **At the moment I feel like I'm treading on eggshells around my
toddler. If I deny him anything, he goes into a massive strop.
What should I do?**

*It sounds like your toddler is starting to rule the roost.
He knows that you do not like seeing him cross and upset
and is using this knowledge to his advantage, which just
goes to show what a clever little lad he is! You need to set
boundaries, and as much as he may push against them, resist
the urge to give in. If you stand firm, your toddler will realize
that he can't always have his own way. It is an important
lesson he needs to learn and one that will hold him in good
stead in the future.*

▶ **When our toddler is being naughty I usually send him to his
room. But recently a friend told me this wasn't a good idea.
Why not?**

*Of course, where you choose to send your toddler for
Timeout when they are misbehaving is up to you, and will
be dictated partly by your accommodation and also by
whether you have other children. That said, you want your
toddler's room to have happy associations, to be a place of
calm and sanctuary, so that come bedtime they are content to
stay there. It is this consideration to which your friend was
probably referring.*

▶ **We have just ditched the high chair, but now I'm really
struggling to keep my toddler sitting at the table until
mealtime is over. How can I make her stay in her seat?**

*You have to be realistic. Forcing your toddler to remain at
the table until everyone has finished will seem like an eternity
to her, and it is not surprising she gets bored and fractious.
Instead, insist that she remain seated while she is eating, but
once she has finished let her get up and go. Also, by making
mealtimes a happy family time, your toddler is more likely to
want to stay put.*

▶ I really want to get my 22-month-old toddler out of nappies before we go on holiday in six weeks' time. Do you think it is possible?

Why set yourself this deadline? By doing so you are in danger of making the process unduly stressful for both you and your toddler. Unless your toddler is ready, there is no point in even starting toilet training, let alone insisting that they adhere to a set schedule. Relax and let your toddler lead the way. Besides, unless you are going somewhere really remote, most places sell disposable nappies, so you do not have to worry about filling up your suitcase with them.

▶ Can daytime and night-time toilet training be cracked at the same time?

It is possible, but only if your toddler instigates it. Some toddlers do go through the night with dry nappies at the same time as they are showing readiness for daytime toilet training, but many more do not. If your toddler falls into the latter category, simply concentrate on achieving daytime dryness first. It is not uncommon for a child to reach the age of six before they are completely dry every night.

▶ I recently took my toddler to a child's birthday party, thinking she'd have a lovely time playing with the other children. Instead she ignored them. Why?

Don't worry, your little girl is not being unfriendly, she just hasn't yet reached the stage in her social development where she is able to play with other children. Instead, she prefers to play alongside them in what is known as parallel play. And while she might have looked as if she was ignoring them, rest assured she was taking everything in, and in a year or so she will be in there playing with the best of them.

▶ My toddler seems to think her baby brother is a plaything. How can I get her to be gentler?

Try not to criticize her or tell her that she's doing something wrong. Toddlers do not automatically know how to behave properly around a newborn and need adults to teach them. Let your toddler practise with a dolly, holding, stroking and cuddling it. Heap lots of praise on her when she is gentle and don't expect her behaviour to improve overnight – it takes a little time for a toddler to learn how to be gentle.

▶ Why has my son started demanding a bottle again now that the baby's arrived?

This is a classic sign of toddler regression and it is a perfectly normal reaction to a new sibling. Put yourself in your toddler's shoes. From being your entire world, he sees the baby now getting much of your attention, while everyone who visits fusses over the new arrival. By making himself more babyish he hopes to put the spotlight back on him. Don't make a big deal about it – he will soon be back to wanting to prove he is a big boy.

▶ I honestly think my two sons, aged 18 months and three years, must hate each other. They do nothing but squabble. What should I do?

Your boys' behaviour is totally natural. They are jockeying for position in the family, and are pushing each other to the limit as they do so. While this process is tiring for you, it is vital for your sons. Sibling rivalry teaches many important life lessons, from managing conflicts, sharing and cooperation to expressing ideas and feelings. Try to avoid stepping in and resolving disputes and do not apportion blame. You can also take comfort in the fact that research shows sibling rivalry only occurs in healthy families.

▶ I'm worried about my daughter, who's terribly shy. She refuses to say hello to people, even when we know them. How can I get her to be less timid?

It is important to accept your toddler's shyness and not to push her into situations that make her feel uncomfortable. Through positive encouragement and support, you can help build your daughter's confidence. Try not to apologize for her shyness and do not talk negatively about it in front of her. The next time you meet someone, rather than insisting that your daughter says 'hello', encourage her to give the other person a smile instead.

Taking it further

In this section a number of organizations are listed that you may find useful.

Association of Child Psychotherapists is an organization that holds a directory of accredited child psychotherapists.
Website: www.acp.uk.net
Email: admin@acp-uk.eua
Tel: +44 (0)20 8458 1609

Childcare Directory is a resource to help parents find childcare and other child-related resources in their area.
Website: www.childcaredirectory.co.uk
Email: info@childcaredirectory.co.uk
Tel: +44 (0)1379 898 535

Cry-sis is a charity that supports families with crying and sleepless children.
Website: www.cry-sis.org.uk
Email: info@cry-sis.org.uk
Advice line: +44 (0)8451 228 669, seven days a week, 10.00 a.m. to 5.00 p.m.

Daycare Trust is a charity that provides information to parents, employers, policymakers and providers.
Website: www.daycaretrust.org.uk
Email: info@daycaretrust.org.uk
Tel: +44 (0)20 7840 3350
Advice line: +44 (0)20 7840 3350, Mondays, Wednesdays and Fridays, 10.00 a.m. to 5.00 p.m.

Eric is a charity that helps families deal positively with childhood continence problems.
Website: www.eric.org.uk

Email: info@eric.org.uk
Tel: +44 (0)117 960 3060
Advice line: +44 (0)845 370 8008, Monday to Friday, 10.00 a.m.
to 4.00 p.m.

Home-Start is a charity that provides support and friendship to
parents of under-fives.
Website: www.home-start.org.uk
Email: info@home-start.org.uk
Tel: +44 (0)116 233 9955

National Literacy Trust is an independent charity that aims to
change lives through literacy, beginning from birth.
Website: www.literacytrust.org.uk
Email: info@literacytrust.org.uk
Tel: +44 (0)20 7587 1842

Parentline Plus is a national charity that works for, and with,
parents.
Website: www.parentlineplus.org.uk
Tel: +44 (0)20 7284 5500
Advice line: +44 (0)808 800 2222, 24 hours, seven days a week

Parenttalk is an organization committed to inspiring parents and
helping make parenthood fun.
Website: www.parenttalk.co.uk
Email: info@parenttalk.co.uk
Tel: + 44 (0)20 7921 4234

Talking Point offers information and advice about speech and
language development in children.
Website: www.talkingpoint.org.uk
Email: info@talkingpoint.org.uk
Tel: +44 (0)845 225 4073

TAMBA: Twins and Multiple Births Association provides
information, a confidential helpline and mutual support network
for families of twins, triplets and more.

Website: www.tamba.org.uk
Email: enquiries@tamba.org.uk
Tel: +44 (0)870 770 3305
Advice line: +44 (0)800 138 0509, Monday to Friday, 10.00 a.m. to 4.00 p.m.

The Children's Project is committed to promoting positive parenting and better outcomes for children.
Website: www.socialbaby.com
Tel: +44 (0)8450 94 54 94

The Infant and Toddler Forum aims to provide practical help and information on infant and toddler nutrition and development.
Website: www.infantandtoddlerforum.org
Tel: +44 (0)20 8971 6408

Index

active play, *230*
active/feisty toddlers, *23, 26–7*
additives and tantrums, *87*
aggression, *85, 131–3*
appetite, *272–3*
art and craft, *229–30*
assertiveness, *40–1*
attention, *69*

babies, helping toddlers accept, *247–9*
battles: choosing, *54–5, 92*
bed, moving from cot to,
 193–4, 274
bedtime routine, *61–2*
 case studies, *61–2, 187*
 difficulties with, *186–7*
 poor sleeping, *183*
behaviour problems: specific,
 131–5, 274–5
biting: case study, *132–3*
bladder control mechanism, *219*
books, *232*
boredom, *69*
boys
 food fussiness, *161*
 imaginary friends, *232*
 talking, *140–1, 155*
 toilet training, *217–18*
 toys, *235–6*
brain development, *6–7*
break-ups, coping with, *265–9*
breath-holding, *89*

car journeys, *74–6, 212*
cautious toddlers, *23, 27–9*
change, coping with, *240, 243–71*
 case studies, *248–9, 253–4, 265,
 268–9*
 childcare, *254–65*
 family break-up, *265–9*
 moving house, *249–54*
 new siblings, *245–9*
childcare, *254–65*
 au pairs, *262*
 case study, *265*
 childminders, *257–8*

kinship care, *258–60*
 nannies, *260–2*
 nurseries, *255–6*
 organizations, *278*
 relatives, *258–60*
choices, giving, *49–50, 92*
clinging, *21*
communication elimination, *203*
comparisons
 family, *32–3*
 other toddlers, *8*
 siblings, *78*
 toilet training, *216–17*
competitiveness, *8, 69*
continence problems: support
 organizations, *278–9*
controlled crying, *184*
creative play, *229–30*
crying: support organizations, *278*

decision making, *49–50*
defiance, *30*
development, *1–17*
 12 to 18 months, *9, 11–12, 13,
 38–40*
 18 to 24 months, *10, 12, 13–14, 40–2*
 24 to 36 months, *10, 12, 14, 42–3*
 brain, *6–7*
 of independence, *38–43*
 mental, *11–12*
 milestones, *7–15*
 physical, *8–11*
 and play, *222–5*
 playing with others, *232–3*
 social and emotional, *12–15*
 toilet training, *209*
developmental play, *232*
diet, *167–71*
discipline, *113–38*
 aggression, *131–3*
 case studies, *117, 119, 121–2, 128*
 consistency in, *120*
 difficulty of, *115–18*
 effective, *118–24*
 methods of, *124–31*
 and personality, *119*

discipline *(Contd)*
  positive reinforcement, *125–8*
  problems, *274–5*
  versus punishment, *114–15*
  reward charts, *126–8*
  role modelling, *123–4*
  smacking, *136*
  timeout, *128–30*
distraction technique, *93*
dressing, *70–1*
dressing up, *231*
drinks, *172*
DVDs and television, *150, 228–9*

E numbers, *87*
early rising, *188–9*
easy/flexible toddlers, *23, 25–6*
eating, *158–78, 272–3*
  case studies, *41–2, 60–1, 93, 160, 176*
  food allergies, *171–2*
  food jags, *159–61*
  foods to be careful about, *170–1*
  fussiness, *158–61*
  and independence, *162*
  mealtimes, *60–1, 93, 166, 173–4, 275*
  offering new foods, *163–5*
  parental influences, *165–7*
  snacks, *169*
  toddler diet, *167–71*
  vegetarian toddler, *175*
embarrassing behaviour, *133–5*
emotions and flashpoints, *68–9*
everyday activities as play, *240*
exploring, *38–9*

family break-up, *265–9*
  case study, *268–9*
family comparisons, *32–3*
feisty toddlers, *23, 26–7*
flashpoints, *67–81*
  avoidance techniques, *92*
  sibling squabbles, *76–9*
  triggers, *70–9*
flexible toddlers, *23, 25–6*
food allergies, *171–2*
food jags, *159–61*
free play versus structured play, *225–6*
frustration, *68, 92*
fussiness, *29*
fussy eaters, *158–78, 273*

games to play, *238–9*
girls
  talking, *140–1*
  toilet training, *217*
  toys, *235*

high activity levels and tantrums, *85*
high intensity character, *85, 161*
hitting, *131–3*
holding close, *97–8*
hunger, *68*

imaginary friends, *232*
incontinence: support organizations, *278–9*
independence, *37–66*
  18 to 24 months, *40–1*
  24 to 36 months, *42–3*
  case studies, *39–40, 41–2, 43, 54–5*
individuality, *19–21*

jealousy, *69*

kicking, *131–3*

labels, avoiding, *29–30*
literacy: support organizations, *278–9*
low adaptability, *85, 161*
low rhythmicity, *85*

mealtimes, *59–61, 166, 275*
  case studies, *60–1, 93*
mental development, *11–12*
  and play, *223–4*
milestones, developmental, *7–15*
misbehaviour, reasons for, *116–18*
moving house, *249–54*
  case study, *253–4*

naps, *190–1, 273–4*
  case study, *191*
naughty step, *98–9*
negative behaviour, *38, 39–40*
neophobia, *158–63*
new baby, *247–9*
new foods chart, *164–5*
night tantrums, *193*
night terrors, *191–3*
nightmares and terrors, *191–3*
'no'
  case studies, *39–40, 52*
  limiting use of, *50–2*
nutrition: support organizations, *280*

outside help
    organizations, *278–80*
    sleeping, *278*
    tantrums, *109–10*
    toilet training, *217*
outside play, *230*

parenting skills, *5*
parenting styles, *130–1*
parenting support organizations,
  279–80
personality, *19–36*
    avoiding labels, *30–2*
    case studies, *20–1, 25–6*
    and discipline, *119*
    and fussy eaters, *161*
    individuality, *19–21*
    self-esteem, *30–2*
    and tantrums, *85–7*
physical development, *8–11*
    and play, *223*
picking your battles: case study, *54–5*
play, *222–42*
    case study, *224–5*
    and development, *222–5*
    in everyday activities, *240*
    free versus structured, *225–6*
    and gender, *235–6*
    importance of, *222–3*
    with other children, *232–3, 276*
    playing with your toddler, *227–8,*
    238–40
    types of, *229–32*
playdates, *233*
playdough recipe, *234*
positive reinforcement, *125–8*
potty training, *see* toilet training
potty versus toilet, *205–6*
pregnancy, *245–6*
pretend play, *224–5, 230–2*
    case study, *14–15*
psychotherapists, *278*
punishment versus discipline, *114–15*
pushchairs: refusing, *3*

quizzes
    personality, *23–5*
    toilet training, *202–3*

reading, *232*
regression, *277*
    case study, *253–4*

    caused by changes, *247, 252, 268, 277*
    toilet training, *211, 213–14*
repetition, *6*
respect and discipline, *121–2*
reward charts, *126–8*
    toilet training, *209–10*
role modelling, *123–4*
routine, *55–64*
    case studies, *57, 64*

safety
    outside, *39, 121*
    toys, *236–7*
self-awareness, *41*
self-esteem, *30–2*
separation anxiety, *39, 40, 43–5*
    case study, *45*
sharing, *68–9, 224*
shopping, *72–4*
shyness, *29, 277*
siblings
    comparisons, *78*
    coping with, *276–7*
    coping with new, *245–9*
    cutting rivalry, *78, 277*
    squabbles, *76–9*
    and tantrums, *104–5*
sleep, *179–98, 273–4*
    babies to toddlers, *180–1*
    bedtime routine, *183*
    from cot to bed, *193–4*
    early rising, *188–9*
    how much, *182–3*
    improving, *183–6*
    naps, *190–1*
    nightmares and terrors, *191–3*
    outside help, *278*
    in parent's bed, *195–6*
    problems, *186–9, 273–4*
    safety, *194*
    sleep diaries, *189*
    training, *183–6*
    understanding, *181–2*
    waking in the night, *188*
sleep training, *183–6*
    case study, *185*
slow-to-warm-up/cautious toddler, *23,*
  27–9
smacking, *136*
snacks, *169*
social and emotional development, *12–15*
social development and play, *224*

soft toys: case study, *43*
speech and language development, *139–41*
sticker charts, *126–8*
structured play versus free play, *225–6*
stubbornness, *29*

taking turns, *14, 77, 224*
talking, *139–57, 144*
    case studies, *142, 152–3*
    dummies, *150–2*
    encouraging, *144, 144–53*
    expressive language, *141–2*
    gender, *140–1*
    language milestones, *142–4*
    modelling words, *146, 153–4*
    problems, *153–5, 279*
    reading, *147–8*
    receptive language, *141–2*
    singing, *148–50*
    socializing, *152–3*
    speech and language development, *139–41*
    television, *150*
tantrums, *82–112, 274–5*
    and additives, *87*
    avoiding, *91–4*
    case studies, *85–6, 90–1, 93, 94–101*
    contributory factors, *86–7*
    coping with, *94–101*
    ignoring, *94–6*
    keeping a record, *103–4*
    myths, *107–8*
    night, *193*
    other toddlers, *105–6*
    outgrowing, *108–9*
    outside help, *109–10*
    and personality, *85, 85–7*
    in public, *101–3*
    and siblings, *104–5*
    signs of, *88–9*
    spectrum of, *89–91*
    timeout, *98–9*
    and twins, *105–6*

    types of, *88*
    what not to do, *100–1*
teeth cleaning, *272*
television and DVDs, *150, 228–9*
temperament, *21–3*
    and sleeping, *180*
'terrible twos', *3–4*
testing limits, *42–3*
timeout, *275*
    discipline, *128–30*
    tantrums, *98–9*
toddler-proofing, *38–9, 46–9, 50*
toilet training, *199–221, 276*
    accidents, *208–9*
    away from home, *210–12*
    bladder control, *219*
    boys, *217–18*
    car journeys, *212*
    case studies, *205–6, 210, 213–17*
    communication, *203*
    development, *209*
    dry nights, *218–19*
    girls, *217*
    incontinence: support organizations, *278–9*
    outside help, *217*
    potty versus toilet, *205–6*
    problems, *213–17*
    process of, *206–8*
    rewards, *209–10*
    timing, *200–4*
    underwear, *209*
toys, *234–8*
travelling, *74–6*
troubleshooting, *268–9, 272–80*
twins
    organizations, *279–80*
    and tantrums, *105–6*

vegetarian toddler, *175*
vocabulary, *40*

waking in the night, *188*
walking, *10–11*